THE PASSION OF JOHN ASPINALL

by the same author

Molière (1969)
Sartre (1969)
Saint-Exupéry (1970)
Rabelais (1971)
Camus – A Study (1973)
Wynyard Hall and the Londonderry Family (1974)
Dreams about H.M. The Queen (1974)
The Dukes (1975)
Now Barabbas was a Rotter: The
Extraordinary Life of Marie Corelli (1978)
The Mistresses of Charles II (1980)
Georgiana, Duchess of Devonshire (1981)
Great Hostesses (1982)
Killing for Company: The Case of Dennis Nilsen (1985)
The Swinging Sixties (1985)

THE PASSION

OF

JOHN ASPINALL

Brian Masters

JONATHAN CAPE
THIRTY-TWO BEDFORD SQUARE LONDON

To the memory of Lady O.

First published 1988
Copyright © 1988 Brian Masters
Jonathan Cape Ltd, 32 Bedford Square, London WC1B 3EL
British Library Cataloguing in Publication Data
Masters, Brian
The passion of John Aspinall.
1. Aspinall, John   2. Zoologists—
Biography
I. Title
591'.092'4   Q431.A8/
ISBN 0-224-02353-5
Phototypeset by Falcon Graphic Art Ltd
Wallington, Surrey
Printed in Great Britain by
Adlard & Son Ltd, Letchworth, Herts.

Contents

Illustrations

The author and publishers are grateful to the following for permission to reproduce illustrations: Keith Lloyd (29); London Express News & Features Services (6, 28); Mail Newspapers plc (3, 20, 31); The Osbert Lancaster Estate and John Murray (page 79); The Photo Source (25); The Press Association (21); Syndication International (11). Other photographs are from John Aspinall's personal album and from private sources.

Preface

It will be perfectly clear to the reader that this book could not have been undertaken without the full and generous co-operation of Mr John Aspinall, who has given me full access to his private papers, absolute discretion as to their use, and complete freedom to make my own assessments and draw my own conclusions. Furthermore, he has devoted many hours of conversation to assist me in the task, and afforded me the warmth and hospitality of his home on scores of occasions. Some felicities of style are due to improvements suggested by Mr Aspinall. It has been altogether a happy experience.

Lady Sarah Aspinall has shown exemplary patience with my intrusions, for which I am most grateful, and Miss Susan Hunt has guided me cheerfully and scrupulously through a confused sequence of papers.

The zoological establishments in San Diego, California; Chicago, Illinois; Denver, Colorado; Dallas, Texas and Los Angeles, California have been among the most helpful in contributing the professional view, as indeed has the Zoological Society of London.

In addition, there have been a great number of people who have been willing to share their reminiscences with me, and I trust they will not deem my gratitude a poor thing if I thank them here alphabetically. They include Mr Gerald Albertini, The Rt Hon. Peter Archer MP, Miss Amanda Aspinall, Dr Robert Aspinall, The Duke of Atholl, Miss Julie Battersea, Mr Tom Begg, Dr Kurt Benirschke, Mr Robin Birley, Mr

Anthony Blond, Mr Robert Boutwood, Mr Claus von
Bülow, Mr Timothy Cassel, The Hon. Mr Alan Clark, Sir
David Crouch MP, Mr Nigel Dempster, The Earl of Derby,
The Duke of Devonshire, Mr Lester Fisher, Mr Edward
Gilbert, Lady Annabel Goldsmith, Mr Edward Goldsmith,
Sir James Goldsmith, Mr Ian Grant, Mr Peter Halliday, Mr
Gary Hart, Mr Warren Iliff, Mr Eric Ingersley-Nielsen, Mr
Philip Jebb, Mr Brian Jenks, Mr Ronald Johnson-Gilbert,
Mr Richard Johnstone-Scott, Mr David Jones, Miss Tessa
Kennedy, Mr Michael Leathers, Mr George Levey, Mr and
Mrs Anthony Little, Mr Michael Lockyer, The Marquess of
Londonderry, Professor Dr Konrad Lorenz, The Master of
Lovat, Mr John Matthew QC, Mr Ian Maxwell-Scott, Mr
Daniel Meinertzhagen, Mr Guy Mountfort, Mrs Tertius
Murray-Thriepland, Mr Digby Neave, Mr James Osborne,
the late Mary Lady Osborne, Mr Kerry Packer, Mr Richard
Parkes, Lord Parmoor, Mr Brian Rathbone, Mr Stuart J.
Ross, Sir Peter Scott, Sir John Stradling-Thomas MP, Mr
Harry Teyn, Dr Warren Thomas, Dr Edwin Wiesinger, Mr
Terry Whittaker. If I have inadvertently omitted anyone, I
ask forgiveness. Some have asked that their help remain
unacknowledged.

Mr Jock Murray deserves a special word of appreciation
for locating the Osbert Lancaster cartoon and affording me
an afternoon of delight searching through the others. Mr
Anthony Blond has generously allowed me access to the
manuscript of his forthcoming autobiography. My editor,
Tom Maschler, offered sage advice with his unerring intuitive
eye, and my copy-editor, Elizabeth Smith, went through the
text with great care. I am grateful for her assiduity and honour
her contribution to what follows.

The description of the Clermont Club 1962-72 is from
memory, as the present owners refused my request to see
the premises.

Finally, it is I hope not improper for me to add a personal
word. I have been aware of John Aspinall's pioneering work
with animals for some twenty years, and long ago cherished
an ambition that I should one day write his biography, chiefly

because I admired what he was trying to do and wanted to bring it to wider public attention. This is not therefore a book entirely without prejudice, for it grew out of a belief in the value of Aspinall's contribution to animal husbandry. To some extent I must consciously proselytize, and would be happy if some readers were convinced by this presentation of one man's quest for harmony between the species. On the other hand, I have striven to give due weight to critical opinion, and to the views of those scholars who dispute Aspinall's aims and methods. Hagiography is more likely to win enemies than friends and thereby thwart its own purpose. I trust that in writing about a man whom I know, I have been able to summon that degree of objectivity which might allow the reader direct access to his personality and commitment. I believe that Aspinall's achievement cannot fail to convince.

London, 1988   Brian Masters

I

From Delhi to Zulus

As far as one knows, there is not a single zoologist among John Aspinall's ancestors. It is likely that his male forebears delighted more in slaughtering animals than in studying them, still less in seeking their company and cherishing their qualities. His extraordinary, almost unique rapport with other primates appears to have come from nowhere at all, to bestow upon him privileges of interspecific contact which few other people can ever enjoy, and to load upon him a burden of responsibility, as spokesman, apologist and passionate defender of all non-human mammals, that few would care to endure. But if Fate chose him, then she is indeed whimsical, for John Aspinall, had he trodden a conventional path, would have been a respectable, unremarkable middle-class businessman living in a dormitory suburb. His past and his upbringing pointed towards unremitting normality, but his character, always disdainful of orthodox expectations, demanded more glamorous expression.

Through his mother, Aspinall is descended from four generations of Anglo-Indians. Mary Grace Horn was the eldest of three daughters of Clement Horn, a construction engineer whose speciality was building bridges. The Horns were originally from Barnet, near London, but as Mary's great-grandfather and grandfather had both lived and worked in India, and she herself was born in Seoni, just outside Nagpur, all her memories and traditions were Indian.

Clement Horn had travelled to Seoni on a bridge-building contract (some of his bridges are still standing today), and shortly after his daughter's birth the family settled in Nagpur, capital of the Central Provinces, virtually in the middle of India. She always regretted that her father had not had the imagination to name her 'Seoni' rather than the more pedestrian 'Mary', but she had little else to lament. She and her two sisters, both born in Nagpur within the next five years, grew up bilingual in English and Hindustani. In common with many other colonial families on the subcontinent, the Horns lived in comparative opulence, with at least twelve indoor servants and a nanny for Mary; by the age of four Mary had already been given her own pony, which she called 'Strawberry'.

In those days, travel to England took three to four weeks by sea, which meant the journey was rarely undertaken. Although Mary was aware that she was English, she did not see England until she was sent to school in Bedford at the age of nine. Even after that, home was still India and her future still lay in Nagpur, which was both a blessing and a curse. The advantage of living in comfort was outweighed, as she grew older, by the gradual realisation that to be female in that society was a definite and insoluble nuisance. Clement Horn, a strict, authoritarian paterfamilias with solidly Victorian principles, made no secret of his deep disappointment at only having daughters, with no male to continue the line of Horns. It was made clear to Mary that the main purpose of her life was to marry, and she determined to do so as soon as she could.

Social life was abundant in Nagpur, with dances almost nightly, and far more eligible young men about than there were marriageable girls. Mary, who by this time was known to all by the nickname 'Polly', was an accomplished dancer who never missed a soirée if she could help it. Once, when staying with her uncle, Stuart Ross, she went to a dance where she spied a young man called Dr Robert Aspinall, of whose reputation as a superb dancer she had previously heard. They met on the dance floor and were married within a fortnight. Mary wanted at all costs to leave the family home and, though her parents did not explicitly push her into marrying, she knew perfectly well they were glad to see her go. The precipitate nature of her courtship with 'Robby' Aspinall and the suddenness of their marriage was to have sad consequences for her happiness and would obliquely influence the character of her second son John.

Robby Aspinall was by no means the most illustrious catch. Unlike Mary, he had no Indian background, but had been born in England, had studied at Guy's Hospital, and joined the Indian Medical Service in search of adventure. Posted to Peshawar, he was appalled at the inadequacy of the hospitals and of the services they were able to offer, particularly in the field of surgery where his skills lay. He was in despondent mood when he met 'Polly' Horn, and he, too, was ready for romance to brighten his life.

Robby applied for compassionate leave, which was granted, and the freshly-married Dr and Mrs Aspinall went to England for seven months. On their return to India, with two days' leave remaining, they stopped in Delhi where Robby reported to his superiors in the Indian Medical Service and convinced them his talents were not properly used in Peshawar. He was immediately given the top posting, Civil Surgeon of Delhi. Mary was not simply pleased with their new status; she had actively urged her husband to seek it.

They lived for seven years in Delhi, progressively aware that their hasty marriage had been a mistake. Mary's ambitious nature found no comforting echo in Robby's more cautious approach to life, and her dissatisfaction found release in flirtation and complaint. In 1924 their first son was born. Named Robert, he was known from the beginning as 'Chips', for reasons which no one can recall. The second son, John, was born in 1926.

Both boys were brought up by an ayah (nanny), with the result that for many years they were more fluent in Hindustani than in English. Though they spent all their childhood together, the marked difference in their characters was apparent at an early stage. Chips took after his father, firm, reliable, but uninspiring, whereas John had far more of his mother's wayward spirit, ever likely to test the response to unconventional behaviour, curious and inquisitive, and not remotely shy. He said whatever came into his head. Even as an infant, he was agreeable company, lively and affectionate, and very attractive, with a shock of blond hair. There grew between Mrs Aspinall and her second son a powerful bond, uncommonly close and confidential, which was never to be impaired. In any fraternal quarrel, no matter how mild, and irrespective of the justice of the case, Mary always took John's side.

There were no signs that John had any particular affinity with animals. Like most Anglo-Indian children, he read and enjoyed Kipling, and, like many, he had the opportunity to experience close contact with animals which in England would be regarded as exotic. Stuart Ross, his great-uncle, gave camping parties at which John would ride elephants, and, as he later wrote, he fed them sugar-cane and was lifted high in their trunks and settled back on the ground without being hurt. 'Even then I was awed by their power and gentleness.' One of his mother's admirers, Tony Benyon, had two tame tigers. On all the evidence, John accepted encounters with these animals as a matter of course, though he admitted that the tigers added to 'Uncle Tony's' prestige in his eyes.

The hero of the family was Great-uncle Fred, married to Mary's Aunt Mabel. He was a hospitable and hearty man who kept open house and arranged for generous gifts to tumble from one's napkin at the start of dinner.

This happy, not very eventful, life continued until John was six years old and was sent with Chips to attend prep school in England. The Aspinalls were not wealthy, but they contrived to save enough to choose a decent, though not famous, school near Eastbourne called Temple Grove (it later moved to Uckfield). On his first day, John was pummelled into a corner by some of the older boys, according to the traditional mores of English boarding-school children, probably because they thought he was too pretty, or maybe merely to assert rights of seniority. Whatever the case, it did John no lasting harm, but fostered in him a deep respect for power and a determination that he, one day, would be in a position to wield it. Far from resenting the confidence of those boys who were able to make their own rules, he admired them and sought to emulate them. Very quickly, he established himself as a character and a maverick, a boy distinguished from the general crowd by a mischievous, rebellious nature which was none the less free from malice.

Once he had settled down at Temple Grove, John found that he could best assert his personality not merely by breaking rules, which, though satisfying, was not very productive, but also by offering his protection, both physical and moral, to boys less blessed with self-confidence than he was. The first of the Aspinall acolytes was a youngster called Anthony Newnham, slightly John's junior, who stood in awe of the seven-year-old's apparent ease in getting what he wanted and doing what he liked. The two boys were inseparable, not because there was any deep bond between them, or because the one confided especially in the other (boys rarely confide anyway), but because John was the leader and Anthony the led, a relationship which suited them both. John took Anthony under his wing, looked after him, helped him face the rough world of others. It is a role he has been playing ever since, with a few interruptions, and those he now protects include whole herds of mammals.

It is not easy to understand whence John derived his remarkable degree of confidence at this age. The love of his mother had given him strength, it is true, but she was now thousands of miles away and he was abandoned, with his brother, in a world peopled by strangers. For a while, during term time, he was able to turn this to advantage, for it was wonderfully romantic to have parents in far-off exotic lands when everyone else came from such places as Hove. But the truth of the situation was plain at the end of term, when the boys from Hove had a home to go to, and the Aspinalls were nomadic. For six years, until he was twelve, John saw his mother at most only once a year, when she made visits to England, and his father not at all. For Robby Aspinall, both boys merely represented cheques to be signed. Mama provided the pocket money of 10s. a term each, which was comfortable though not exorbitant (£1 a term in those days would have been a fortune). They certainly did not feel they mattered much to their father. Chips secretly felt rather ashamed that his family was not like others. In John's case, he nursed a quiet ambition that his mother should one day receive the admiration she deserved, and his pride not be apologetic.

For the first few years, Chips and John spent their summer holidays with their grandparents, Mr and Mrs Clement Horn, who had by then deserted India and settled in retirement, first at Broadwater Road, Worthing, and later at Goring-on-Sea. Having wielded considerable authority in India, the Horns accepted their loss of status without complaint. No one knew much about them, or deferred to them in any special way. But their grandsons naturally held them in awe. Clement Horn was a Victorian martinet whose word was final and whom nobody gainsaid. Biblically educated, he believed firmly in Heaven and Hell and would invoke either when cause allowed. The boys were instructed to behave on all occasions 'like a sahib'. At the same time, Clement was creative; he was both a talented painter, who had painted every single picture which hung in the house, and, more important for John, a bewitching teller of stories. It was at grandfather's elbow that John first felt the power of a good story, with substance, point and *dénouement*, and recognised that, while bald truth might be accurate, an embellished parable could hold an audience rapt. Before he was ten, John was himself an incipient raconteur, mining books for good tales which he would use to win attention from other boys.

As for grandmother, she was soft and indulgent, and when mother came over from India for part of the summer holidays the two women combined to make life agreeable for the children.

Though Chips and John were certainly not spoilt, they enjoyed more personal freedom than other boys of their age, perhaps to compensate for their lack of a permanent

family. Provided they behaved themselves with due for-
mality indoors, very few restrictions were placed upon them
outside. They were permitted, for example, to ride off on
their bicycles and explore the countryside long before their
contemporaries at Temple Grove enjoyed such privileges.
They were essentially country boys, surrounded by fields and
woods and in communion with the natural things with which
the land abounded. For John in particular, this richness held
an apparently endless fascination. He collected slow-worms,
grass-snakes, frogs, and kept a jackdaw at Temple Grove.
None of this is unusual for little boys, but John appeared to
know these creatures better than others did, and they to know
him, moreover. On one bizarre occasion during a family
picnic, which included cousins, on the beach at Goring,
the honey-pot attracted a swarm of wasps which descended
upon the group, causing all to flee, adults and children alike.
Only John remained, unperturbed and fearless, as the wasps
whizzed and buzzed around him, some even settling upon
him. They did him no harm.

Not that there was anything saintly about John's behaviour
towards the animal world. He and Chips both plundered
birds' nests regularly, but John would always temper the
deprivation by insisting on leaving one or two eggs behind,
for honour's sake.

When the other two school holidays came round, at Easter
and Christmas, and Mrs Aspinall remained at home in India,
she paid for Chips and John to stay as guests at Palfrey Farm
on the Petworth estate, run by Jack and Eileen Pring. For
several years John spent his holidays there, in company with
other children, including at least once his cousin Ian Grant
(son of Mary's sister), and the cumulative experience had a
considerable effect upon his personality.

In the first place, Farmer Pring fulfilled the role of surrogate father. One does not have to be a Freudian to recognise
that by this time John felt a very real need for paternal influence. It was curious that he never found cause to mention
his father; it was as if he were dead, or had never existed.
Farmer Pring filled the gap to perfection. Having no sons

himself (he had two daughters, Barbara and Helen), he had a special fondness for John, with his liveliness and spirit, and John in turn nurtured a very high regard for him. He was the dominant kind of father, masculine and self-reliant, able to turn his hand to anything and teach by example rather than precept. Pring employed only two workers on the 110-acre farm, managing the rest entirely alone. He would get up at 4.30 in the morning (waking John with the sound of his stropping the cut-throat razor) and milk the cows in time to take three churns of milk to the end of the mile-long drive to await collection. John was happiest when he was asked to help in these raw tasks, and felt useful when told to undertake any physical work, as well as proud to be doing so at the side of such an admirable man of such sterling character.

Then, also, Farmer Pring had a close relationship with every animal on the land he tenanted, treating each with respect and care, rather than regarding them as mere instruments of profit to be exploited. Each cow, each chicken had its own name, and some cows could be milked only by Pring himself, refusing to accept anyone else. There was a huge white boar called Esau, with which John established a private friendship, for Esau would allow him to ride through stinging nettles on his back. 'Esau's taken a liking to you, John,' said Farmer Pring. That one could be *liked* by an animal was a new concept to John, and one that he found thrilling. The words sang in his mind, though it would be many years until he would develop the tune beyond anything Farmer Pring envisaged. Much later, he wrote of Jack Pring, 'I loved his smell and his brittle temper and the feeling of safety by association that he gave me. I relished also the satisfaction that comes from a friendship with an animal feared by others.'

John also learned the weird code of the farming world, that some animals can be murdered, and others cannot. Robins, thrushes and blackbirds were out of bounds, dependent on man's protection, whereas sparrows and pigeons were fair game. John accepted all this without question, and was a fierce little hunter in his time. He had not reached an age where he could challenge such arbitrary choices, and felt no guilt in killing those creatures which the farmer decreed one could.

A final, tiny influence of Jack Pring's was to offer the first opportunity for John Aspinall to gamble. Quite innocently, with no idea what potent seeds he was sowing, he bet John £1 that he could not ride his bicycle all the way to Petworth and back in his pyjamas. John took on the bet, and won. He was then about eleven, and though he obviously wanted to win so as to shine in Jack's estimation, he took very quick note that it was a convenient way to make money.

Back at Temple Grove, Chips and John made light of their strange pseudo-orphan condition by never drawing attention to it. After all, summers at Goring and other holidays with the Prings did not constitute deprivation; they were enormous fun. Yet it was obvious to them both that their lives were unusual, not like those of others, and no boy wants to be so different that he invites disdain. Chips and John reacted in quite different ways. For Chips, it was romantic and exciting to have parents in distant lands; he turned embarrassment to advantage, showed off the exotic stamps on letters he received, and boasted of the important position which his father held in life. He attempted to show that fundamentally he was not so different at all. John, however, decided that he would never have cause for resentment, would never bargain for entry into any little group and never ask for friendship and risk having it refused. He became more than ever rebellious and difficult to handle, behaving according to his own lights and no one else's. Far from concealing his difference, he advertised it, and soon found that other boys came begging admission into his own little club. Secrecy, he discovered, was a solid fortress, and exhibitionism a powerful magnet. He also took some refuge in books. He read widely and copiously, as if hoping to find in print some parallel to his own position, some echo of his history or representation of his own embryonic attitudes to the world. Within a year, as we shall see, he was to find just such a book.

It is also interesting that while Chips was collecting British colonial stamps at this time, John showed a preference for stamps from the French colonies; these were nearly always decorated with beautiful pictures of animals.

At the age of twelve, John Aspinall was an attractive, incorrigibly scruffy, beguiling child. With his blond hair and blue eyes, extravagant personality, vitality and vigour, and easy conversation, he was pursued, at a very discreet distance, by men who would have liked to adopt him. The faint aura of loneliness which he could not entirely dispel made the cocktail irresistible. Fortunately, at this age John was completely unaware of the effect he produced and never knew that he had such admirers. One might say this was his only blind spot as far as self-projection is concerned, for otherwise all his life he has been in firm control of the effects his charm could achieve.

Chips naturally left prep school first and went to Felstead. When it was John's turn, he joined his brother there for one term, where he greatly impressed the headmaster, Mr Bickerstaffe, who in later years frequently enquired after his progress. The reason for John's removal was simple. Mama was divorced and remarried, and there were now sufficient funds to send her favoured son to a major public school.

When Mary Aspinall first told her children that she and their father were to be divorced, they both 'blubbed', to use the vernacular of the day, in the back of the taxi. They were not so upset at losing a father they never knew, but were sorry for their mother to be exposed to calumny. In those days, divorce among the middle classes, so keen to uphold appearances, was a disastrous admission of defeat. Mary explained to the boys that Robby had not been 'kind' to her; that was all they needed to know, and they were not of an age to suspect a partial view.

Fortunately for Mary, the gods turned all their best omens upon her. Sailing towards England in the autumn of 1937, the divorce and India behind her, she was feeling particularly dejected and forlorn. She was determined to make a life for herself and her sons somehow, but could not yet see the way. One evening, she went to the deserted top deck and sat on a coil of rope, pondering the past and the future, how she had made so many mistakes in her life and whether she was going to be able to manage. She began to sob. Gradually she realised there was someone else on the deck, a man, who presently came over and sat beside her, gently enquiring into her distress and offering some comfort. He was George Osborne, a bachelor in his mid-forties and a distinguished ex-soldier who had twice been wounded in the First World War and twice mentioned in despatches. He was also the heir to a baronetcy which dated from 1639, with a country house in Sussex. In February 1938, George and Mary were married.

There is no need to exaggerate George Osborne's qualities, for every account of him depicts a man of extraordinary generosity of spirit. He was kind, good, attentive, never losing his temper, or saying or doing anything which could cause unhappiness to those around him. He was certainly a saviour to Mary, but, more pertinent to this story, he provided the first real home for Chips and John Aspinall, when they were respectively fourteen and twelve, and his total, unreserved acceptance of them as his wife's children, and candidates for his protection, had a profound influence on John's moral perceptions. George's loyalty to John's mother, and his status as provider and supporter, appealed to John's maturing values and earned his devotion and unqualified respect. George Osborne did both boys a power of good.

For reasons of prestige (which mattered very much to Mary), John had been sent to Rugby, an ancient and revered public school which had a reputation for turning out not politicians, as Eton did, but professional men with a highly-developed work ethic and a Christian sense of duty. For these reasons, Old Rugbeians usually disappear back into the soup of the general population as barristers and civil servants, whereas Old Etonians compel attention all their lives. Rugby was not the best choice for John Aspinall, but no doubt it was hoped the strict traditions of the place might tame his unruly behaviour.

John went off to Rugby with no qualms, largely because he was permitted to take with him a pet jackdaw he had recently befriended and which stayed with him for two years. 'The fact that he could recognise me from 500 yards high in the sky and fly down and perch on my shoulders made me inordinately proud. On one occasion, on a summer afternoon, he landed on my shoulder when I was batting for the school.'

John's first year was spent in Cotton House, where he shared rooms with John Stradling-Thomas, later to be a Tory MP, a knight and a Government whip. Within days he was almost constantly being whacked by Head of House, Hardy, for minor but regular infringement of rules. Far from being abashed, John would show off the strokes he had received, throwing Hardy into a fury of indignation. Eventually, announcing that he would whack Aspinall no longer, Hardy sent him to the butler, Elsworthy, who devised devilish schemes for punishment, such as moving hundredweights of coke, cleaning the floor beneath it, and moving the coke back again.

In May 1941, he transferred to Whitelaw House, where he remained for the rest of his school career. It was here that John made the first really strong impression of his life. He was universally liked, both by boys and teachers, and it would be safe to say he had no enemies, not only because he was entertaining company, but also because he never bullied anyone or made a victim of another boy. One contemporary recalls, 'He was never cruel throughout his time there, and there are very few people about whom one can truthfully say that.' Consequently, his gregarious nature was not denied; people wanted to be with him.

He was also by now a strong, accomplished athlete and, at sixteen, a formidable presence, broad, tough, commanding, cheerful. He worked hard to get his Rugby XV cap, and was openly pleased when he succeeded in 1943. As an athlete he was good but not graceful, better noticed for heavyweight presence than for fleetness of foot. Still, he relished achievement and recognition.

John Aspinall was already an exhibitionist, whether by design or genetic inheritance. He knew it paid to show off and it earned a great deal of attention. Whitelaw House was proud of him because he was so obviously different from everyone else, so *outré* and confident, in the grand manner. Even his untidiness had something splendid about it – never just a sock out of place but an entire sartorial shambles. When other boys were shy about their bodies and would hide them at every turn, Aspinall was supremely indifferent to such concerns and would walk about naked in the dormitory without even noticing it. He carried his exhibitionism right to the edge of the permissible, and was forgiven because of his charm and his style. 'If he had been anyone other than who he was, he would have been intolerable,' was how one of his fellow pupils put the matter.

Rugby did nothing to curb his enthusiasm for disruptive behaviour. It was not that he set out deliberately to challenge authority, simply that he did not recognise its existence. That others should know better what was good for him, for the expression of his nature, was a concept he found appalling, and he ignored rules if they ran counter to his understanding of what he wanted to do and how he wanted to do it. In the forty years that have since elapsed, this attitude has been amended in no way, as the Gaming Board, the World Wildlife Fund, the Department of the Environment, zoo-keepers and casino owners the world over can testify.

Subversive or mischievous conduct in boys may seem innocent enough, even laudable, but it can be hugely irritating to others. John Aspinall was a member of the OTC, or School Cadets, but he was a hopeless boy to have in one's platoon. On one occasion, when they were supposed to be attacking a farmhouse, Aspinall's section was discovered dozing beneath a tree. There was no doubt that he was lazy (a fault that he has never even tried to eradicate in the years since), but he was also iconoclastic. Adolescent boys pretending to storm a deserted farmhouse in Lincolnshire in order to mould their character struck him as supremely silly, so he didn't do it. He was quite able to participate fully in activities both scholastic and extra-curricular, as his being selected for the Rugby XV demonstrates, but only he would choose those activities or enthusiasms, no one else.

He could not be pushed, and he responded to discipline with contempt.

It took considerable courage, 'guts', to continue flouting rules which everyone else respected, in the certain knowledge that he would be punished. Aspinall saw punishment as perfectly logical, but the anticipation of it was no deterrent. He would still do what he wanted, and not apologise if his choice conflicted with established practice, or complain at the consequences. Inevitably, his attitude was regarded as slap-happy, irresponsible and cocky by the Head of House, a deeply conventional and rather prim boy called Nigel Power, who was the only person to disapprove strongly of Aspinall. He was unable to appreciate the qualities of this madcap individual who was simply, in his view, a bad team member. Nor could he understand why the House appeared to be proud of him, when they should want to disclaim him. Power's frustration reached a peak, and with his help Aspinall made history of a sort by being the first boy in living memory to be quad-flogged at Rugby.

This ancient, strangely hieratic custom was the maximum punishment which could be inflicted. It involved dragging the boy out after bedtime into the centre of the quadrangle, in the chill air, while the Head of House repeatedly ran at high speed down the steps and across the quad to thump the miscreant on the backside in full view of other members of House, who stood in silent witness of the chastisement. It was brutal and it was humiliating, but more than anything it was ritualistic. When Aspinall was flogged, neither Power nor any of his prefects knew that the priestly atmosphere of the occasion was appreciated by none more than Aspinall himself. His insatiable appetite for reading had led him to a discovery which, as we shall see, had profoundly affected the way he viewed the world, and ritual played a significant role in this view.

Indiscipline naturally impressed the younger boys, who were open-mouthed in wonderment at the spartan bravery of this lad who seemed to fear nothing. And yet, oddly, he did not attract a following, a gang of admirers, because he dealt with people as individuals and kept them at a fair distance. To those of his contemporaries who looked more acutely at their companion, it was clear that he did not find personal relationships at all easy. Aspinall was entertaining, but not entirely natural; confident with words, ill at ease with people. In a strange way he was even vulnerable, and some thought they discerned a sadness in his life, a large area of emptiness from which something essential was missing, something all other boys had but for lack of which he had to compensate by inventing, creating a flood of anecdote, and absorbing stories from books to use as ammunition in keeping the others amused. One boy distinctly remembers feeling sorry for him.

During his four years at Rugby, he adopted the name 'Jonas V. Aspinall', on the grounds that John was too prosaic (the V is genuine enough, standing for 'Victor'). His exhibitionism, too, was a way of acting out a fantasy, and he appeared to be more of a dreamer than a thinker. He created mythologies and was swept along by their grandeur. He was fascinated by the power of words to seduce and was already creating literature with his sentences, in the manner of ancient tellers of epic tales. His stories were not banal, but rich in adverb, adjective and incident, theatrical in their effect. It was impossible, however, to engage him in any discussion about matters of substance. He was, for instance, completely indifferent to the progress of the war, which other boys followed daily. Still less was he willing to talk about anything personal. So reticent was he about his family and upbringing that no one realised he was born in India. He did not, in those four years, cultivate any particular friendship, any bond which could survive the fruitless banter of schoolboy chumminess. Such bonds would be forged later; as yet, he had not encountered anyone he could recognise as being like himself, a maverick and a misfit.

Once he journeyed to London with a boy called Ronald Johnson-Gilbert (now secretary of the Royal College of

Surgeons), to see a cricket match at Lord's. On Aspinall's advice, they stayed at the Cumberland Hotel at 10s.6d. each for the night, and Johnson-Gilbert felt that since Aspinall knew all about hotels and must therefore be worldly, there was no telling what else he might be inveigled into, and was nervous lest he might be dragged to a nightclub or the like. Aspinall was not merely showing off in going to an hotel; he had a glimpse of the kind of life he would want to lead when he grew up.

In the end, he was too big a fish, too extravagant a character for Rugby to handle with any success. He resisted attempts to shape him into a mould of which the English middle classes would approve, and in 1943 his mother and stepfather received a letter suggesting that John might not want to return for the new term, that the school had no more to offer him. He was not exactly expelled, but the letter was a tactful way of saying that he would do better to avoid the possibility. Mary Osborne, to whom John was the most perfect of children, always helpful and obliging, ever ready to lend a hand with the washing-up at home, did not take in the import of the letter and thought the school must be mad to suggest he would not wish to go back. He had gently to tell her what the authorities really meant.

As for himself, he had no regrets whatever. Though an avid reader, he was not to any degree an academic, and was unwilling to give of his time and energy to the study of a subject which did not interest him. He came top in Geography, History and English, winning the essay prize in the latter, but coming close to bottom in everything else. What did fire him was not a set-book, not part of any agenda, but something which excited such an intensity of interest that it was to stay with him for the rest of his life and have a profound influence upon his emerging ethical values.

By chance, one day at the very beginning of his Rugby career, when he was thirteen years old, John Aspinall had taken down from the library shelf a book called *Nada the Lily*, by H. Rider Haggard. Written in the full-blown Haggard style, with grand exhortatory sentences and pages of local colour, it was an adventure story with an added dimension, for it opened Aspinall's eyes to a world so different from the one he knew, so much more romantic and impressive, on a scale so super-human, that he was entranced. Moreover, he experienced for the first time that strange heart-beat of recognition; much of what he had secretly thought and imagined was there in those pages before him. He saw a reflection.

Nada the Lily is the story of Umslopogaas, illegitimate son of the great Zulu king Shaka, banished with his mother from the kraal when a mere child and brought up by another tribe. Umslopogaas and his mother are for a long time ill-treated, spurned and excluded from Zulu society. The boy swears vengeance for his shame and for the humiliation his mother is made to endure. After many an adventure, Umslopogaas is carried off in the jaws of a lioness and is thought to be dead, but he secretly prospers, grows strong and brave, and pairs up with another outcast and child of nature, Galazi the wolf-man, whose howl is answered by all the wolves of the mountain.

In a highly pertinent passage, Umslopogaas is attacked by ravenous wolves who threaten to tear him apart and are inches away from his flesh. They suddenly halt, fawn and lick him. 'Umslopogaas, looking into their red eyes, felt his heart become as the heart of a wolf, and he, too, lifted up his head and howled, and the she-wolves howled in answer.' Twenty-five years after he first read it, this passage, apart from the initial attack, became reality in John Aspinall's life.

Eventually, Umslopogaas grows into a fine man, physically impressive and mentally alert, able to take the measure of people and outwit them. He has cunning, but he also has honour, and makes no excuses to avoid keeping a promise. He can argue his way out of an awkward situation and, with all cards apparently stacked against him, can emerge triumphant to the wonder of all. On one occasion, he is about to be executed and is instead rewarded, due entirely to his 'gift of the gab'.

He becomes a fierce and merciless warrior before whom all run in terror, and spares no time to appreciate the attractions of his women, who can have a dangerous influence, 'for the greatest men grow small enough in their own huts'. Most significant of all, Umslopogaas is solitary because he is unusual, out of the common run. 'The tree that stands by itself on a plain thinks itself tall and that there is no shade to equal its shade.'

From that day when he discovered *Nada the Lily*, John Aspinall devoured every book he could get hold of, first by Rider Haggard, second on the history and character of the Zulu people. (Today he has one of the finest collections in England of Haggard first editions.) His fascination with the Zulus knew no bounds. They were known to be excellent raconteurs. All their literature was oral, and the gift of bringing the past to life in conversation was one they all shared. Aspinall continued this tradition and throughout his schooldays enthralled other boys so much with Zulu lore and accounts of battles and personalities, that even those who can remember nothing else about him recall the Zulu obsession. He even went so far as to claim his mother was a Zulu princess, and some of the younger boys, perhaps unaware that his blond hair, blue eyes and a fair skin were inconvenient evidence, believed him.

Umslopogaas was based upon a real character, and his natural father, Shaka, was the greatest of all Zulus, founding the Zulu nation in the nineteenth century. Before the advance of European civilisation blindly and stupidly destroyed them, the Zulus were a remarkable race, dignified in bearing, noble in thought, learned in natural sciences, with a vast unwritten language and refinement of manners which would make many an Englishman seem vulgar by comparison.

A characteristic of Zulu culture which particularly caught Aspinall's interest, and which he was to emulate in years to come, was their extraordinary habit of hospitality. An emissary from a neighbouring or distant kraal, a visiting family, even a passing stranger, would be entertained warmly and lavishly, with many a special treat in food or display provided for the occasion. It was part of their ethic of honouring a friend, and honour was an important concept in their canon. The feasts Shaka gave when he was on his way to supreme power surpassed in splendour and munificence anything that had been given before.

As Aspinall developed his expertise in Zulu history, he realised there was a great deal in the personality of Shaka which appealed to him. It is interesting to observe the echoes of this personality and the strength of mind which fuels it sprinkled throughout Aspinall's subsequent career; the young reader hoarded his hero.

Shaka, thought by many to be a military genius equal to Alexander, by others to be a cruel tyrant as ruthless as Napoleon, was shaped by a harsh, healthy childhood, working all day in the open veld until the age of sixteen under a regimen designed to weed out the weak and produce strong virile manhood. He grew up with the Zulu's strict regard for hierarchy, little boys subservient to big boys, adolescents to men, men to the chief of the kraal, the chief to the king, and women of course subservient to all. Like all Zulu boys, Shaka was educated by nature, studying plants, trees, insects, rocks, weather, the medicinal uses of herbs, and so on, and afterwards learning the martial arts.

Shaka was a rebellious child who sought to dominate those around him, but was utterly devoted to his mother. Like Haggard's characters in *Nada the Lily*, for many years Shaka and his mother were destitute vagrants, homeless and dependent upon the kindness of others. Shaka nursed a fierce determination that he would never have to live in that state when he became a man, and swore he would take revenge on those who had condemned him to such a condition. Poverty, he decided, was an intolerable disgrace. On the other hand, he felt undying gratitude to the foster father who rescued him from isolation. He grew into a brave adolescent of striking physique who surpassed all others of his age in his feats, was disdainful alike of danger and of weakness, and cultivated an iron will, both to protect himself against hurt and to bring his aims to conclusion. He could make others do his bidding by sheer force of will.

Yet Shaka was not a snob. Once in power, he promoted those he favoured strictly according to merit; he was totally blind to their riches and their social standing alike. This, too, has always been true of Aspinall. Shaka was generous to people whose spirit he admired and who had fallen upon hard times, and he made a conscious decision to have nothing to do with women until his power was established and consolidated. It was a question of priorities, and their order was not to be compromised. One suspects Aspinall made a similar decision at a similar age.

Finally, it is attested by many chroniclers, including some who knew Shaka at first hand, that he was not nearly as ferocious as he liked to appear. There was something of the artist in him, demonstrated by his love of popular singing music, and his wit. Moreover, he was secretly sensitive. Behind that façade of iron discipline lurked an emotional and sentimental man.

Zulu customs as a whole, and the character of Shaka in particular, dominated Aspinall's attention from the age of thirteen. Whether consciously or not, his own personality was considerably influenced by his reading, as indeed happens to most of us. But the consistency of Aspinall's fascination with the subject is rare; he admired the values and habits of the Zulus to such an extent that they seeped into his view of himself. He was a different person for having discovered *Nada the Lily*.

That discovery was now more than three years ago. Back home with the Osbornes, John went about his country tasks contentedly, shooting those creatures that were permitted, leaving others unmolested, without a thought as to the justification of this arbitrary line. (The Zulus were quite vicious to their animals, so there were no lessons to be learned in that regard.) George Osborne only decreed that no shooting should take place on Sundays; otherwise he was easy-going and malleable.

John and his brother Chips decided to turn their knowledge of guns to good use. They would buy guns from people they encountered shooting at Barnham, advertise them in the *Exchange and Mart*, and sell them at a profit. It sometimes worked the other way, finding a bargain in the paper and selling it to a local dealer. In addition, they shot partridges, pheasants and hares and sold them to the local butcher. The rate was 2s. for a rabbit and 5s. for a hare, both handsome dividends during the war. In effect, these were the first two 'businesses' set up by Aspinall. He was sixteen and a half years old.

On the other hand, Chips was the more resourceful entrepreneur of the two at this stage. It was he who made the money, John who did his bidding. John was too dreamy and idealistic, too much the romantic, to grasp the practical steps towards profit. One of Chips's ruses was to advertise in *The Times* inviting interested parties to send £1 in return for which they would receive enlightenment on the mysteries of how to make soap. Hundreds of letters arrived at prep school. They were answered with a page copied from the *Encyclopaedia Britannica*.

The first of four Osborne children was born in 1943. Thereafter the house would be full of babies, when Chips was already a man and John was approaching twenty. It was almost as if they were living in someone else's house. John took refuge as ever in reading, and his latest interest, not remotely allied in style or content to the Zulus, was the life and works of Oscar Wilde. Before long, he was able to quote passages at random from the plays, as well as from the poems of Lord Alfred Douglas. Their homosexuality was of no interest to him (it is doubtful if, at that stage, he understood it), although he was infuriated by the pitiless destruction of Wilde by the upper classes. It was Wilde's style that entranced him, his florid appearance, self-confidence, ability to stand out and be different from everyone else, and especially his success in holding an audience spellbound with his stories. Wilde the raconteur endeared himself to Aspinall, and Wilde's wisdom, revealed in sparkling paradox, intoxicated him. At about this time, John decided that he would himself be a poet. He had written only one poem, published in Rugby's school magazine, on the death of a Zulu chieftain, but he knew he was destined to be a misfit in society, and imagined that poetry would be his route to glory as well as his means of self-expression.

However, what he should do with his immediate future was becoming a pressing matter. Chips was by now a medical student and thereby exempted from military service, but the Second World War was still far from over. John made a sudden, uncharacteristic decision. He volunteered. His patriotism was not in doubt, and he was not tempted in any way by the doctrines of pacifism, but, for a man who bridled at the very thought of organised authority thwarting his will, it was inexplicable that he should seek entry into the most obtuse society of all. Probably he did not anticipate quite what it would be like. And he had to do something, after all.

Aspinall joined the Royal Marines at the age of seventeen and a half and stayed with them for nearly three years. As a recruit, he was first posted to Deal, which was conveniently close to his stepfather, Colonel Osborne, who commanded the garrison at Dover. Almost as soon as he arrived, however, the Colonel was posted elsewhere.

On his first day he was issued with kit and given a groundsheet on which he was required to place the various items in a strictly ordained pattern for inspection the following day. In barracks, some of the recruits found themselves short of certain items and began to panic. One after another, they asked Aspinall ('Jonas' was too posh for them, so they called him 'Blondie') if he could spare a second pair of socks, or whatever, with which requests he willingly complied. The next day his stock was seriously depleted, and the men thought him insane to be so indifferent to the trouble he was about to face. His solution to the problem was novel. He offered what was left of his kit to all and sundry until there was nothing left. When the Captain-Adjutant, nicknamed 'Chang' after a comic-strip monster, began his solemn kit inspection, danger seemed very close. Aspinall, questioned as to the disappearance of his entire kit, calmly explained that he had never been issued with any. Chang, indignant at such a lapse in good order, gave instructions that a kit be supplied immediately.

Aspinall went next to Eastney Barracks in Portsmouth, then joined the Intelligence Section of the 30th Battalion, serving in England and on the Maas river in southern Holland. He declined to be an officer, and remained a plain marine throughout, with pay of £1 a week, supplemented by another £1 from his mother.

This was not an eventful or profitable passage in Aspinall's career, nor did his experience have much influence upon his character. He always marched at the back of the platoon because he found it difficult to keep step. Once he was discovered on a verge reading Sir Edwin Arnold's translation from the Persian poets. When questioned, he said he suffered from the poetic temperament. He could indulge in fairly well-controlled sobs if he found a gruelling route march to be pointless and nasty.

Aspinall was not suited to military life and never contemplated following the example of his stepfather. Still less was he attracted by medicine, Robby Aspinall's profession, which his brother Chips had already chosen as his life's work. He was frankly too lazy for serious study, too averse to hard work. None of his family yet understood that he needed to be his own man, that he could not be standardised. A friend of his aunt arranged an interview for him with Burmah Oil. It was the normal expectation that someone from his background should join a large firm and work his way up through the hierarchy over a number of years. John went for the interview, and was offered a post whenever he cared to take it up, but it was remarked upon that he had spent the entire interview crushing a handkerchief in his fist. What the board did not realise was that he was itching to get out. He knew perfectly well that there was not the slightest possibility of his working in such an organisation; he recognised his own faults, and acknowledged that he lacked the right qualities to hold down a job in any hierarchical establishment. He could not 'slot in'.

With congenital idleness, a knack for attracting or causing controversy, and a propensity to speak his mind, John Aspinall was indeed difficult to place. Something had occurred, however, which was to make the task easier. His only friend from this time in the Marines, Desmond Dunphy, had played a role in his destiny of which neither of them yet suspected the importance. Dunphy knew how to handle a pack of playing cards.

2
Oxford

At a rare family gathering in 1947, John Aspinall met his cousin Stuart J. Ross, son of his mother's sister, and confided his indecision and uncertainties about his future. As he was deep in the grip of his Oscar Wilde obsession and saw himself as a writer, Ross suggested that an Oxford degree in English Literature would give him the background to support an interest in the theatre, as well as a platform for a career in Letters. It was Ross who pursued the matter further when Aspinall declared his enthusiasm, by gathering information about grants and vacancies, and finally advising him to send an application to Jesus College, where Stuart Ross *père* had been a student. By a happy coincidence, the Master of Jesus, Sir Frederick Ogilvy, was an old Rugbeian, which made it virtually certain that Aspinall would find a place if he could pass the relatively simple entrance examination. He did.

Unfortunately, Jesus College did not provide the atmosphere which suited the disposition of 'Jonas V. Aspinall'. In fact, it was decidedly dull, not at all chic and very near the bottom of the list socially. It had a reputation for being stuffed with earnest Welsh schoolmasters. Aspinall's suspicions were confirmed when he arrived with his bags at the beginning of term and was allocated a room sharing with a gloomy, lack-lustre undergraduate for whom he did not care at all. He stayed there one night, then packed his bags again and moved to digs in Walton Street for 15s. a week, bed and cooked breakfast.

When one considers what would come later, it is interesting that Aspinall's finances at Oxford were notably modest. As an ex-serviceman he received a government grant of £70 a term, supplemented by an annual allowance of £40 from his distant father, Robby Aspinall. The combined resources were not enough to enable him to compete with most undergraduates, especially the kind towards whom he would instinctively move, and he frequently gave the impression of being quite broke.

Impressions mattered to Aspinall at this time, and this was not one he wished to encourage. He was an aesthete of sorts, but the impecunious, wasted, suffering variety did not appeal to him. His admiration for Wilde and Lord Alfred Douglas was at its peak, so he set out to celebrate their style in his own person. He wore a salmon-pink suit and gold waistcoat, carried an ebony cane and snuff-box, and often tucked Lord Alfred's poems under his arm. With his fine looks, long blond hair and arresting physique, he cut a magnificent figure in the High Street, and there were quite a few undergraduates who noticed him, and wondered who he was. Some (who later became friends) thought he was obviously a man to avoid.

While Aspinall's admiration for the poetry of Alfred Douglas was perfectly genuine, and indeed he himself wrote a poem, his second, which was published in *Cherwell*, it would be misleading to depict him as a full-blooded literary lion in the manner of his contemporary at Oxford, Kenneth Tynan, who breathed literature every day. Serious study and textual analysis bored him; he knew what he liked, and that was sufficient. In fact, throughout his three years at Oxford Aspinall did not attend a single lecture. He kept his weekly appointment with his tutor, but more often than not the paper he delivered for consideration was copied from some one else so blatantly that its familiarity was obvious. In short, John Aspinall did not care for work, and in the Oxford of those days no one seemed to mind. The days when university education was to become a matter of passing examinations and acquiring qualifications had not yet come, and a nineteenth-century ideal of education by absorption of mood still applied. Aspinall was not the only undergraduate to take a dim view of study; on the contrary, the swot was a rarity.

The poem he published in the *Cherwell* on 26 April 1948 was entitled *Lines in Support of the Old Look for Gentlemen.* It is not fanciful to see in this foppish, nicely-turned confection some intimation of the Aspinall to come. Impatience is there, especially with the unwarranted pre-eminence of the female, and also a crude desire to be noticed in some way; apocalyptic pessimism, too, all done with clever alliteration and some bold internal rhymes. As Aspinall did not go up to Oxford until October 1947, and did not write again during his undergraduate career, it is clear the poetic impulse was quickly stifled by other considerations after his second term. Here it is:

> The time has come! We must emerge
> In silks and satins, banish serge
> And hessian, away with hispid tweed!
> Are we not men, and can we not be freed
> From all those tortures that infest
> Our frontage, that burlesque the best
> And boldest lineations we possess?
> Just think of that monopoly of dress
> Which females hold – the gilded gold
> Of costume that was ours of old –
> Ye gods! Now all is gone and we are left
> Of all that's rare and beautiful, bereft.
>
> Oh twisted fate! Oh bitter gall
> That women should deny us all . . .
> It is not right – indeed 'twill not be borne
> That they indulge their whims while we are shorn
> Of all that taffeta and lace,
> Of all that finery and grace
> We knew so well and in such style enjoyed,

With such finesse, superb aplomb, employed.
But now that Decadence is here –
Alas! it seems for always – where
Is that brave spirit we most surely need
To dam the deluge and deny this greed:
A Brummel or an Oscar Wilde
To be by half the world reviled,
And yet to roll an epoch back - a sage
To herald in, once more, the satin age?

                                        Jonas V. Aspinall

In his first few months, Aspinall's impact upon Oxford was therefore that of a dandy, a showman who bent his energies upon making an effect. He seemed to be born to have an audience. His *élan vital* was extraordinarily beguiling and infectious, and it was not long before his reputation as a raconteur had spread through the colleges. When he told a story he could enthrall his audience into rapt attention. His subject matter was drawn from mythology, ancient Nordic tales, and especially Zulu character and history, and his detailed knowledge in these fields could not be challenged. Like an actor, or more particularly an epic narrator in the oral tradition, Aspinall was adept at giving life to his story, vivifying it with adjectives and adverbs which made the human element shine clear; there was never anything inanimate in an Aspinall narrative.

It was noticeable, also, that there was purpose to these long tales of heroism. Aspinall was emotionally committed to the mythology of courage which they celebrated, and convinced that the core of man's condition and fate was contained in antique wisdom passed down through countless generations, rather than in polished literature. As he told his tales, he wanted to reveal truths truer than the surface reality of his narrative, to unveil essences, and watch the effect as his audience was suddenly smitten by insight. The real nature of man and his place in the world, his capacity for extreme courage and total inherited wisdom, these were the themes which moved Aspinall and inspired his skill. There was something positively Nietzschean in these enthusiasms, which would become sharper and, in the opinion of some, more brutal, as Aspinall grew older. They also foreshadow one aspect of his apparently intuitive understanding of animals.

But that is to anticipate. At this stage, there is no evidence that John Aspinall had any philosophy whatever with regard to animal life. Nevertheless, something crucial did now occur which altered his own life for good, and would one day enable animals to prosper.

His friend from the Marines, Desmond Dunphy, had gone up to Oxford at the same time. He was at Oriel, a notch or two up from Jesus, where he occasionally held a game of poker and Aspinall, who had never played, sat quietly and watched. One might safely call this a turning-point. Aspinall witnessed ten whole games with careful attention before he decided he would attempt to play, and from that moment, with the cards in his hand, he knew that he had found his métier, the one occupation which would call upon all the reserves of courage and cunning which he so admired. Very quickly, he was betting on horses and dogs as well, and was on the alert for any gambling group in other colleges against whom he could pit his skills.

The game at Oriel was hopelessly modest, with stakes seldom higher than 1s. a time. It was considered a disaster, for example, when a Cambridge man called Younghusband visited, and cleaned them out with the takings of £18.

In his rooms in the High Street, Digby Neave, certainly as good a player as Dunphy, also held a regular poker game. These were the two best card-players in Oxford, but Aspinall soon recognised that the excellence of the card-player mattered less than his wealth, and he was anxious to move up the social scale to mingle with those young men who could bet seriously.

At Balliol there was a tall, willowy and beautiful young man called John Pollock, who had won an Open Scholarship to this intellectually demanding college at the age of fifteen, and was obviously the genius of his generation. Equally clear was it that he was already on the way down to ruin and desolation, being irrevocably neurotic and self-indulgent. He and Anthony Blond, a witty, dark, mercurial boy from the Marks family (of Marks and Spencer) on his mother's side, gave the first big post-war party at Oxford, at which the guests saw their first lemons for many years. Pollock and Blond both gambled, but not well, which Aspinall was quick to observe.

From Corpus Christi came Milo Cripps, charming and clever, perhaps too partial to drink, who was another punter. He later took rooms at 167 Walton Street, which was to become the centre of Oxford's gambling fraternity and a magnet for all kinds of eccentric. Also, there was the son of a well-to-do couturière in the West End of London, called 'Bouncer'. Pollock, one of the few to be truly enamoured of literature, gave him this nickname because, he said, like the Ancient Mariner, 'he stoppeth one in three' – in other words his cheques habitually bounced. But the one gambler who outshone them all, the only truly heroic and reckless punter in a class with the wild men of the eighteenth century who played with fortunes and estates, was a man Aspinall noticed one day at Mr Ormerod's.

'Captain' Ormerod was a mountain of a man, over 20 stone in weight and just as tough as he looked, who ran the local bookmaker's shop in the backstreets between Cornmarket and the Mitre Hotel. Of course, his dealings were entirely illegal and had to be operated with the utmost discretion, which the undergraduates were only too happy to respect. John Aspinall went there regularly to place his bets.

On this particular occasion there was another under-graduate at Captain Ormerod's. Aspinall noticed that he was smartly dressed, impressively arrogant of speech, and, most important of all, was placing bets at £5 or £10 a throw, far in excess of anything John and his friends were used to in everyday gambling. (This would be equivalent today to somewhere between £200 and £500, an astonishing amount for an undergraduate to play with.)

Aspinall waited until the stranger had left, then asked Captain Ormerod who it was. 'That's Mr Ian Maxwell-Scott,' said Ormerod with the hint of a sneer. 'Arrogant young man. Runs a poker game at Balliol.'

Arrogant or not, he was obviously someone to court, and Aspinall calculated how best to make his acquaintance. The next time he went to Ormerod's he lingered behind, having placed his bets, and waited for Maxwell-Scott to show up. When he arrived, Aspinall left him alone for a while, then approached him with the kind of brash confidence which already came easily to him. 'You're Maxwell-Scott, aren't you? Poker player. We run a game at Oriel. Why don't you come and play with us?' Naturally, Maxwell-Scott scorned the proposal, because Oriel's game was markedly smaller than his at Balliol. Aspinall knew perfectly well that he would refuse, even before he asked, but he bargained that the man's code of honour as a gentleman would oblige him to extend an invitation the other way. He did. Both Aspinall and Dunphy were at the next poker game at Balliol, hosted by Maxwell-Scott (and including Alan Clark, son of the art historian Kenneth Clark), and Aspinall was on his way. 'I knew,' he has said, 'that I was absolutely happy in this ambience, surrounded by gamblers. It was where I belonged.'

Of all the people Aspinall met at Oxford, no one has been more intimately involved with the progress of his fate than Ian Maxwell-Scott, although their relative fortunes have, in the course of years, dramatically altered – in a way, they have changed places. Maxwell-Scott had more than one cause to be proud of his ancestry. In the first place, he was a great-great-grandson of Sir Walter Scott, and nephew to the man who still owned Abbotsford. Secondly, his was one of the oldest and most respected Catholic families in the land, tracing its heritage back to the kings of Connaught in the sixth century, and more recently, allied by various marriages to the Dukes of Norfolk. Indeed, there was hardly a family in the Catholic aristocracy to which he was not related. His father had been aide-de-camp to the late King George V, and he had himself followed his father's example with a career in the army. Unfortunately, his father had died in 1942, leaving Ian in the hands of trustees who were disposed to allow him too much licence. Had his father lived, his son's life would almost certainly have taken a different course.

Or would it? His attraction to gambling was not lightweight. It was not a hobby to be chosen from among many, but a compulsion of almost medical proportions, and perhaps incapable of correction. At any rate, when he went up to Balliol to study law, he never had the remotest intention of studying; his addiction to racing and the card-table had already taken precedence. (Besides which, his tutor was a bridge-player!) He was a romantic gambler, with a recklessness which defied belief and which had been rare in England for many years. It is important to understand the difference between Maxwell-Scott's romanticism and Aspinall's entirely realistic, business-like approach to gambling, for therein lies the cause of the decline of the one and the ascendancy of the other. Maxwell-Scott was a true hedonist, who found almost sensual pleasure in placing bets, and moreover preferred to play cards with people who were better than he was. He derived more sheer fun from the experience of risking a loss, tilting at windmills, than winning. His poker game at Balliol was distinguished by very high stakes and very poor players. For Aspinall, by now a cool, cerebral player with a magician's touch, they were sitting ducks.

Maxwell-Scott was extravagant in other ways. Happiest with a good meal and a choice claret (he is today one of England's most knowledgeable experts on wine), either after the races or before the cards, he ran up a staggering £400 buttery bill at college in one term (nearly £20,000 in today's money), and limply explained to his trustees that writing paper and books were *so* expensive. Thereafter Balliol limited his permitted expenditure to £100 a term.

The stories of Maxwell-Scott's gambling exploits do not deserve to be ignored by social historians, though doubtless they will make moralists shiver with indignation. Once he was driving to the races when he had a quite serious accident. No one else was involved and no one was in sight on the lonely country road. Maxwell-Scott should have received urgent medical attention, but his priorities determined other arrangements. A policeman drew up on a motorbike and offered to take the injured man to the nearest hospital. Maxwell-Scott required a telephone kiosk first. There he put through a call to his bookie and placed a bet on Brown Alligator at Kempton Park. Only afterwards did he consent to being taken to hospital. The horse won. On another occasion he visited London and stayed at the flat of a friend in Dolphin Square. The friend was out of town, leaving him free use of his home. Finding that he was out of cash, Maxwell-Scott took the entire wardrobe of his friend to the pawnbrokers, and put the proceeds on a horse. It won. He was then able to retrieve the clothes and put them back in the flat.

This, then, was the man who became John Aspinall's closest friend at Oxford. They could hardly have made a more disparate pair, Maxwell-Scott the languid, rich, confident aristocrat, Aspinall the cheeky, ebullient, entertaining *arriviste*, with an infectious braying laugh and hardly a penny to his name. At this stage, and for some years to come, it was certainly Aspinall the acolyte to Maxwell-Scott's sage. Today, Maxwell-Scott is the only person left who still calls him 'Jonas'.

Under his influence, Aspinall grew somewhat reckless himself. He once placed his entire grant, the £70 green government cheque, on a horse in the 2000 Guineas owned by Aly Khan and called Palestine. Odds were 2–7, so when it won he only came away with £90, but the risk was enormous. He shortly had a reputation as a tipster, and even his tutor, weary of asking him to do any work, would make the best of the situation and gain some tips for himself. It did not always work so neatly. There was one egregious snob and social climber who occupied Oscar Wilde's old rooms at Magdalen, and organised a First of June party to which he had asked far too many other undergraduates. He hadn't enough money to pay for the champagne, so asked Aspinall for a tip, and was given a horse called Golden Crocodile at Sandown. It was beaten by a head. The result was a social catastrophe for the poor man so bitter that it was written up in *Cherwell* as 'The Glorious Thirst of June'. Heavily embossed invitation cards had specified champagne, and guests were offered cider cup.

Such frivolities were not, on the whole, Aspinall's style, and as time went on he concentrated his energies more and more on the cards. He was fast becoming a mascot of one of the more outrageous sets in Oxford. There were other 'sets' of course, often better known. The Strawberry Set included Lord Blandford (later Duke of Marlborough), Richard Cochrane, Tony Berry (later Sir Anthony Berry, one of the fatalities of the Brighton Bomb in 1984), and Colin Tennant (later Lord Glenconner). Then there was the intellectual crowd which gathered around Kenneth Tynan, holding court at the Randolph Hotel and laying plans for the artistic conquest of London with earnest readings from Verlaine. Aspinall attended one of Tynan's meetings and impressed him with his rendering of a passage from *Dorian Gray*, but the artistic set possessed a vagueness which left him impatient. The set to which John Aspinall belonged was not socially smart like the first nor intellectually demanding like the second. Moreover, it centred not round a person, but an address, the rather *louche*, irregular lodging-house at 167 Walton Street which had more in common with Isherwood's pre-war Berlin than austere post-war Britain. It was here that Maxwell-Scott and Aspinall found the style which suited them and where Aspinall was to meet two brothers who were, in startlingly different ways, to have an even more profound and enduring effect upon his life. These were the Goldsmith boys.

The landlady of 167 Walton Street was a former vaudeville artist of uncertain age called Maxie, small, lumpy, with blonde hair (probably dyed) tied in a bun at the back, and red-rimmed eyes. Maxie was fond of her regular tipple. Her career in the theatre had prepared her magnificently for the job of landlady to several boisterous undergraduates, as she had herself lived in digs all over the country, and furthermore had learnt to appreciate the advantage of tolerance. Battling within her was another characteristic which antedated her theatrical experience, a determination not to be taken for granted. She often had cause to summon her anger, which could best be placated by an extra bottle of gin. Thus, Maxie was a curious mixture of screaming harridan ('Who do you think you are, making this mess on my carpet?'), and amused, maternal protector ('Lord love-a-duck, what these educated young gents get up to!').

What they got up to at 167 Walton Street was really quite a lot. On the top floor were two highly effete youths called David Borgia Duck and Martin Jones, at that time fascists and Firbank followers, in a room painted black with candles, lots of silver, and pictures of Franco and Mussolini on the walls. Below lived Jocelyn Baines (future biographer of Conrad, and suicide), often with a mistress. An occasional inhabitant was Toby Rowe, who even at that age ran a Raymond-Chandler-type bar called White's, with a restaurant upstairs, dedicated to selling drink to already drunken students. (White's had been an Oxford magnet in the High Street since the war.) Rowe later opened London's first homosexual club, the Rockingham in Soho, of which all the Walton Street gang, including Maxwell-Scott and Aspinall, were honorary members.

In the first-floor front room lived Milo Cripps (later Lord Parmoor), and it was in this room that Aspinall perfected his technique at poker. Once a week for eighteen months they met here, Pollock, Neave, 'Bouncer', Dunphy, Maxwell-Scott, and a new man from Magdalen called Teddy Goldsmith, an extraordinary restless spirit, forever pacing the room in an effort to expend surplus energy. From a rich Franco-German family, Goldsmith could afford to lose rather more than the others, but that was not as important as his endearing indifference and absent-mindedness. At eighteen, he was younger than the rest, but his intelligence was sharper. Goldsmith was the first person to give Aspinall the nickname 'Aspers', a neat sobriquet which has proved durable.

When Teddy's younger brother Jimmy Goldsmith, aged sixteen, appeared in Oxford having grown tired of Eton, he was immediately adopted into the group, where he flourished for a while. Jimmy later became one of the world's best backgammon players (indeed, it might be said that he plays backgammon still, on a colossal scale, with businesses). Aspers recognised in this ambitious youngster a kindred spirit – strong will, iron resolution, non-conformity to expected patterns of behaviour – an outsider through choice. Jimmy, too, spotted that Aspers was very much his own man, and it is possible that they saw in each other some kind of *Übermensch*.

Twenty years later, Teddy was the most trenchant ecologist in Britain, educating an entire generation in the wicked folly of man's spoliation of the planet and his betrayal of his trusteeship for all other plants and animals. Jimmy was busy making several fortunes with a view to exerting influence through wealth. They could hardly have been more dissimilar, yet in an odd way they each echo an aspect of John Aspinall's personality, and just as they have never been able to work as a team, so he has never quite reconciled the opposite demands of these two springs of personality.

The poker game in Milo Cripps's rooms had been in operation for some weeks before Aspers became a part of it, but he very shortly dominated the table. His technique was scarcely credible, and was based on a scrupulous examination of human nature. He seemed possessed of a unique microscope to look into the soul of his opponent and understand his psychology. He knew what card a man would play before he had decided to play it, because he knew his temperament and character. He was in control. He also appreciated the limits to which people would go, and pushed them just to the edge of that barrier with enormous charm. Being interested in the qualities of courage and deceit, he loved to *dare* people (although he always knew their response), and enjoyed the element of bluff (though he often sensed when the bluff would be called).

At times it seemed Aspinall's powers were uncanny, magical. No matter who dealt, or shuffled, or led, he appeared to know what cards were on the table and what were to come. 'Drawing to an inside straight' is a particularly risky business in poker. It means that one is looking for a missing middle card which would complete a straight run; a card at either end has a better chance of appearing, but the odds against the middle one turning up are more than 12–1. Aspers treated this nerve-racking situation with supreme nonchalance (or at least, that is what he showed). While everyone else sweated silently, he would surprisingly, coolly, turn up and show all four cards, ask the dealer to serve him a fifth, then refuse to look at it. Nevertheless he bet on it, and he won. That level of bluff and control made Aspinall a fearsome opponent and earned him a glamorous reputation. He understood that it was important and exhilarating to inject an element of folly into the game, which he did with panache and apparent indifference to the outcome.

He would not have said so, and probably the thought did not even occur to him, but what Aspinall was doing was putting existentialist principles to practical use. The idea that a man is not the sum of his essences, but creates himself daily by his acts, is one that accords well with Zulu attitudes and was most brilliantly embodied in Shaka, who not only created himself, but by a sequence of innovative decisions altered the character of the Zulu nation. Shaka was an example of the supremacy of will. At the card-table, John Aspinall also used his will in order to win. In fact, it was the challenge to will-power which attracted him to poker in the first place. He was the existentialist player *par excellence*. It is worth pausing to remember this, as Aspinall is very much the sum of his acts if anyone is, so that the technique of his poker has been applied to his life, and he has resolutely refused to be lumbered with any 'essences', immutable characteristics to drag with one through life like so much baggage. He has 'created' himself as he has gone along, in true Sartrean fashion. It is also important because the same penetrating understanding of another's psychology that enables him to predict responses has been brought to bear in his dealings with animals, and the same effort of will, bluff, and control has helped him 'dare' the animals to let him be their companion.

Nor must one forget that there is nothing cruel or even unpleasant about this challenging stance. The animals have accepted Aspinall because they *like* him, and forty years ago the gamblers who assembled in the front first floor room at 167 Walton Street to be worked over by Aspers, did so cheerfully, beguiled by his charm. Teddy Goldsmith and Milo Cripps lost modest amounts to Aspers week after week, and loved it. One who was there has said, 'He gets a man to like him, looks him in the eye, plays his hand, takes money from him, and the man enjoys it.' Or again, 'Aspers knew the price of a masochistic thrill and wouldn't overcharge for it.'

Of course, the gaming did get out of hand long before the end of term, when credit was crossing the table in lieu of cash. 'I'll see you for £200,' from a boy who couldn't pay his bus fare. John Pollock started losing a great deal of money, which everyone knew he didn't have, so that the credits happily exchanged were like something out of Alice's Wonderland. On one occasion, Desmond Dunphy lost £250 to Baines and Cripps, which he paid with a cheque drawn on a bank in Croydon. Wisely, the winners hired a taxi and took it all the way from Oxford to Croydon to cash the cheque before it was reduced to mere paper. (Cripps bought a Henry Moore drawing with the proceeds.)

On the way to the races, Maxwell-Scott decided to stand everyone lunch in a hotel restaurant. When the bill came, he discovered he had insufficient funds to cover it, so he declared his intention of using the table-cloth as a cheque. This was, as it happened, perfectly legal. The amount was written on the table-cloth, adding something by way of a generous tip, and adding also the cost of the table-cloth itself. A 2d. stamp was stuck on it, and Maxwell-Scott signed over the stamp, folded the cloth, and left it for the hotel proprietor to despatch to Maxwell-Scott's bank in London. It was the first, and presumably the last, bouncing table-cloth in the bank's history. Maxwell-Scott generally exhausted his allowance after the first few weeks of term.

He and Aspinall would then buy books on credit from Blackwell's and sell them in London at half-price, simply in order to generate some cash; their parents would have to pick up the bill some four months later.

Aspinall's cousin Stuart Ross was also at Oxford in these days, one of the few to be engaged in serious study. He was reading Philosophy, Politics and Economics at Pembroke College, and good-naturedly called on Aspers at his lodgings several times, to be told unfailingly by the landlady that 'Mr Aspinall was at the races.' He gave up. One day, however, Aspers turned up at Pembroke, full of affability and interest in Ross's academic career, and after a lengthy chat, just as he was going to the door, let drop, as casually as he could, 'I suppose you couldn't lend me fifteen pounds, could you? To get a good degree I need a lot of text-books, but the money has run out.' Ross also needed text-books, and he was at least likely to read them, so he refused. The story, flimsy enough on the face of it, is interesting for its sequel. Some thirty years later, when Aspinall learned that his cousin had fallen on hard times, he equipped his entire house with all the paraphernalia necessary for his work, and paid off all his debts, on the grounds that Ross had been very kind to him at Oxford, though they had rarely met since.

The merry-go-round continued for the best part of eighteen months. A drunken breakfast at Walton Street would be prepared by the long-suffering Maxie for her household of eccentrics. (With gamblers, 'queers' and fascists distributed on different floors, and a constant flow of brilliant repartee between the three, it was soon the most unusual house in Oxford.) Then the inveterate gamblers would play poker in the morning, go to the races in the afternoon, dog-racing at Littlemore in the evening, and perhaps another card game until late at night. Aspinall was fundamentally changed by his meeting with Maxwell-Scott and his adherence to the raffish set at No. 167. In place of the salmon-pink suit, he now sported, metaphorically that is, plus-fours; in place of the ebony cane, he carried a copy of *Sporting Life*; in place of the sonnets of Lord Alfred Douglas he was reading the Form Book; and in place of the snuff-box in a waistcoat pocket there were betting slips. The transformation was complete.

It will no doubt seem strange to a later, less inhibited generation that very few of these robust and energetic

young men had any sexual experience whatever, nor any
compelling need for it. At 167 Walton Street sex played a
part in the imaginations of the inhabitants and visitors, but
none in reality. There were a few exceptions, remarkable for
being exceptional. Everyone knew that Jocelyn Baines had a
mistress, as also did an elegant Belgian baron called Peebles
Friesen, but these were the only two who could be identified.
John Pollock's homosexual adventures were fascinating, if
only because he challenged convention to indulge his chosen
way of life, and triumphed. But the rest?

There were a number of ladies available for decora-
tive purposes – Hilary Sarson of the vinegar family; Sarah
Macmillan, niece of the Duke of Devonshire; Antonia
Pakenham, large and weighed down with heavy beads and
bangles, who would one day be Lady Antonia Fraser. There
was also a pushy, persistent girl called Margaret, anxious
to be admitted to parties, who later married a man called
Thatcher and was Britain's first woman Prime Minister.
Aspers himself was sometimes seen with a beautiful girl
by the name of Ann Braithwaite, eye-catching and elegant.
She was a trophy more than a mate, and he once felt bound,
at the age of twenty-three, to ask Anthony Blond how one
should kiss a girl. At twenty-five he was free enough to boast
that he was still virginal, and not fear derision. With all these
men, high spirits and self-conscious sophistication blended
astonishingly with bald naïvety, but with Aspers there was
another dimension; he knew that to make a mark in the world
he must not dally with women before time. They would have
their place, but must not be allowed to dominate attention or
deflect a man from his ambition.

Aspinall's Oxford career did not end in glory; neither did
it end with a whimper. There are various versions of the day
he and Maxwell-Scott missed their examinations, all hilarious
and vivid. The exams happened, by dreadful mischance, to
coincide with Royal Ascot. Of course, there was no doubt
in their minds which event must take precedence. Aspinall
went so far as to enquire whether the date of the examination
might be changed! That was out of the question. One hot

day in the summer of 1950, then, two students turned up
in the examination hall unaccountably dressed in severe grey
overcoats which they refused to remove. Each in turn told the
elderly invigilator that he felt giddy and unwell, and tottered
so dangerously that it looked as if he were about to faint. The
invigilator, either solicitous for their welfare or fearful of the
consequences, earnestly advised them both to retire to their
lodgings until they felt better. With weary gratitude they
trundled out, then nipped round the corner to a waiting hired
Daimler, which promptly drove them to Ascot.

Maxwell-Scott was granted the rare award of an *aegrotat*.
John Aspinall received nothing at all.

Others in the Walton Street Set did better, despite their
boast of being 'failures', a cover for the truth, which was
that they were all outsiders in their various ways; few would
progress to an ordinary career.

Back at home, Aspinall busied himself with gardening
chores. George Osborne had since inherited the baronetcy
and was now Sir George, and his wife, now Lady Osborne,
would henceforth be known by everyone, including her son
John, as 'Lady O.' They had moved from Uckfield to the
family home of the Osbornes, a handsome old house at
Framfield called The Grange, in 95 acres of grounds which
boasted a garden, two tennis courts, a small lake, and two
little woods. The house was noisy with young children, as
Lady O. had borne Sir George two sons and two daughters
by this time, and Aspinall was the lone representative of
her former marriage, Chips having moved on to pursue
his medical career. Anthony Blond called upon him at the
Grange, and found him in the garden lifting a huge trunk of
ancient wood which three men together could not budge. He
was a man of enormous strength and determination, but still
without a properly focused aim.

Life at Framfield was in no sense luxurious. There were
two cooks, Ada and Mary, and two gardeners, Old Weaver
(aged seventy) and Young Weaver (fifty), but that still left a
lot of work for Lady O. herself. Her four Osborne children,
Peter, Jennifer, James and Carol, each had specified stations

in the house which they had to run to with a bucket at times
of heavy rainfall, such was the condition of the roof. They
had only two family holidays throughout their childhood, in
Truro, so they were hardly spoilt. Their one great pride and
fascination was in their glamorous older brother, who, with
his leonine appearance – a mane of hair above a vast double-
breasted overcoat topped by wide beaver collar – made him
unlike anyone else they knew. He told them a bedtime story,
mischievously entitled 'Next Instalment', which related terrifying tales of the school bully, and would withhold the next
instalment if they declined one of his 'dares' – for instance to
dive into the makeshift swimming-pool for 10s. By this mixture of bribery and braggadocio, John taught all his siblings
to swim and to ride. Good Sir George was perplexed by his
startling stepson, landed upon him as a bonus to marriage,
and did not know what to make of him. Nevertheless, he
determined to try and steer the headstrong young man
towards stability.

Sir George had one influential neighbour at the Grange,
who lived in a very modern, avant-garde house nearby. He
was Sir William Emsley Carr, proprietor of the *News of the
World* and a figure of some eminence in the newspaper world.
An interview with the great man was arranged for John, who
took the train up to London and saw him in his private office.
Gruff and blunt, Sir William asked him simply, 'Well, what
do you want to do?' Aspinall said he wanted to be the racing
correspondent on the *News of the World*. Sir William called
in a tired, stooped, shabby man in his fifties, a typical Fleet
Street hack. 'That was Mercury,' he said. 'Do you want to
be like him? He's at the top of his profession, so that's all
you can expect.'

Despite this discouragement, a job was arranged for
Aspinall as understudy to James Park, the doyen of London's
racing correspondents, on the *Evening Standard*. It was his
part to attend race meetings and cable the results back to Fleet
Street, a task he undertook cheerfully, though he did not care
for the regulation that racing correspondents must not bet,
and generally disregarded it. One day, Park announced that

he would have to go away, and Aspinall must stand in for him at the Epsom Spring Meeting, where the very important Great Metropolitan Handicap was due to run the next day. 'You write the article, and you make the selection for our readers as to which horse will win.'

There was a horse in the race belonging to the Aga Khan called Eclat, which loved running second. Aspinall wrote that he found it impossible to predict which horse would win, but he could virtually guarantee Eclat would be second. The editor was furious; no tipster had ever recommended the *second* in a race; Aspinall must be out of his mind. As it happened, the winner was a 33–1 outsider, Burnt Brown, tipped by no one, and Eclat came in second at 100–8, so Aspinall's tip may well have been a coup. But it was too late. He was fired before he could get into print, and his Fleet Street career had lasted precisely six weeks. It was perhaps the only time that Aspinall declined to stick his neck out.

He nevertheless had some success privately. On behalf of a new friend, Gerry Albertini, he bought a horse which made some money for them both, called Simon de Montfort. (He could not afford to buy anything for himself.) It cost £300 and won three races in a row, at Wolverhampton, Hurst Park and Wincanton, netting for its owner nearly £16,000, of which Aspinall received a cut. At Leicester the horse won by fifteen lengths. As a result of going to the races virtually every day since coming down from Oxford and mixing with wealthy punters, he was building a reputation as an expert on long-distance hurdle racing. When times were bad, he would retire to Framfield Grange and recuperate there.

The Osbornes despaired of his ever settling down to a proper job. He seemed to regard himself as unemployable, a misfit, but Lady O., brought up in the hard-working colonial administrative class, would not accept what she considered defeatism, and constantly nagged him to find a niche in the commercial world. He was now twenty-six, far too old to treat life in such a cavalier fashion. The job on the *Evening Standard* had fallen through; he must make another attempt.

Eventually, Sir George had to find a job for him behind his back. Another friend, Colonel Hughie Boyes, treated John in an avuncular fashion and took an interest when Sir George told him of their predicament one day while they were out shooting together. Colonel Boyes, whose business was in Nigerian tin, arranged an appointment for Aspinall with John Holt and Company, a shipping line and West African trader in Liverpool, and even paid his fare of £7.10s. Aspers felt he had run out of excuses, so set off glumly for Liverpool, with the exhortation ringing in his ears, 'Don't let Hughie down.'

The interview went disastrously well for Aspinall. The last thing he wanted was a real job, but nothing he said was able to cloud their enthusiasm. The Colonel had prepared the way with a fulsome recommendation of the young man's merits and character. Now, the board was further impressed by his having been to Rugby, by his having played in the first XV, by his having volunteered for the Royal Marines. It was going too well. Why had he volunteered? Because he had been asked to leave Rugby. Even better! Beaming smiles greeted every confession of unconventionality. To what rank did he rise in the Marines? None; he got himself demobbed because he was doing too nicely and did not envisage sitting examinations and staying another year. He did not want a military career. Then what? Oxford. Degree? No, the finals coincided with Royal Ascot and he fancied a horse in the Gold Cup called Supertello. It won at 7–1. What an enterprising young man!

Back at Framfield, both Boyes and Aspinall received letters from John Holt and Company. Boyes was warmly thanked for having introduced the Company to such an extremely promising and charming young man. Aspinall was told that he had been accepted, and was congratulated on his appointment. He was to work for the next three years in Lagos, and would learn the business from the bottom, starting as a salesman in the Chief Store. He should report to Southampton in two weeks' time, when the ship was due to sail for Africa. The letter enclosed all necessary tickets for the journey, and furthermore a cheque for £123.10s. to purchase tropical clothes; the cheque could be used only at Austin Reed.

Aspinall was, for once, at a loss. He felt trapped, condemned, about to be exiled. There was never any doubt in his mind that he would have to wriggle out of the commitment somehow, even if it meant risking the displeasure of his stepfather, a man who was consistently good to him and whom he admired. There appeared to be no delicate way of escape; Aspinall certainly chose the most mischievous.

He duly presented himself at Austin Reed and selected a salesman whom he thought might be open to mild corruption. He persuaded the salesman to give him cash for the cheque and at the same time prepare a receipt which he would sign to confirm that he had in fact bought tropical clothes. In return for this favour, Aspinall would be happy to accept a mere £90, instead of the full amount for which the cheque was drawn.

With the £90 in his pocket, he backed five winners in a row, and was soon in sufficient funds to send the £123.10s. back to John Holt and Company. He felt his luck changed from that moment. More important, he knew that he would never again be interviewed for anything. Wherever his future lay, it was not in any corporate organisation, not in any team, and not for any regular salary. He would follow no existing path; he would instead cut one for himself.

There then occurred a strange meeting, so improbable and so dramatic that it might easily have appeared in particularly extravagant fiction. It served to remind John Aspinall once more that he was unlike other men, and with reason. But first we must depict events which led to this meeting.

Since coming down from Oxford, Aspinall's finances had remained erratic, unsteady. He still had no money of his own, and was often in debt through a combination of high living and small gambling. Mixing in circles where everyone had debts, and was bailed out in classical fashion by rich parents, he was undoubtedly living beyond his means without in any way causing himself unnecessary anxiety. He would be well-off one month, and spending lavishly, then back in debt the next, and looking for help. In both conditions he was cheerful, and never once felt that debts would sweep him away, an attitude both attractive and, in the years to come when he would have to weather several catastrophes, highly beneficial. Moreover, he always paid his debts back, and conversely never expected those who owed him money to pay until they were able. The habit of paying 'on the dot', so commonplace in the commercial world, has always been foreign to his nature.

His stepfather helped out whenever he could, without recrimination or advice (and Aspinall has ever since paid him back a thousand times over by looking after George's descendants, his own half-brothers and -sisters), but his means were strictly limited. One day he decided to approach his own father, Robert Aspinall, now retired in England. Summoned to meet him at the East India Sports Club, John went with some curiosity but no trepidation to an encounter with a man he barely knew, who had in the past supported him and his mother financially. He determined to come straight to the point. Oxford had left him with debts from which he had not fully recovered, he explained.

'What do you come to me for?' asked Robby.

'I was hoping, sir, you might find your way to lending me £2,000 for a few months.'

'I will do nothing of the sort. It's time you knew that you will never be able to come to me with stories of this kind. You're nothing to do with me at all. I'm not your father, you see. I'm afraid that from now on you are on your own.'

Aspinall left the East India Sports Club in a state of elation. He was not hurt, angry, ashamed, nor in any way bowled over by the news. But he was undeniably excited, and consumed with curiosity. He had already discovered that Colonel Aspinall had assumed his surname; he had been born Stivala, of Maltese stock, and had chosen the name Aspinall for no discernible reason, presumably to evade the stigma of sounding foreign. That was interesting enough, but the news that Robert Stivala Aspinall was only his putative father was irresistible.

He took the train straight down to Framfield and confronted his mother. Lady O. at first denied the imputation and called her first husband a scoundrel and rogue. There were loud sobs and much slamming of doors. Aspinall calmed her and told her there was nothing whatever for her to be ashamed of, but she must understand that he naturally would like to know who was his father. Nobody would blame her. Reassured, she told for the first time the story of her second son's conception.

His father had been a penniless professional soldier, and irresistibly handsome. She had been lonely and unhappy, she said, and could not gather the strength to turn him away. There was never any future in the affair, and they had not met frequently. John had been conceived after a dance one evening, beneath a tamarisk tree. Robby had been told eventually, and had taken it well, continuing to send John through Rugby despite his knowledge that they had no affinity. The man's name was George McIlree Bruce (nicknamed 'McKay') and he was serving in India with the 2nd battalion, the Lincolnshire Regiment when he met 'Polly' Aspinall in 1925.

With this scant information, Aspinall set about tracking down his natural father, to the intense surprise of Lady O., who had never suspected his latent depth of interest in ancestry and identity. Poring through the army lists and tracing his career in various archives, after some weeks he had pieced together a more or less ample picture.

George McIlree Stanton Bruce had been born in Canada in 1896, then educated at Haileybury and Sandhurst. He served in France during the First World War, was wounded twice and awarded the MC. His Commanding Officer selected him as proxy Company Commander to take over his position and duties if he should ever fall in battle, a sure indication of the regard in which he was held. After service in India, he was selected to raise the Malay Regiment in 1933, and was its Commander until 1938, when he was honoured with the OBE. His training of the Malay Regiment brought forth fine fruit when that regiment distinguished itself in the Second World War. Bruce was afterwards entrusted with raising and training the 82nd West African Division, which he subsequently led.

He appeared to be living quietly in retirement somewhere on a small pension; though he had risen to the rank of Major-General, his pension was that of a major. Aspinall traced his most recent address, a flat in Campden Hill Square, London, and with no warning or announcement presented himself at the door of the flat one day towards the end of 1952.

When the door opened, John Aspinall saw himself aged sixty-three, 'like Dorian Gray come to life'. Bruce stood under a light and could be seen clearly, whereas Aspinall was hidden in the gloom of the corridor.

'Who are you?' he asked.

'I'm your son.'

At this, Bruce took him by the elbow and motioned him in under the light. 'Good God,' he said, 'You're Polly's boy, aren't you?' It was not really a question, and he did not need to wait for an answer. 'This calls for a celebration.' Indeed it did; Bruce had never once seen his son in twenty-six years. He went straight to the cupboard and produced his cherished stock, just half a bottle of whisky.

The details of the conversation that took place that day need not concern us. Just three circumstances are significant. The Major-General occupied himself in retirement by painting meticulously detailed regimental portraits, finely drawn and absolutely correct figures in uniforms of all periods. These he showed to his son, letting slip the comment that he sent them occasionally to a shop in Bond Street, Fores, where they stayed for years on end; few seemed interested in their purchase, but never mind, he was happy painting them. They were priced at 4 guineas.

Days later, Aspinall went to the shop posing as a Greek. He expressed interest in the regimental portraits which were not exactly on display but hiding in a corner. There were twelve of them. The Greek stranger bought the whole collection on the spot, for cash, and commissioned some more for delivery as early as possible.

The next time Aspinall visited his father, the old man was in an especially good mood. 'We've got something else to celebrate today,' he said. 'Some Greek lunatic has bought all my pictures and wants more of the things.' This time there was a whole bottle of whisky in the cupboard. He died a few years later without ever having discovered the true identity of the purchaser. Today, John Aspinall still has five of the portraits, others having been given to his children; they are his only family heirlooms.

He confessed he really loved Sir George when he realised, following this strange encounter, what the man had had to accept.

Aspinall also discovered two circumstances of his ancestry which were of interest. Firstly, his grandfather had been a big tin-horn gambler in Canada. Secondly, the Bruces had emigrated to Canada from Scotland. Their original home had been Wick in Caithness, an area peopled almost entirely by those of Nordic descent, with scarcely a smattering of Celtic blood or influence. This explained Aspinall's striking blue eyes and blond hair, and possibly much more than that. The Nordic approach to animals was in direct opposition to that inherited from the Judaeo-Christian tradition. Whereas two millennia of Christian doctrine had taught that animals were soulless and therefore inferior to man, who alone was made in the image of God, the much older traditions of Old Norse literature, reflecting the attitudes of generations, always showed animals as equals, worthy of respect and admiration, even capable of teaching man some lessons, if he would but heed them.

3
The Floating Gambler

Aspinall continued to hang around race-courses for some months until Ian Maxwell-Scott came up with a proposal. Though Maxwell-Scott had managed to throw away most of his money at Oxford, he was still the ultimate part-beneficiary of a family trust of which his mother had control. He now persuaded her to chip some of it off for immediate use so that he could set himself up in business. The 'business' he had in mind was that of course bookie, peregrinating from one meeting to another throughout the season, and his proposal was that Aspinall should help him.

Not being overwhelmed with alternatives, Aspinall accepted. Maxwell-Scott's book was called 'Mittens', an allusion to his habit of wearing them at every race, and it began inauspiciously hidden in the back row of bookies in the Silver Ring, the least fashionable ring of the course. The top class of clientele went to the Club Enclosure, after which there was Tattersall's, which cost £1.10s. for entrance, and below that the Silver Ring, entry into which was gained with a mere 10s. and which was thronged with the great mass of ordinary punters, the *hoi polloi* of the race-track. Here there were five rows of bookies, almost entirely Jewish, and Mittens had to struggle to be noticed or heard amid the din, with its board and its tickets and its two posh young men lurking at the back. From this pitch, farthest away from the stands and the punters, the only way to claim attention was to offer better prices than those in front. If the favourite in the race was running at odds of 6–4, Mittens would shout out 13–8 and hope to pull in enough customers to compensate for the slightly higher odds they were offering.

The history of Mittens was short and sad. Maxwell-Scott was such a 'goer', so inveterate a punter, that he would leave Aspinall in charge of the pitch and run around the ring placing bets with other bookies. He had a considerable flair for long-shot betting, especially in the National Hunt. After an entire afternoon of this activity, he would go off to spend the evening dog-racing (not the act of a careful man), then would join a floating game of *chemin-de-fer* run by a man called German Willy, which was well known to be crooked. Aspinall, who at this stage had not yet played in a 'chemmy' game, remonstrated with his friend, who merely replied that there was no other game in town. As a result, whatever profits Maxwell-Scott made with Mittens in the afternoon dissolved before the end of the evening. His final collapse came when, after only a few weeks, he met with a blizzard of eleven out of twelve favourites winning in two days at Kempton, which effectively wiped him out.

Aspinall then took over his equipment, consisting of hod, board, umbrella and various bits and pieces which make a bookie, and with £500 generously advanced by his stepfather started his own book called 'Aspers', with tickets proudly bearing the motto 'Aspers never owes'. He also inherited Maxwell-Scott's chalkie and clerk (Alf and Ted) as well as his tick-tack man. 'Aspers' did rather better than 'Mittens', lasting a total of seven months in 1953, despite energetic attempts by other bookies to freeze him out. Some of his old Oxford friends, like Anthony Blond or Alan Clark, would turn up to laugh at Aspers slumming in the Silver Ring, but in a small way he was successful. Several thousand pounds were made in profit, though Aspinall had little to show for it, not because he speculated on the dogs like Maxwell-Scott, but because he enjoyed spending on good living. The switch from 'Mittens' to 'Aspers' on the race-track may be said to symbolise the alteration in the relative fortunes of the two friends, and to mark the beginning of Aspinall's ascendancy.

For another seven months Aspinall and Maxwell-Scott, with astonishing cheek and nerve for their age, stayed in one of London's most exclusive hotels, the Ritz, where they occupied Room 505 just down the corridor from the multi-millionaire Gulbenkian's suite – 501, 502, and 503. In this room, presumably unknown to the management, they ran a small game of husband-and-wife poker, the takings from which enabled them to pay their bills, at least for a while. At other times, they would move out temporarily and hold the game at the more banal Park Lane Hotel. Anthony Blond remembers one evening when he was playing at the Ritz and Maxwell-Scott's voice was heard from Piccadilly below, screaming for money. Aspinall went to the window, detached a £1 note from his pocket and let it float down on the air. Unfortunately, a busker spotted it coming, and waved up his gratitude for such largesse to the window above; but he had not noticed the needy Maxwell-Scott, with a nose like a greyhound who snatched it from his imminent grasp and hurtled down the street. (Another Maxwell-Scott incident dates from this time. He is alleged to have given a cheque in return for the cash in the collection box at the Brompton Oratory, after a mass he attended; the fate of the cheque is unknown.)

As well as poker, a great deal of betting on horses operated from this room, through the discreet agency of a messenger-boy called Bishop, who regularly sped along the long corridor to place bets on behalf of Messrs Aspinall and Maxwell-Scott. Thirty years later, the artful Bishop became head receptionist in charge of the hotel's main restaurant.

The Manager of the Ritz, Mr Schwentner, gradually realised that the account for Room 505 was not always paid on time, and that the funds for eventual settlement came from sources of irregular fertility. He took to the habit of waiting at the bottom of the stairs for the young gentlemen to appear and accosting them directly. One day the bill outstanding had reached the impossible sum of £700, far beyond their ability to recoup from poker, and Mr Schwentner presented them with an ultimatum: either they pay up within forty-eight hours or they would be out on the street!

Aspinall knew perfectly well that the situation which now faced them was dire indeed. Maxwell-Scott, on the other hand, neither recognised the imminent likelihood of disgrace nor seemed to care about the consequences. It was left to Aspinall to come up with the solution. He raised £150 by cashing cheques with a series of trusting (or tolerant) night-club owners, and declared his intention of putting the whole lot on a horse called Rock Spring, due to race at Wye, which would raise enough to cover the debt comfortably. Leaving instructions with Maxwell-Scott to get in touch with four friends who could come to their rescue if the horse did not win, he boarded the train for Kent while Maxwell-Scott remained behind in the Ritz with four telephone numbers and addresses. The four presumptive knights-errant were Jimmy Goldsmith, Richard Parkes, Olga Deterding and Gerry Albertini.

Rock Spring almost saved the day. He won by a short head, but an objection that he bumped the horse which came in second was upheld and victory was snatched from his (and Aspinall's) grasp. Aspinall spent the one-and-a-half-hour train journey back to London in utter gloom and dejection, until he realised that one of his four chums would by now have been traced and would produce the wherewithal for survival.

The Hall Porter at the Ritz, Victor Legge, was a reliable ally. He always tried to warn Aspinall if the Manager was lurking in wait so that a circuitous route to the room could avoid an unwelcome encounter. On this occasion, it was made clear that his only safe option was to use the service stairs at the back of the hotel; even then, he crept up the staircase like a furtive adulterer. When he came to the corridor, he saw half a dozen waiters loaded down with platters bearing viands, pheasants, salmon, champagne, buckets of ice, which he assumed were destined for Gulbenkian. Until, that is, he watched the waiters take the whole feast to Room 505.

Perhaps Maxwell-Scott was celebrating his successful hunt and was entertaining Deterding, Goldsmith, Parkes and Albertini to dinner by way of thanks? Not a bit! He was lying in bed partaking of a final private supper, and complaining the while about the quality of the pheasant. Moreover, he had made no effort the whole day long to find any of the four musketeers. Besides, only one of them was in England, Richard Parkes, and no one knew quite where. Aspinall was now deep in real consternation. He had only £30 left, barely enough to pay for the food in the room, let alone the enormous account. Just then, by one of those most fortuitous coincidences which make life attractive to a gambler, Victor called up from the desk below and said there was a gentleman to see them, should he show him up or say they were out? The gentleman's name was Parkes.

It need hardly be said that Richard Parkes was given the most genuinely-felt welcome of his life that evening. He opened the proceedings by asking Aspinall to cash a cheque for £20, to which he speedily assented over dinner that night. Aspinall in return suggested that he and Parkes should set up a new book together. They could call it Jonathan and Carlyle (the first for 'John' Aspinall, the second for Richard Edward 'Carlyle' Parkes), and the resonant name might help them acquire a more wealthy clientele than they had counted upon in earlier ventures. They would need about £1,000 to start it up. Aspinall would make all the arrangements. Could Parkes perhaps provide the capital?

Richard Parkes handed over a cheque for £1,000, out of which, the next morning, with some arrogance, they paid Mr Schwentner in full and cleared the account. Schwentner was almost as furious to be paid as he would have been had they not paid, as he had for months resisted the assurances of Victor and Bishop that those rascals in 505 would come through in the end, and was not happy to be proven wrong. He was cheated of the sweet vengeance of having them removed by force.

Jonathan and Carlyle was not to be a bookmaker on course, as 'Mittens' and 'Aspers' had been, but an S.P. (Starting

Price) office in London with some cachet, dependent for its business upon the establishment of reputation among the gambling fraternity rather than casual trade. Essential to its success was the right choice of address, and on this point Aspinall made a disastrous error at the very beginning. He was offered premises at 33 Dryden Chambers, opposite Bourne and Hollingsworth in Oxford Street, with two rooms and several telephones. The address had a nice ring about it, and the rent was remarkably cheap; on both counts he felt he had found a bargain, and took it.

What he did not know was that Dryden Chambers had acquired a bad reputation. The address was so well known that many punters hesitated to place bets with any book-maker in the building; of all the houses in London, Aspinall could scarcely have chosen one less suited to his plans. When he and Maxwell-Scott attempted to open up trade accounts with other bookmakers, according to established custom, they discovered that Dryden Chambers was an obstacle to negotiations which it would require all Aspinall's charm to overcome. They did overcome it, after a fashion, but were reduced to hustling round dog-tracks in the evening to pick up business, and had so little genuine trade they were obliged to punt themselves. It was an oddly clumsy start to the career of London's most famous casino proprietor.

One good client they secured through the recommenda-tion of Victor, the porter at the Ritz, was a French-Canadian called Jean Carique. Suave and sophisticated, he worked with four or five large and respectable bookmakers, but he also placed a number of bets with Aspinall every day, not because he could rely upon the best odds, but because he liked the man and admired his pluck. He enjoyed Aspinall's stories and used often to give him lunch just to hear them. If it were not for Jean Carique, Jonathan and Carlyle would have folded much earlier than it did. A number of rogues had, at the very beginning, almost sunk the operation by not paying up for bets they had placed. Sometimes Lady O. would sit in the office and loudly berate people who won too frequently, following them into the street. Fleeing, they called her 'Al Capone with a shopping basket'.

At the other end of the market, they were assisted by an artful dodger of an Irishman called Aubrey Wallace, whose sister later opened the Casanova Casino. Known as 'Gunboat' Wallace after a notably hopeless film character, because everything he touched turned to dross, he was employed by Aspinall to tour the markets of Billingsgate and Smithfield picking up small bets from the porters. This was strictly illegal, of course, but Jonathan and Carlyle were in theory ignorant of Gunboat's methods and only knew that he turned up regularly with a tin box containing cash which he then invested on horses. They would naturally assume the money was his.

Gunboat Wallace had a habit of turning up late, panting, a few minutes after the first race had finished. It did not take long to work out what he had been doing. He would write the name of the winner of the first race on many of the betting slips before he handed them in to Aspinall, and leave with a handsome profit. This little scheme also cost the firm a substantial amount of money. With one thing and another, Jonathan and Carlyle was lucky to last six months, before Aspinall was obliged to seek other ways of making a living.

Groping towards a way of achieving the life style that he wanted – mixing with big spenders, dining out, above all being able to act as lavish and impressive host to his friends – Aspinall had already realised that he could not continue to buck the odds all his life. He had made the progression from punter to bookie, from risking his own money to risking other people's, had crossed from one side of the gambling world to the other. In this sense, John Aspinall was never a gambler in thrall to a compulsion, and from 1954 onwards he played less and less (except, much later, when times were bad and a risk was preferable to oblivion). He was, moreover, still a poor man, with no capital whatever. Had he been a saver instead of a spender, he could by now have accumulated enough to afford himself a very comfortable life indeed, which would alone have been a remarkable achievement after the £1 a week he had been used to only six years before. But a 'comfortable' life did not entice him, nor, despite appearances, was money important enough to be cherished, flattered and protected in this way. He looked for life in the grand manner, outgoing and hedonistic but unselfconscious, and the idea of saving up for a rainy day never crossed his mind. He had to find a way whereby he could make an income from gambling on a regular basis.

In 1955 Aspinall began to organise gambling parties in a flat he took in Hans Crescent, behind Harrods. The games were baccarat and roulette, and the system was that one of his rich friends would finance the evening, provide the bank and all the costs, while he would take care of the organisation, invite guests, arrange food, and so on. At the end of the evening he and the backer would split the profit, if any. It was fraught with chance, for the roulette wheel is notoriously risky. Some nights they would lose more than they won on other nights. There seemed to be no security or permanence in this method, though Aspinall knew that he was approaching the formula that would direct his fortune; it needed one small permutation to make it perfect. Also, of course, the parties were so successful from a social point of view, so well organised and run, that he laid the foundations in this year for the reputation that would ultimately bring him the best clientele. The rich and the aristocratic were beginning to hear of John Aspinall, and to welcome news of one of his parties.

The nascent regard for Aspinall's abilities suffered a harsh setback unwittingly at the hands of his old friend from Oxford, Anthony Blond. When Blond's parents were away in New York, he and his brother decided to give an enormous party at the parental home, a lush Tudor manor outside East Grinstead. Food, drink, waiters, girlfriends, all were laid on with abandon. Aspinall was invited and urged to bring friends with him, so he turned up with Maxwell-Scott, Vere Harmsworth, Gerry Albertini and others, and also the kit necessary for roulette and twenty-one. Blond had set aside one very elegant room for the gambling, but he was apprehensive and on edge. Although he had permission from his parents for the party, he had not mentioned that it would include a gambling-room, for which permission would almost certainly have been withheld. For him, anyway, the gambling was an incidental, additional treat, whereas for Aspinall it was the main purpose of the evening.

Everyone appeared to win at Aspinall's twenty-one game, including Blond's Uncle Jack, who walked out of the room with £40. Aspinall was down by several hundred pounds and needed another hour or two to recoup. At one o'clock in the morning he produced the kit for *chemin-de-fer*, and Blond became increasingly worried. His mother's loyal butler, Ripley, threatened to telephone New York and reveal all, which Blond dare not risk in any circumstances. As Ripley was stone deaf, it is unlikely that he would have carried out his threat, but the danger was nevertheless present. Blond went into the room and confiscated the cards. More cards were produced, more were confiscated. Aspinall could scarcely believe what was happening. Blond was telling everyone to get out, to go to an adjacent room where there was some television to watch (television then being a relatively new toy), and Aspinall was yelling that he must not remove the crowd and leave them stranded. In what Anthony Blond calls 'an atmosphere of appalling ill-will', Aspinall and Maxwell-Scott drove off into the night, cursing him.

The humiliation as well as the financial loss was a severe blow to Aspinall. He was made to look foolish, his reputation undercut and left wobbling, his losses large enough to set him back a few months. It was also one of the first occasions when he allowed his latent fierce temper to show. Aspinall has been known to go berserk at times, to work himself up into a blather of verbal assault, turn red in the face, and leave his opponent reeling with astonishment and fear. Some have suspected the attack may be self-induced. Whatever the case, it was made clear to all present then that John Aspinall, for all his charm, was a dangerous man to cross. Despite his admiration for those qualities of nobility and magnanimity he discovered in the course of his mythomania, he did not always call upon them in himself when disappointment was bitter or disloyalty harsh.

Aspinall more or less stumbled into the crucial decision of his life, the solution he had been groping for, by accident. Under a statute dating from 1854, the law did not allow games of chance to occur in the same place habitually, a regulation which effectively condemned gamblers to the condition of itinerants, and made them dependent upon someone with organising ability to plan and see a game through. Very few such people were in evidence. One who now came into Aspinall's ken was Leslie Price, universally known as 'The Vicar', mainly because he looked and talked like one.

The Vicar organised games of *chemin-de-fer* for the upper-middle-class clientele, solid citizens with money but little glamour. Towards the end of 1955, he met Aspinall at the races and invited him to a game in a flat on the top floor of a house in Park Lane, south of Curzon Street and near where the Hilton Hotel now stands. Aspinall accepted, though he had no money at all and would need to borrow in order to participate. He went to the game with two friends, Dominick Elwes, a bright, handsome, and extremely entertaining man, and Dominick's current girlfriend, Sarah Chester-Beatty, who later married Lord Brooke. This was the first professional *chemin-de-fer* game Aspinall had ever attended.

The players that evening were Stephen O'Flaherty, a highly successful businessman with the concession for Bentley and Volkswagen in Ireland; Susan Pulbrook, wife of Sir Eustace Pulbrook, the chairman of Lloyds; Johnnie Phrantzes, attaché at the Greek Embassy and a somewhat Byzantine figure; Johnnie Holbeach, the gin heir; and Nick Ackroyd, stockbroker. Aspinall and Elwes naturally lost and were obliged to borrow from Sarah in order to pay; she gave £300 to Aspinall and £100 to Elwes (who was understandably peeved that it was not the other way round). But the loss was as nothing compared to the lessons which Aspinall learnt that night or the vision which opened up before him.

With his peculiarly hypnotic sing-song voice, the Vicar took Aspinall aside and explained the attractions of the system. 'Very nice little game,' he intoned, '£1,000 a week tax-free, thirty times a year, £30,000, can't complain, sorry about your loss, doesn't matter, come again, see you next Thursday.' At the back of the table was a slot, called the *cagnotte*, down which automatically disappeared 22 per cent of the money staked, which went directly to the Vicar. Aspinall opportunistically realised that, as long as everyone paid up (an important proviso, as we shall see), the organiser was bound to win. At last he had found the one certain way to make a living in the gambling world. He would start 'chemmy' games himself, but would do them better than anyone else.

The Vicar, who doubtless thought his comments would encourage Aspinall to bring in some rich punters and had no idea that he would instead purloin the idea for himself, said that one should on no account skimp on the food. 'Only the best, spoil them a bit, Fortnum and Mason's, keep up the standard' – this to show that Aspinall's rich friends would be well looked after. On the contrary, Aspinall was thinking that shop food was very poor form, and that if (when) he gave chemmy parties, he would make sure the food was home-cooked and superior to anything the punters could obtain in shops, hotels, restaurants, or anyone else's parties. He would engage the help of Lady O., who was a superb cook by any measure and, as a team, mother and son would transform the London gambling scene by introducing style and quality to an activity still thought by many to be sleazy, largely due to the necessity always to keep one step within the law. Even the punters were made to feel shifty. Aspinall determined he would change all that. It was a conscious and a final decision, without which none of what followed, in spheres far removed from gambling, would have been possible.

It also changed Lady O.'s life. As stand-by to her son, she enjoyed herself in this raffish world as never before. It was not only the pleasure of piling hampers on to the London train from Framfield (including soda siphons from the local pub which little James had to collect), but the excitement of grasping for the best. She felt released. It was a rare example of filial influence.

Typically, Aspinall went for his object with total commitment. For his first chemmy game he took a flat in Upper Brook Street, in Mayfair, and spent some time and thought decorating it so as to make himself appear prosperous and discerning. He still, at this stage, had not a penny in the bank, so he went to the Leger Art Gallery and showed serious interest in a Canaletto and a Pannini, each selling for a little over £1,000. He said he would consider buying them but wanted first to see if they looked well in his décor, and would gladly receive them on approval. With an address in Mayfair there was no difficulty in arranging this. Thus the first chemmy game Aspinall ever organised took place beneath a borrowed Canaletto in a rented flat, but the effect was genuine enough, and the punters, believing the paintings to be personal property, felt things were on the up and up.

There was a farcical postscript to this début. A few weeks later Aspinall was giving a cocktail party for friends and a whole crowd of potential punters whom it was important to impress, when a pair of removal men in overalls turned up unexpectedly. They had been sent by the Leger Gallery to retrieve the two paintings which the tenant clearly had no intention of buying, and they would brook no resistance or delay. Aspinall had quickly to pretend that he had *ordered* the men to take his paintings away for cleaning!

The profit from this first venture was £1,350, which Aspinall deployed entirely on the next game to make it better and yet more attractive, neither banking nor saving anything. He employed staff to serve and minister (including one man, Bert Payne, who is still working for him thirty years later), and offered a lavish reception before the game began. Lady O. introduced her game pie, which over the next two years was to become quite famous. At this second game the profit was £3,200, a staggering amount to Aspinall, which he once more used to invest in the quality of the third party. He bought more comfortable chairs, spent hugely on the appurtenances of the evening, had the tables repolished, the baize renewed, and emerged at the end with a profit of £5,000. With each game there appeared fresh faces, new punters, who were beginning to hear of Aspinall's reputation and were prepared to play for high stakes in return for an evening of luxurious entertainment.

The reason for the success of these early games and the rapid rise of John Aspinall's star was not only the attention to detail and the creation of style, but also the participation in the games of Aspinall himself. He was such an unlikely figure in a world which had hitherto attracted only seedy characters (and which had thereby kept most of the aristocracy away). He was relaxed, amusing, and intelligent. He told funny stories, long anecdotes and epic tales with such verve and vitality that he made the evening 'feel' civilised and natural long before the games were started. It was just like giving a dinner party for sophisticated friends, with much talk and exchange of news, idle gossip or urgent affairs of the moment. Nobody was made to feel that he was in a disreputable house, or that there was anything to apologise for. The chatter went on during the games as well, Aspinall always taking the initiative as the leading raconteur, spreading an atmosphere of fun and sociability so that no one was in a hurry to leave, all the while slotting his percentage down the middle.

Aspinall's pile-driving through the British aristocracy and separating younger sons from more money than they ought perhaps to have had access to, thus began as a conquest by charm, the seduction by the bard who hypnotises his audience, the irresistible pull of the Pied Piper, in an ambience made purposeful by the provision of luxury. (A friend later remarked that parents and trustees viewed Aspinall's arrival on the London scene as comparable with the disembarkation of Lenin at Helsinki Station in 1917.) His grand design and his strategy were brilliant, save for one fatal flaw: he had to sink his trust in the anticipated behaviour of gentlemen, and had to hope that all his punters would honour a debt. The flaw manifested itself with his fourth chemmy game, which almost brought total ruin in its wake.

In order not to flout the terms of the 1854 Gaming Act, which stipulated that private gambling should not occur at the same venue more than twice, Aspinall shifted addresses to remain within the law, not escape from it. The fourth game was moved farther along Upper Brook Street. So well known were Aspinall's evenings by this time, that a clutch of what used to be called 'swells' announced their intention of participating. They included Hugh Fraser, Bill Stirling, John Coulandris and Geoffrey Keating. Someone suggested an additional guest: a fabulously rich Oriental princess. Aspinall had never met her, and was from the beginning a little hesitant, but could see no good reason to refuse. The princess then declared that she would not be present in person, but would send her business manager, Mr P.G., to bet on her behalf. She would guarantee him for £10,000.

This was truly a vast amount of money in 1956, and there is something rather beguiling in the rough confidence of this 29-year-old who had been penniless a matter of months earlier and was now handling huge sums. Even he was reluctant, however, to accept the guarantee of someone he did not know in the smallest degree, and was only persuaded to assent when a third party said he would back it up, in other words guarantee the guarantee so that Aspinall was doubly protected.

The game was a notable success, largely because everyone appeared to be winning and was visibly happy with the way the evening was proceeding. The host had some very contented punters, except, of course, for one. There had to be a loser, and that was the mysterious royal representative. His losses mounted to dangerous heights. When they passed the £10,000 mark, and he was pleading for more credit, Aspinall asked the second guarantor what he should do. Stop him? 'No, give him another five,' was the rather careless reply, innocent of any disaster looming. In the end, P.G. lost a total of £16,400, which he paid by cheque. Aspinall paid out to the winners also with a series of cheques.

Almost inevitably, P.G.'s cheque bounced, causing Aspinall's payments to the big winners to be equally worthless. (He paid smaller winners to the tune of £5,000, which was all he had.) The reputation so carefully nurtured seemed set to be destroyed irretrievably in one night, the glimpse of Aladdin's Cave and a life of sybaritic bliss whisked away like a discarded bus ticket on the wind. He made strenuous efforts to recover the money without success. P.G. couldn't pay; the 'third party' wouldn't pay; no one could get anywhere near the princess, who should pay. It was stalemate. Friends commiserated with Aspinall, but implied that if you will move in a dangerous world you must expect to encounter danger.

Assuming that he would be unwelcome in any of the circles in London he would want to frequent, and knowing that the chemmy games which held such promise were at an end, at least for the time being, Aspinall went to the South of France. There in a casino he spotted an American, who was playing in a studied nonchalant manner for very high stakes, and struck up conversation with him. His name was Eddie Gilbert, a man made in the mould which was bound to appeal to John Aspinall – robust, aggressive and individual, with a rich vein of scorn for whatever was established practice. An outsider by nature, Gilbert was destined always to outrage the insiders, and his handling of his business affairs on a grand scale and with grand disregard of the rules would more than once place him behind the insiders' bars.

Aspinall warmed to him and his evident self-reliance, while Gilbert enjoyed chatting to this agreeable young Englishman. Their rapport laid the foundation for an easy but firm friendship. In the course of conversation Aspinall told the story of his ruin, which he obstinately believed would be temporary, and Gilbert listened with some attention. He then invited Aspinall to play at a neighbouring table on his behalf, and handed him a few thousand dollars for the purpose, which he quickly transformed into several more thousand. His wizardry with cards and his control of emotion were never more useful than now. Gilbert was so impressed he gave Aspinall a handsome percentage of his winnings, enabling him to return to England with something in his hands. He was *en route* once more.

Back in London, Aspinall sought out his two rich friends, Gerry Albertini and Richard Parkes. Both were what is loosely described as 'young men about town'. Albertini, of mixed Spanish, Cuban and Irish ancestry, was an American citizen whose money derived from his family's railway investments in the US. Parkes, who read law at Christ Church, Oxford, was the son of a wealthy builder who owned dog-racing tracks. One had already rescued Aspinall at a previous crucial crossroad in his life, and with the money he now brought back from France he stood them both a handsome lunch at the Dorchester Hotel. He also told them the miserable tale of his still unpaid debts to punters, and asked if they could lend him the money to pay these off so that he might start up the chemmy games again. He offered them a high percentage of the profits on all his future activities, which they declined on the grounds that friendship was more solid than investment. Albertini gave him £10,000 and Parkes, who could not resist the reflection that it was the most expensive lunch invitation he had ever accepted, came up with £5,000. Thus armed, Aspinall called his creditors (Keating, Stirling, Fraser *et alii*) on the telephone and invited them all to come and see him. Three months had passed since the disastrous fourth game of *chemin-de-fer*.

Aspinall learnt an important lesson on this occasion. The creditors were so astonished to be repaid, he had the distinct impression they had all but forgotten about the matter. The corollary of this was their entirely disproportionate and fulsome gratitude, which would have been tepid had he paid his debt to them on the spot. He learnt that among the people he was courting, if you paid your debts immediately, they were taken for granted; if you disappeared and paid them much later, when they had ceased to be expected, you were deemed to be a very impressive and honourable fellow. Furthermore, they assumed he must have borrowed from a moneylender at extortionate rates, and he did not disabuse them, their incipient feeling of guilt being quite useful.

They asked if there was anything they could do for him. Well, perhaps, said Aspinall. He was thinking of re-launching the chemmy games. It might be quite helpful if, just for the first one or two, they might like to show up for an hour. It would assist in putting the word around that the games were resumed and Aspinall himself back in circulation. Of course they would! Only too happy! What's more, they'd bring other people along and get the whole show under way again. It was important for Aspinall that he be well thought of by the big figures in the gambling world, by the heavy punters and members of London's most stuffy gentlemen's clubs. Inadvertently, just when he feared he had spoiled his chances by the catastrophe of the fourth game, he had in fact restored them by his show of honour; misfortune had been turned to advantage.

Nor was that the only lesson. Another incident, which ought by conventional standards to have turned people against him, worked again in his favour. He was sitting in Upper Brook Street one evening with his friend Mark Birley, Birley's wife, Lady Annabel, and his new escort Jane Hastings. Annabel and Mark were invincibly aristocratic and unlikely to be moved by any bourgeois considerations of taste. Peter West telephoned from Les Ambassadeurs, London's smartest night-club at Hyde Park Corner. West asked to speak to Aspers, and told him that not only was Mr P.G. present in the club, but he was actually with the Oriental princess herself. They were entertaining an American couple. Aspers should get down there at once.

Aspinall was reluctant to comply. He had solved the problem and would make the money back with his chemmy games. He was loath to indulge in a public squabble, which would doubtless result if he were to confront P.G. But Birley pressed him to have a brandy and make the short walk down the road to the night-club to get the thing over with; he would accompany him, in fact they all would.

It was a big night at Les Ambassadeurs. The première of Sam Spiegel's latest film had taken place and the subsequent party was being held there. International film-stars and multi-millionaire backers were crammed round every table. The princess's table was on the right, partially hidden behind a column. Aspinall went up and spoke quietly to P.G., suggesting that they had matters to discuss. P.G. said yes, after dinner. Aspinall withdrew.

Back at the bar, Birley was not at all satisfied, and continued to goad Aspinall into action. He should not be 'fobbed off' in this manner, but should demand settlement there and then, not despite the presence of the princess, but because of it. Aspinall's ever-latent capacity for a display of berserk behaviour was dangerously provoked. He went back to the table at a high pitch of emotional excitement, and announced that he was not prepared to sit and wait for three hours but demanded they talk immediately. P.G. turned to him and said, 'You bother me,' whereupon Aspinall pulled him by the head and dragged the man, the tablecloth, and all the tablecloth's burdens on to the floor.

What followed was fast and farcical. Four or five waiters tried to pull Aspinall off his prey and restrain him; the

princess screamed that she was pregnant, on hearing which intelligence the gallant, ever-vigilant and deeply masculine film-star Robert Mitchum piled in and began punching Aspinall; whereupon Annabel and Jane joined the fray with waving handbags and flailing fists. The incident was resolved in a matter of minutes, but it was long enough to make the newspapers the following morning, the first occasion they had taken real note of John Aspinall. It was not an introduction to public attention which boded well for the future, even when dignified with a cartoon by Osbert Lancaster.

What really mattered was the response of Aspinall's would-be clients. They had none of the middle-class horror of violence in public places, none of the Victorian virtues of decency and reticence and respect for the proprieties, no wish for decorous concealment or self-control. Theirs was an eighteenth-century attitude, full-blooded, emotional, retributive: the man was a cad, a bounder, and Aspinall was quite right to give him a thrashing. He shouldn't be allowed to get away with it! The lesson for Aspinall, his second in a month, was useful, too. He thought that his attack on P.G. might ruin him socially, that he may have made a fatal blunder in allowing himself to get wrought up. But no! He found himself being congratulated by the very kind of people he wished to attract to his games. The oddest aspect of all this was that Aspinall should still have been so steeped in conventional values that he was surprised by their congratulations.

The eighteen months between the summer of 1956 and the beginning of 1958, the period of the notorious 'floating' chemmy games which were responsible for a change in the law, were the most fruitful of John Aspinall's life thus far, and the foundation of his first fortune. But they were preceded by three more mundane events which, in differing degrees, were to have far-reaching effects upon his future direction: he got married, he befriended a wild animal, and he bought a house in the country.

Contrary to the public image which was beginning to emerge, Aspinall was never in any real sense a 'playboy'. Indeed, he was abstemious in the two areas where one normally expects playboys to be prodigal, in so far as he was neither a drunkard nor a womaniser. It came as a small surprise when, at nearly thirty, he suddenly married one of the young women he had recently been escorting, for he did not appear to be the marrying kind. At root, however, he was a man profoundly oriented to the family tradition, and anyone who could discern beyond the amusing stories and the financial ambitions saw that his vision of himself demanded he be a provider and protector, that he would not reach maturity until there were people dependent upon him and until he could cater for that dependence. Whether he saw himself as a chieftain in the Zulu mould or an eighteenth-century Whig landowner is almost beside the point; these are both romantic notions which he has always been happy to indulge. What matters is that beneath the appearance of selfish hedonism lay a thoughtful man who secretly and surprisingly deplored the aimlessness of his life, though he affected to admire or tolerate it in others.

Marriage offered purpose and the prospect of someone else to strive for. That the bride was also one of the most beautiful women in London was for Aspinall a welcome bonus. As it happened, the alliance did no harm for her socially, either. Naomi Jane Hastings came from Tomintoul, a tiny village near Aviemore in Inverness-shire, Scotland, where she had worked as a beater for very little money and lived a simple rustic life. Her peerless unblemished beauty attracted the attention of visitors from London and she was persuaded to journey south, fare paid, to launch herself as a model. This Jane did, and was modelling clothes at a fashion show which meandered amongst the tables in Fortnum and Mason's tea-room when John Aspinall was sitting quietly alone reading *Sporting Life*. Encouraged by an elderly lady at a neighbouring table, Aspinall fixed the haughty and disdainful beauty with his eye and eventually gathered courage to ask her to the races.

Their first day together was at Sandown. Aspinall gave Jane £100 to bet with, and was impressed when she spent it immediately and asked for more; nonchalance of this order endeared her to him. Together with Richard Parkes, she accompanied him on the lucky journey to the South of France when Eddie Gilbert came to the rescue, and was part of the uproarious scene at Les Ambassadeurs. Very soon Jane was a magnet for photographers and such a high-spirited member of the new Mayfair crowd that she was generally known as the 'Spirit of Park Lane'. Scarcely anyone denied that her 'inner glow', her radiance, were phenomenal. When it became known that the captivating model was to marry the maverick blond gambler, those adept at creating gossip called it the Wedding of the Year.

As was becoming predictable in any event to which Aspinall contributed, the wedding was at once marvellously impressive, superbly arranged, and deeply farcical. It came at a time when Aspinall was virtually destitute, after the disaster of his fourth chemmy game and before their subsequent restitution, a circumstance which in no way did he allow to curtail the extravagance of the occasion.

While the wedding ceremony was in progress, bailiffs turned up and thundered at the door. Obviously in pursuit of the bridegroom, the two strangers caused pandemonium in Caxton Hall as they burst in waving writs which they attempted to serve. Mr and Mrs Aspinall did not wait to be identified. They made their escape through a side door into a taxi hailed by Albertini, while the bailiffs, spotting a blond blue-eyed young man in the congregation, served their writs somewhat aggressively on Dominick Elwes.

Aspinall was literally without a penny and could not afford a honeymoon, but decided rather perversely to take his bride to the Connaught Hotel for two nights instead, which he could not afford either. The Manager of the Connaught, one of the most chic and expensive hotels in the world, was utterly charming to the newly-weds, not to say obsequious. So happy was he that this beautiful young couple should celebrate their union in the Connaught that he welcomed them personally and sent champagne up to their large suite with the compliments of the house. He politely discussed with Aspinall the latter's plans to give a cocktail party in his suite the following day by way of a wedding reception; there were to be eighty guests, and they would all proceed to the Dorchester for dinner afterwards.

In the morning the Manager received a palpable shock on opening his daily newspaper, wherein it was disclosed that his delightful guests were broke. He flew up to their suite and gave instructions they must pay their bill immediately or leave. Aspinall pointed out that he could do neither. He could not possibly leave with eighty people coming that evening for drinks, and if the Manager were to insist on turning them out on the street the day after their wedding, the resulting pub-licity would be even worse, for the Connaught as much as for the married couple; the Manager would appear heartless in the *Daily Express*! Aspinall had every intention of paying the bill the next day, as he would borrow wildly from his own guests at the cocktail party, though he did not admit so much to the Manager. As it happened, Gerry Albertini gave him a wedding present of £500, which more than covered the account. The Manager's sigh of relief could be heard even by the doorman.

With the re-establishment of the chemmy games, Aspinall began to make money again. He and Jane took a flat in Eaton Place on two floors, first floor and basement, with exclusive use of a small back garden. In other parts of London it would have been called a 'maisonette'. They had staff to look after them and a valuable butler, Bob, who also served at table. Bob's only shortcoming was a terror of tigers, not a fault which would normally preclude an honourable career in charge of the wine-cellar, but the Eaton Place household became distinctly unorthodox in the course of 1956.

For no absolutely compelling reason, Aspinall began frequenting Palmer's Pet Shop in Regent's Park, where wild animals and zoo animals were a speciality. One day he paid £20 for a capuchin monkey and brought it home to his astonished wife. (This animal, 'Dead Loss' or 'Deddy', is in 1988 probably the oldest capuchin monkey in the world.) There soon followed a beautiful tigress, 'Tara', bought from the same shop, who struck very lucky, as it turned out, with her purchaser; her genes continue in over one hundred and fifty descendants of the third generation, whereas she might well have ended up a film-star's pet with no progeny at all. Finally, Aspinall surpassed himself and bought a pair of eight-month-old Himalayan bears, 'Esau' and 'Ayesha'.

It is impossible with hindsight to identify the deep, firm flow of motive which prompted the absolutely crucial decision to make these animals part of his life, a decision the implications of which he did not foresee, or its importance suspect. There had been clues, tiny clues, in Aspinall's past which might have pointed in such a direction, but might equally well have pointed to a dozen other routes. He was certainly unaware of them. He was not realising a long-cherished ambition. He did not envisage grandiose plans of expansion. He did not yet know very much about the dangers which even then were threatening the survival of all living things on the planet, with the glaring exception of mankind. Nor was buying the animals a mere 'stunt', a way to *épater les bourgeois*, although it is fair to say that Aspinall was still an extrovert who would enjoy showing off to friends by doing something totally unconventional. There was something behind the purchase, something indefinable. In the presence of these proud, secretive, untameable creatures, he felt *moved*. As he later wrote, 'I liked dogs and cats but they did not stir my imagination. It is difficult to be uplifted by a Dalmatian or a budgerigar.' These are the words of a man who has stumbled upon his own religion.

In the meantime, this rather awkward foursome had to be accommodated in the Eaton Place flat. Tara was given a room upstairs (i.e. on the ground floor) but for nearly all purposes had free run of the flat. In the back garden Aspinall built an enclosure to be shared by the two bears and the monkey, which worked surprisingly well. Esau and Ayesha occupied the floor of the enclosure, while Deddy swung about at the top, occasionally descending to groom the bears by sitting on their heads and meticulously picking off old bits of skin. They did not object, for like all mammals they positively enjoyed being groomed.

In the house, Tara practised her hunting technique by nipping heels, as she would in the wild have gone for hamstringing antelopes, or for knocking one foot of her 'prey' in front of the other, causing it to trip up or even fall over. This was all very amusing and harmless, but it did not bring a smile to Bob's face. Once bitten on the ankle as he was serving potted shrimp, he immediately gave in his notice.

Some of Aspinall's friends likewise sought assurances before they would venture to his flat. Lord Worsley (now Lord Yarborough) would not approach the bears, but being unfortunately short-sighted he might on occasion share a sofa with them unknowingly, or be content with the information that they were Labrador dogs. A lunch was once interrupted by Deddy defecating on the table-cloth.

Neighbours were even less happy, and complaints flooded in. Aspinall could not very well take an Indian tigress on the lead in Belgravia during the daytime, but late at night he would give her exercise around the square. This practice came to an abrupt halt one evening when a huge, fierce Alsatian dog spotted Tara from a distance, growled, came hurtling towards her, only to realise too late that it was no puppy, tried to stop itself advancing, skidded to land in front of her, and was despatched with one swipe of the paw and one bite in the neck. Aspinall quietly dumped the corpse of the rash unthinking brute down someone else's basement stairs.

After only a matter of weeks it was obvious that the Aspinalls could not continue to live in a central London flat with two bears, a tigress and a monkey. It was essential they find a place in the country where there would be space and privacy, as much for the animals' sake as for that of the outraged Belgravia neighbours. Aspinall's first thought was to live in Sussex, where his slender family roots still called him, but after looking at sixteen houses in vain, he saw by chance an advertisement for a house near Canterbury in Kent. Approached by a handsome straight avenue of lime trees, many of which had fallen down over the years to block the path, so that one had to clamber across giant horizontal tree-trunks to get to the house at all, Howletts was in a dreadful condition, dilapidated, sad, wet, its exterior stucco walls shamefully neglected. But it was romantic, it had 38 acres of parkland, and with renovation one could see that the original eighteenth-century elegance of the mansion might be recaptured.

The price for the freehold of Howletts was £6,000. Even by the standards of 1956 this was not expensive, but Aspinall could not meet it. He had enough to pay the deposit of £600. He then went to Newmarket and placed a bet on Prelone in the Cesarewitch Handicap. It won, and with the proceeds Aspinall bought Howletts outright.

4
Howletts and Bow Street

The reason for the almost totally derelict state of Howletts was curious. The previous owner, a wealthy Australian called Ramsey, had bought the mansion before the First World War and looked after it reasonably well for the first ten years. An amateur pilot, he also built Bekesbourne Airport nearby, the brick hangar of which still stands (and is nowadays used as a fruit store). When he reached the age of seventy, Ramsey thought he had done enough and would not survive much longer, so he decided to retire from active life and retire also from worrying about the house. Alas for Howletts, he lived to the age of ninety-seven, leaving twenty-seven years of neglect behind him. His executors seriously considered that there was nothing they could do with the crumbling old mansion but demolish it or convert it into a warehouse. Such was their plan if a purchaser was not found quickly.

The owner of the adjacent orchards was a member of the most powerful family in the area, the Mounts. Archbishop Ramsey used to say that Canterbury was 'a city surrounded by seven Mounts'. This Mr Mount wanted to purchase Howletts. He would have bulldozed the house to make room for more orchards, but as he refused to go above £5,500, Howletts was saved by his caution.

When John Aspinall first saw Howletts it was difficult to imagine the Palladian purity of its line, quite simply because it was largely obscured by subsequent additions. The space between the four magnificent pillars of its portico had been filled in, giving the house the appearance of a squat, bumpy box. But behind all this lay the only surviving example of the work of Sir John Leach, an architect of the mid eighteenth century.

Leach had been a pupil of the architect Sir Robert Taylor and had built Howletts in 1787-9 for an East India merchant, Isaac Baugh, before prematurely giving up architecture for the law. Elected to Parliament, he rose to become a Privy Councillor and Master of the Rolls. On the death of Isaac Baugh, Howletts was acquired, rather appropriately as it turned out, by the famous gambler Sir Thomas Dering. In true Regency style Dering lost the whole estate one evening playing faro at White's Club, whereupon it fell into the hands of a money-lender called Abraham Gipps. Gipps's heirs founded Martin's Bank and held on to Howletts until almost modern times. (A less welcome association was with Stephen Hales, the prominent scientist who performed gruesome experiments on animals. He was born at Howletts – in an earlier house on the site – in 1677.)

The house presented Aspinall with his first challenge in restoration, the first of a handful of achievements for which his contemporaries have given him little credit. Philip Jebb, a young architect introduced by the brother of Dominick Elwes, was unknown and untried. That made him all the more attractive to Aspinall, who engaged him to resurrect Howletts. It was a gruelling task, for the house was so riddled with dry rot that all the wall plaster and all the floorboards had to be replaced. Aspinall said what he had in mind, but gave a free hand as far as finance was concerned, a fruitful encouragement to talent. Philip Jebb's work cost £80,000, paid in four stages, so that the house developed like a play in four acts. At the last stage, the great John Fowler was brought in to mastermind the interior decoration and re-create the feel of eighteenth-century elegance which the house demanded. Russell Page was employed to advise on the park and gardens. The entire restoration took five years, during which time the Aspinalls moved in, their children Amanda Jane

and Damian Androcles were born, and the animal population grew apace. Now, Howletts is a listed building, and
the Spanish chestnuts, ilexes and Cedars of Lebanon which
have graced its surroundings for centuries are likewise under
a protection order.

The name is ancient and much revered by local people.
Variously spelt from 'Owlet' in Tudor times to the modern
version, folk tradition holds that it must in no circumstances
be changed. Aspinall was rather too vocal in a nearby
tea-shop on one of his early visits, loudly announcing his
intention of giving the place a more suitable name, but had
quickly to withdraw this when a lined, witch-like old woman
felt bound to warn him of the most dire consequences: ''e
that changes the name of the mansion will bring ill-luck upon
'isself,' she intoned. With his natural respect for inherited
wisdom rather than acquired knowledge, Aspinall never
hesitated in accepting her advice.

It was fortunate that the restoration of Howletts coincided
with the most fruitful period of Aspinall's floating chemmy
games. The games took place every ten days or so, with
a total of about thirty in one year. Lady O. was relieved
of her duties in keeping accounts and was placed in sole
charge of the justly renowned refreshments, though as often
as not she would play herself. As the games grew more and
more famous, so they attracted the biggest gamblers in the
country – the Newmarket landowning set – and they became
unbelievably smart occasions. The Duke of Devonshire and
the Earl of Derby were both regular punters, as were scores
of the rich and the titled. It might have seemed all too heady
for the middle-class colonial son, but apparently not. As one
put it, Aspinall fitted in like a round peg in a round hole, as
if custom-made. Furthermore, there was not the smallest
suggestion of snobbery about him, which the titled in Britain, normally smothered and stifled by obsequiousness, find
irresistibly refreshing.

Only one drawback occasionally spoiled the lush gilded
atmosphere of an Aspinall evening: it sometimes appeared
that there were too many people playing for the 'house'.

This was an unfortunate impression, made inevitable by the nature of *chemin-de-fer* itself. There were nine seats at the table, each punter playing against all the others, winning not from the house but from another punter. The house players (Aspinall, Lady O., Maxwell-Scott) were known as 'Blues', and they would play simply to make up the numbers, affording the 'Reds' (real punters) some people to play against. Blues would gradually be withdrawn from the table as more Reds turned up in the course of the evening, until, ideally, all nine players were clients. Indeed, it would hardly be in Aspinall's interest to have too many from the house, as his income depended entirely upon the number of Reds.

It was a foolproof system, for it did not matter who won or lost or how often, as they were not winning from Aspinall himself. He, meanwhile, took his certain percentage down the slot whatever happened. As the punters played for ever higher stakes, so Aspinall's guaranteed income grew ever more inflated. It was estimated that he could have made as much as £350,000 during those eighteen months. Some of this profit was spent making the evenings more attractive than before, some was spent on the restoration of Howletts, and some was used for the foundation of what would one day become the most successful and unusual private zoo in the world.

The relationship between Aspinall and the Inland Revenue was necessarily equivocal. As his activities were of questionable legality, there could be no taxable income arising from them; on the other hand, Treasury officials knew perfectly well there was an income. They reached an agreement with Aspinall whereby he *volunteered* to pay a regular sum into the coffers, which he levied on his own theoretically non-existent income.

Sometimes Aspinall's entertainments were in Claus von Bülow's flat, sometimes in David Hicks's, often in flats that were offered by friends. The Mayfair police knew of these activities and appreciated that the gamblers kept lawful by being nomadic. But the press was another matter. On one occasion a newspaper was alerted and sent photographers to wait patiently outside for hours. In the middle of the night Aspinall, Lord Derby and other guests escaped by climbing over the roof and making an exit through the bedroom of a startled neighbour, while Lady O. was concealed in a laundry basket and carried unseen on to the lorry which arrived to collect the hired furniture. The police were reduced to setting constables on the trail of people they thought might possibly be on their way to an Aspinall game, to see where they led them, and to make sure it was not an 'habitual' house.

This comedy could not last forever. At the end of 1957 the Chairman of a multinational corporation offered a luxury flat overlooking Hyde Park on the north side, which was taken in the name of Lady Osborne, as Aspinall's name was rather too well known by this time. Lady O.'s tenancy of the flat in Hyde Park Street was legal from 5 December, a Thursday, and although she never slept there, John started to give dinner parties on Thursdays which were inevitably followed by all-night sessions of chemmy. The one circumstance her wily son failed to take into account was that north of the park they would be within the precinct of the Paddington police, a quite different collection of officers from those in Belgravia. The Paddington police were less *au fait* with the demands of the 1854 Act, and more hostile to the amusements of the smart set.

After several weeks of surreptitious observation, the Paddington station decided to pounce. A detective inspector, mindful of his need to secure eye-witness evidence of the iniquity he suspected was going on inside the flat, climbed the fire escape on to a window-sill which he found gave him a restricted view into the dining-room. Clinging precariously to a grille he managed to watch the activity inside through a small gap at the top of the curtains, and was delighted to see a green baize table-top, some playing cards and some chips. By dint of squeezing and squinting he thought he could even make out that the cards and chips were being passed from one hand to another.

He told the Chief Inspector and it was apparent to them both that under the provisions of the Gaming Act (1845)* they had the right to enter the premises and investigate further. (They had a warrant in readiness, signed by the Commissioner of Police.) They knocked on the door. It was opened rather grandly by a waiter in full white tie and tails, with the air of someone used to receiving royalty.

The detectives and constables walked in and made their arrests almost immediately. John Aspinall was charged with keeping a common gaming-house ('Young man,' intoned Lady O., 'there was nothing common here until you walked in.') Lady O. herself was charged with permitting her premises to be used for the purpose of unlawful gaming, and one John Burke with assisting in the preparation of a room for gaming. Aspinall pointed out that all those present were intimate friends and had been invited, but the officers were unmoved. Twenty-one other people present, bearing surnames that echo through the centuries of Britain's nobility (Cavendish-Bentinck, Mond, Pelham, Hoare, Willoughby, Fane, Sergison-Brooke), were charged with being found on the premises.

The entire caravan was marched off to the police station to be formally cautioned and charged, including the chauffeur, James Meadarklan, and the still impressively dressed waiter, Robert Richardson. Jane Aspinall gave her occupation as 'housewife', while Lady O., determined loftily to ignore the whole silly proceedings, said nothing ('occupation declined'

---

*The police were given power of entry and search of premises where they suspected illegal gaming might be taking place, under Section 3 of the Gaming Act 1845. The later Gaming Houses Act 1854 made it an offence to assist in keeping a common gaming house, and further stipulated that the question as to whether a house was being used for this purpose should be a matter of law for the judge to decide, not a matter of fact for the jury. A common gaming house was, in law, one where a large number of persons habitually congregated for the purpose of gaming, the crucial word being *habitually* – excessive gaming *per se* was not unlawful. It was under this Act that most modern prosecutions were launched. The penalty upon conviction was a fine of £500 or a year's imprisonment. Under Section 4 of the Gaming Act 1802, a conviction carried the possible penalty of public flogging.

on the charge-sheet). Sixteen people consented to be bound over in the sum of £25 each, not to frequent gaming-houses and to be of good behaviour for the next twelve months. The housewife, chauffeur and waiter were remanded to appear at Bow Street Magistrates' Court on their own bail of £10 each, as were the three major miscreants on bail of £50 each.

One of the officers thought he might pose a crafty question to gather more evidence as to the purpose of the lease on 1 Hyde Park Street, and asked Lady O. if she would care to say what rent she was paying. 'I certainly should not,' came the withering reply.

The hearing at Bow Street took two days. Sebag Shaw, prosecuting, said that some might think the 1854 Act was archaic, but that was not the matter at issue; it was the law and had to be honoured. For the defence, Gilbert Beyfus QC said there would be no question of a plea other than Not Guilty and that all three defendants (the more minor cases being adjourned without dates being set for trials) would elect to go for trial by jury; he submitted, however, that there was no case to answer. The submission was rejected and the defendants were committed for trial at the London Sessions on 18 March 1958.

The subsequent trial, though without dramatic incident or inspiring speech, had an effect so far beyond the particular that it led directly to legislation which immediately and measurably altered social life in England. This was to be John Aspinall's contribution towards fashioning English mores in the second half of the twentieth century, though it would be foolish to contend that he had any such grandiose idea in mind. But the fact remains that no future historian can afford to neglect the profound changes that overtook the betting scene within the next three years as a result of what became known (and is recorded in Hansard) as 'Aspinall's Law'. On trial at the London Sessions in 1958 were, in a sense, the entirely anachronistic regulations governing gambling in England. However, Aspinall's activities over the previous months had been building up to a confrontation with the law, and one or the other would have to give way.

It was again Gilbert Beyfus QC who led for the defence. As it is impossible to believe that the remarks of this experienced, even famous, barrister derived from naïvety, one must assume that he wanted to make the law sound, as well as look, an ass. 'There is no shred of evidence,' he said, 'to suggest that anyone even so much as played a game of patience in that flat.' The purpose of the gathering of so many people was to give a house-warming party for Lady Osborne. Could anyone doubt that such was the intention? 'Take a careful look at the accused . . . ' ('Hear, hear!' shouted Lady O. in a flowered hat.)

Assuming a more solemn visage, Beyfus went on to point out that there were two elements missing in the indictment which would need to be present under the 1854 Act: the element of habituality and the element of business lucre or gain. 'Every single club in St James's with a bridge-table is a common gaming-house,' he added, 'although the police prefer not to prosecute.'

Council then conferred, and the judge (Mr Cassel) turned to address the jury. 'There is going to be a long legal submission,' he said, 'probably wrangle is a better word, with regard to this case. You, fortunately, do not have to listen to it. I do.' The jury were then dismissed until the following day. Beyfus addressed the court in camera for more than two hours, as a result of which, when the jury were called back in on 19 March, the judge told them he was dismissing all charges, and he instructed them to return formal verdicts of Not Guilty. He would not, however, grant costs. 'I think it was a case which had properly to be investigated.' Although there was no evidence of unlawful gaming within the meaning of Section 4 of the 1854 Gaming Act, 'if you hold a party like that, you must run the risk of the police coming in to arrest you.'

That was the end of that; it was also the beginning. For now that private gambling had been modestly sanctioned by the authorities (the case being reported in *The Times*), a great many other people began to hold chemmy evenings, albeit furtively and none with the style of Aspinall, and it was to prevent this proliferation that moves were made in Parliament to change the law.

Meanwhile, Aspinall himself thought it better to be inconspicuous for a while. Not only had there been the slightly damaging publicity of the trial to discourage many of his potential punters, some of whom would rather forego the pleasure of a flutter and a taste of Lady O.'s game pie than risk exposure and obloquy, but rumours affecting Aspinall's own reputation were beginning to circulate in society. There was never any suggestion that he was less than scrupulously honest, never a hint of suspicion that he might permit cheating; indeed, this was one of the firmest rocks upon which his success so far had been founded, as gambling promoters were, on the whole, a thoroughly reprobate lot without a moral between them. One of the reasons the aristocracy went to Aspinall was that they knew they could trust him.

On the other hand, he was thought to be too prone to allow thoughtless younger sons with too much money, or whose fathers had too much money, to get progressively more drunk and lose whatever judgment they might have had. In other words, he was profiting from young men's weakness and could justifiably be termed an entirely *amoral* man when he stood behind (or even near) the green baize. There were some who thought him predatory, setting out to catch a ripe young purse before its contents were needlessly banked, and in years to come he was certainly to use people who were attractive by virtue of their name or fame to entice others into the web.

Aspinall has always countered the accusation of amorality in the shrewdest possible way, by hurling it at himself before anyone else can. Many years later, in a letter to a Cabinet Minister whose son had foolishly run into debt at the tables, he wrote, 'I would happily separate any drunken youth from the maximum he could handle, or his family could handle, without the slightest compunction.' To which one must add that Aspinall placed not the smallest degree of pressure on the young man in question, nor indicated that the debt would

have to be settled at some time in the future. Indeed, he
behaved entirely as if the debt had never occurred, and lent
the young man a further £1,500 to pay his bookmakers; this,
too, was never seen again.

Aspinall was frequently chastised for extending too much
credit in these early days when there were no legal restrictions
placed upon such clever generosity, but as his *Spectator* profile
pointed out in 1985, there is the world of difference between
extending credit and trying to collect from the loser. The
same columnist said that Aspinall had never 'put the arm' on
anyone who owed him money, 'in fact he has gone so far as to
feed and nurture people who owe him hundreds of thousands
and have absolutely no intention of ever paying.'

We anticipate by some years, but since the reputation
for pursuing the ruin of friends at the green table was
first whispered around 1959 and first began to hang on
John Aspinall at that time, it is as well to explore the truth
of the allegation here. It also has a bearing upon the second,
and in my view far more significant half of his life, when he
became seriously involved with the breeding of wild animals.
If Aspinall was slow to discourage punters from losing their
shirts, he was equally slow to press his advantage when they
did. Those in trouble soon discovered that he was the least
greedy of men, and those in need could come to him for
assistance. To this day, there is a small crowd of people
who continue to depend upon him long after the reason for
their call upon his generosity has been forgotten. His attitude
towards money has always been pragmatic; it is to be used,
not accumulated in the usurer's fashion nor adored for its
own sake in the Swiss manner. He will give or lend when
he has the means, and when he is himself close to penury, as
he has been on at least three occasions, he will look to others
to give or lend. He is neither an embarrassed borrower nor a
sanctimonious lender.

When he came to run his own casino, this absence of
venality distinguished him from other casino owners whose
ruthlessness went far beyond the brutal, and accounted in
some measure for his success. Aspinall followed the code

which came naturally to him and applied it in his games. In his obsessive adherence to the principle of loyalty, he found the code of the English gentleman unequal to his demands and jettisoned it in favour of a more primitive one.

Besides, he was quick to point out that when the loss of a fortune at the tables was lamented, it was generally forgotten that one man's misfortune was another man's gain. The money did not disappear, was not wasted; it merely moved around and changed hands. There is no room for sentimentality in such a view. Life is always harsh, and some people must go under.

One who did was Henry Vyner, a second son who rather unexpectedly inherited a large estate in Yorkshire, including Studley Royal and Fountains Abbey, when his elder brother was killed. Vyner lost a great deal of money at Aspinall's games, probably over £33,000 on one particular evening, but the gossip which suggested Aspinall had ruined him was quite false. With his endearing habit of laughing every time he lost, Vyner could fairly be said to have giggled his way through a fortune; the fortune in question was pocket money, however. His eventual ruin, and the loss of his entire estate, came ten years later when he entered into unwise financial arrangements about which, ironically, Aspinall had advised him to be very cautious.

Above all, it was important for Aspinall that gambling should be fun, should enhance enjoyment. If ever it risked becoming a nightmare of bad judgment and misery, then its *raison d'être* would evaporate. Aspinall certainly did not want his 'guests' to be unhappy. Indeed, contrary to received opinion, he frequently worked surreptitiously to prevent some of his clients from losing too much, more than once refunding incautious young men on condition they did not come to the club again.

There was also the question of his personal enjoyment. He positively relished the company of big gamblers, and even today would still rather spend time with a big gambler who happened also to be a bore, than with a sophisticated and witty man whose life was circumscribed by excessive caution.

Indeed, for him a big gambler *cannot* be a bore, as the very fact of his gambling invests him with interest and glamour. A big gambler is a big person, with panache, individuality, style, as worthy of Aspinall's love and admiration as Shaka the Zulu or Oscar Wilde. Similarly, tigers, elephants and gorillas are large in character, self-possessed and awesomely confident. Part of Aspinall's secret in achieving an unexampled communion with large primates would reside in his respect for them, his avoidance of all sentimentality, and his ability never to bear a grudge, the very same characteristics which were in evidence in his dealings with gamblers. Many an experienced handler of animals has yet to acknowledge the value of these attitudes.

Of course, Aspinall was himself still very much a novice at this stage and made many mistakes, one of which almost cost him his life. The bears, Esau and Ayesha, were now happily established in their own large enclosure at Howletts and Aspinall would regularly join them for play and jousting. It was good-humoured though occasionally rough, and if both jumped upon him at once (mysteriously enough, because they liked to suck his neck), he would collapse beneath their combined weight. One day in 1959 he went in without his keys, jumping down from the high wall which enclosed their area. Thirty yards away, Esau was trying to mate with Ayesha, who would not co-operate. Perhaps frustrated, perhaps jealous, perhaps simply angry, Esau turned and charged towards Aspinall with ferocious abandon of all his previous trust. There was no doubt that he meant to tear the man apart.

Aspinall darted from one oak-tree to another in an attempt to exhaust the enraged animal, then threw him his coat, which he proceeded to rip to shreds within seconds, roaring the while. With each rush Esau came closer, and Aspinall was now using his own ebbing strength to shout for help. No one heard. Ayesha distracted Esau long enough for Aspinall to make a dash for the wall beyond the ditch, hurling himself at it and landing with shoulders and elbows at the top. By now the engagement had lasted some ten minutes and Aspinall was too weary to summon the strength to pull himself up over the wall; instead, he slowly sank down into the ditch, where he was defenceless. Esau again approached, slowly and menacingly. Aspinall gave up shouting for rescue, deciding instead to conserve his powers for the final encounter. He threw rocks at the bear, but failed to halt its relentless advance. 'I remember at the time giving myself a twenty-to-one chance of survival,' Aspinall wrote. 'I was determined to die fighting, a crude flint in either hand.'

His mother-in-law, Mrs Hastings, and Richard Parkes were in the cottage 100 yards away. They finally thought the roaring was unusually protracted and went to investigate. When they saw the prey cornered and exhausted, they quickly brought out saucepans and dustbin lids, creating such a din that Esau was made to withdraw and Aspinall could be dragged to safety. He then collapsed into sobs for some minutes, clasping the hands of his rescuers. 'I could scarcely believe my good fortune.' He retired to bed to recuperate.

Aspinall never went in with the bears after that day. The delicate hierarchical balance had been destroyed; Esau could not thereafter be relied upon to observe the rules of trust which had formerly applied. It was one of Aspinall's first lessons in the exigencies of territory among animals when the male is busy expressing his right of precedence. Today, though keepers regularly spend an hour shut in with a full family group of nineteen gorillas, they forgo the pleasure if there is any sign of incipient romance, and are singularly uncomfortable when a female gorilla, as sometimes happens, tries to flirt with one of them.

Aspinall was spending more time at Howletts than before, both because work on the house was proceeding apace, and because the abortive trial of February 1958 obliged him to pause and consider forthcoming strategy. He turned his attentions to the development of another of his ambitions, to be a host in the grand manner. For some months he had been visiting Paris where he saw the impact of stylish entertaining upon socialites and quickly appreciated how welcome would be such sybaritic delights in London, where 'society' had been starved of these pleasures for years. Costume balls and fêtes were given in surviving private houses of *fin de siècle* opulence, such as the Hotel Lambert, home of Arturo Willshaw. Aspinall had initially been shy of attending such occasions, oddly enough, because he was afraid of 'dressing up' and making a fool of himself, a far cry from the exhibitionist fop of early Oxford days. Aspinall sometimes stayed with the wealthy Danish banker Eric Ingersley-Nielsen in la rue de Cherche-Midi, where servants and chauffeurs were part of daily life. A simple dinner party might include up to thirty people. And of course the Goldsmith brothers had their maternal home in Paris.

To attempt a big party in London would afford Aspinall the opportunity to show that he was still around and still able to organise the best gambling evenings in the metropolis, despite recent competition. He decided to give the biggest and most extravagant party London had seen since before the war, the first of many 'feasts' he was to preside over in the coming years.

The venue chosen for this exhibition was a sumptuous flat in Belgrave Square rented by Claus von Bülow. Aspinall did not deign to take expense into his calculations. The total cost was over £10,000, which allowed £35 per guest, and this in the days when a decent restaurant meal for two would cost under £2. An eighteen-piece orchestra, said to be the favourite 'band' of Aristotle Onassis, was flown in from Monte Carlo, and such was the competition among the noble aristocrats of Britain to secure an invitation that five private detectives were hired to make sure the excluded remained so. The final coup of the party was the production of a giant pack of cards which Aspinall cut and dealt to each departing guest and on which was announced the date of his next gambling party.

The occasion was so successful that it quickly earned the sobriquet of The Social Event of 1959 (despite the *faux pas* of chucking out the American actor Van Heflin, whom nobody recognised; he was later re-admitted). Aspinall had managed to make himself and his entertainments sought after, valued and admired. There was no longer any question of his being accepted into the magic circle of Top People, rather it was they who wished to be accepted on to Aspinall's guest list; you were not really a Top Person if you were unwelcome. Of course, with the masterly British habit of having it both ways, born of centuries of practice in subtle social snubs and embraces, the nobility who jostled to attend an Aspinall party rarely invited him to one of their country seats. He was someone to take from, not give to. If Aspinall was aware of these nuances, he showed no sign of concern. He preferred, anyway, being the host.

With success naturally came publicity. Aspinall showed he was a clever operator in what later became known as Public Relations and this characteristic inevitably attracted the attention of gossip columnists. His long unhappy struggle with the press, which hardly became easier when his achievements with animal husbandry were acknowledged, began with a moralistic article by Paul Johnson in the *New Statesman* which appeared shortly after the Belgravia party. Entitled 'Aspers' Little Shindig', it sought to castigate the appalling inequalities of British society, drawing contrasts between the working man who could barely make ends meet and saw his reasonable requests for financial advancement treated with contempt, and on the other hand the privilege and waste of Ascot and the venality of property developers. Johnson considered that John Aspinall, said to 'make' £50,000 a year tax-free, symbolised the rottenness which was poisoning Britain and the 'exotic creatures' who fed from the carcass.

'The benefits they derive bear no relation to what they contribute,' he wrote, 'nor to the economic well-being of the nation. Their manner of life throws into a fearful perspective the moral criteria of a society which recently jailed a widow for concealing the fact that she had supplemented her dole by taking in sewing.' After quoting Disraeli's vision of the Two Nations of England – the rich and the poor – being united by a sense of social responsibility in the possessing class, Mr

Johnson rounded upon Aspinall and his empty-headed guests as a 'squirming, social scrum' which would be swept into oblivion by time and history.

Johnson was clearly premature in his prediction, but his was a valid point of view, and it accurately expressed the resentment, even contempt, which Aspinall was beginning to arouse in those quarters where his reputation penetrated. It was perfectly true that he had no social conscience in the usual sense, that the luxury of his entertainments and profligacy of his spending were on a scale insulting to the impoverished and deprived. Gradually the picture took shape of a heartless reprehensible playboy, giggling to the bank and indifferent to human values. A little of this was justified, though in a far more profound sense than was then realised.

On the superficial level, the 'playboy' image was lent much support by stories which filtered through to London of Aspinall's escapades abroad in the company of his relatively new friend Eddie Gilbert, whom he had first met on that fateful day in Monte Carlo some three years earlier. The friendship had developed into a real bond, buttressed on Aspinall's part by something akin to a schoolboy hero-worship for the glittering, amusing American. Gilbert was at this time at the peak of his success. Known as 'The Wonder-Boy of Wall Street', Gilbert had amassed a fortune of many millions in a very short time, based on speculative investment in the lumber trade. To Aspinall, it seemed he could do no wrong, and his qualities of cheerfulness in the face of daunting risk and loyalty to the concept of friendship were precisely those he most admired. Besides, as Aspinall was busy inventing a 'court' in his own style, a Court Jester was an appropriate addition, and Eddie fitted this role with ease.

During these years before 1962, Aspinall's fortunes were by no means set upon an unhampered upward path, despite the evidence of extravagance. There were times when his ambitious spending left the purse dangerously empty, and it was then that Eddie Gilbert could be relied upon to come to the rescue as he had in Monte Carlo. On one occasion Aspinall took a house at Ascot where he gave a gambling party which included Lord Derby, Richard Parkes, Colonel Bill Stirling and Gilbert. Eddie won nearly £60,000 that night, gallantly accepting his winnings in promissory notes. Had he insisted on being paid, Aspinall would almost certainly have been ruined (although for how long is a moot point). It took him six months actually to touch the money he had won, which he then promptly lost again anyway. The point is that he was prepared to wait, and his patience was worth a mint.

Eddie could also be subtle and sensitive. He did not embarrass his friend by offering to give large sums, as he knew Aspinall was always struggling to keep up the pace he had set himself and would lose face if the struggle were to show. Eddie sensed when Aspinall was broke by the way he behaved, and would then suggest some absurd bet which he knew would be taken up, and moreover which Aspinall was bound to win, for Eddie was careful not to propose anything which the other man might lose. These random bets continued on and off for some six years and were often so fanciful that they compared in outrageousness with the eighteenth-century bets placed at Brooks's when, for instance, one member would bet another that a certain fly crawling up a window-pane would or would not reach the top.

Among the bets Aspinall accepted were for $2,000 he would eat a bowl of flowers in the Hotel de Paris, or that he would completely undress in the lobby of an hotel in Monte Carlo and walk outside to the street for three minutes. Aspinall was ready to accept any challenge, and Eddie happy to oblige with an excuse, although on occasion Aspinall's recklessness was so extreme that he had to be restrained. He accepted a bet to swim across the Loire river which flowed with such force that, despite his strength, the effort might very well have killed him, so Eddie paid up rather than allow him to take the risk. He also accepted a bet, for another $2,000, to consume an entire 2 pounds of butter, and was half-way through before he was released from the wager and carried home in a somewhat frail condition. Once, Eddie saved his life when his eagerness overcame his judgment. Staying at Gilbert's house on Cap Martin, the hat of a lady guest blew into the Mediterranean. A fierce mistral was raging, with wind and horizontal rain churning up the waters. Aspinall bet he could retrieve the hat for a certain inflated sum, and dived in. Having swum out successfully, he appeared to experience some difficulty in getting back against the current. Laughter gave way to serious alarm when it was realised he was in real danger, and Eddie swam out to assist him. When they were close enough to shore, a lifebuoy was hurled on to the water, and both men, exhausted, limped to safety.

Aspinall's wife Jane was equally a source of great strength during these see-saw years. She stood by him in adversity, selling her jewellery whenever funds were needed and waiting for him impulsively to buy replacements when funds were at hand (when she would spend as recklessly as he). She was what his friends called 'game', and so totally did she admire him that there was nothing she would not do to support him. Some likened the pair to the notorious American couple Bonnie and Clyde, and it was suspected that Aspinall required her to flirt with gamblers in order to prolong their presence at the green table. (Quite erroneous, as it happens; he cannot bear flirtation.) On the other hand, her emotional needs were greater than his, and his unusual attitude towards women, born of a theoretic view of their place in the hierarchy of a primate society, made scant allowance for sentiment. Other women found themselves attracted by his cavalier regard for them, and were generally warned off by wise counsel; it was said that John Aspinall did not take women seriously.

More pointedly, it was also said that he was peculiarly adroit in using all his friends and social contacts as ammunition in his cunning strategy to reach the summits he had set for himself. None of them appeared to object to being so used. He was shortly to require all his skill, and all their acquiescence, in his boldest venture so far. For the new Gaming Act of 1960 for the first time in the twentieth century opened the door to the establishment of legal casinos

in London, and, after continuing with his floating games for
a year or more, Aspinall realised that if he did not want to be
left stranded as a fossil of the previous Act, he would have to
open a club of his own. Naturally, it would need to be better
than all the others.

5

The Clermont Club

Paragraph 412 of the Report of the Royal Commission on Betting and Gaming recommended that the law be amended 'to prevent persons being induced to play for high stakes for the profit of the promoter'. The phrasing might well have been chosen with John Aspinall in mind, but in fact the Commission's Report had been delivered some nine years before and had lain neglected by successive governments reluctant to tackle such a serpentine subject. It was generally accepted that a Statute which made the playing of slydethrift (or 'shove ha'penny') a punishable offence was archaic and ridiculous, yet the fear persisted that any relaxation of legal prohibitions could transform sedate and decorous England into a sordid den of gamblers bereft of all morality. Aspinall's spectacular success in recent years had, however, lent urgency to the problem, and it was largely to clip his wings that the Government drafted Section II of its Betting and Gaming Bill, presented to Parliament by the Home Secretary, R.A. Butler, on 16 November 1959.

Both Mr Butler and the Lord Chancellor (Lord Kilmuir), who introduced the Bill to the Lords on 23 May 1960, were at pains to point out that gambling was virtually as old as mankind and could never be entirely eradicated. A citizen of Pompeii had recorded on a wall that he had won 855 denarii on a trip to Nuceria, and loaded dice were found beneath the ashes there. The astralagus, or knuckle-bone, was the forerunner of dice, and archaeologists had found these bones used for gambling purposes even as far back as the sixteenth century BC. Therefore moral indignation was beside the point. It was important to bring betting and gaming legislation into line with twentieth century social habits and requirements, to make a fresh start and sweep away all previous laws on the subject.

Notwithstanding this sage advice, some Members still felt the need to demonstrate their allegiance against the Devil, and Mr George Thomas, the strictly Nonconformist Labour Member who would one day be Speaker of the House of Commons, made a glorious *faux pas* in declaring righteously that he 'regarded sin as a gamble'.

The main provisions of Section II were contained in paragraphs 15 and 16: 'that premises shall not be a common gaming-house by reason of the carrying on of gaming thereon'; that the chances should be equally favourable to all the players and not especially favourable to the promoter (i.e. anyone must be able to hold the bank); and that 'no money or money's worth which any of the players puts down as stakes, or pays by way of losses, or exchanges for tokens used in playing the game, is disposed of otherwise than by payment to a player as winnings'. In other words, Aspinall and his like would no longer be permitted to take a percentage down the *cagnotte*; all the money must be won by someone.

On the other hand, if the premises on which the game was taking place was a club, then it was perfectly proper to charge an annual subscription and/or to prescribe a minimum stake, provided only that the players had joined the club at least twenty-four hours before, and that the club was not 'of a merely temporary character'.

The absurdly flaccid drafting of Section II was expected by the legislators, unbelievably, to pull in the reins on big-time gambling. Mr W. Rees-Davies told the Commons that this part of the Bill was inserted 'to stop this country from becoming a casino country'. 'If people want to play these games,' he added, 'let them go to France!' Rarely can the effect of legislation have been so distant from its promise.

Only one MP, Sir Frank Soskice, correctly foresaw the future. He lamented that the law which prohibited premises being used habitually for gaming was to be thrown overboard. 'A person may, in effect, game as much as he likes, for stakes as high as he likes, as long as he likes and where he likes, without any restriction whatever, subject to two conditions.' This, he thought, was extremely dangerous, 'containing the seeds of great ill'. If the sole safeguards were that the game should be fair and the promoter should not take a cut, then 'an awful lot of people are going to be fleeced'.

In the House of Lords, Lord Mancroft also spotted danger. 'I suspect we are building one law for the rich and one law for the very rich,' he warned, but then added, oddly, 'but that does not matter.'

The Bill became law on 29 July 1960, and the England of bingo halls, betting shops and casinos was launched. The first to take advantage of the new Act was a character of dubious reputation called John Mills, a Polish immigrant who had been a heavyweight boxing champion and who, at 6 feet 6 inches and with a sinister moustache, still looked as if he could be troublesome in dispute. Within weeks of Mills opening his Cercle Club at Les Ambassadeurs the word was circulating that his croupiers were not acting entirely in accordance with the 'fairness' clause enshrined in the new law. One evening Lord Derby lost £165,000 in what was suspiciously regarded as a 'bent' game; the evening has passed into the lore of gambling history. (A few years later, Lord Derby broke the habit of a lifetime, and never gambled again.)

The casinos which Mr Rees-Davies had fondly sought to banish from England's shores proliferated; more than fifty opened in the space of less than two years, and a new service was provided by London's incoming tour operators. As soon as a group of tourists landed, their coach took them to a casino on the way to their hotel so that they might join and be at the tables the following day. Some casinos encouraged this traffic by being particularly nice to the guides.

John Aspinall was not, of course, in competition with such lowly clubs as these, but he was slow to see that he could not continue with his lucrative private games for very long, when punters were being enticed by attractive premises each trying to out-do the other in sparkle. He was not perturbed by the clause requiring that all the money staked by the players should be returned to the winners, for he had already devised a scheme which would permit compliance and still afford him an income. Gamblers bought two kinds of chips when they played at his games: one colour to play with, and one to be used as a tip for the croupier (or for Aspinall himself), after a winning bank. All his regulars were aware of the system and made no objection. Moreover, it was perfectly legal.

When the richly apparelled gaming-house Crockford's opened in 1961, Aspinall at last realised he would have to make a move. His turnover had diminished dramatically and he needed to catch up if he were to maintain his position. Two major difficulties stood in the way. First, he must find a suitable property, and second, he must pay for it. Despite the ruse with chips donated by his punters, Aspinall's income from 1960 to 1962 was virtually nil, and he could not possibly open a club to receive the kind of clientele he would wish in anything but the most opulent surroundings at the smartest address. It was important that his club should be quite unlike the others. In the event, it was.

At 44 Berkeley Square stood a town house of such mag-nificence that it was regarded by estate agents as a 'white elephant'. Prospective purchasers were discouraged by heavy legal protection which forbade any structural alterations inside or out and the house had lain empty, forsaken, and rather seedy for a number of years. The previous owner's family had inhabited it for nearly a century, leaving behind a mouldy atmosphere of Victorian comfort which invited wholesale renovation. When Aspinall saw it he knew immediately that beneath the dust was precisely the style of eighteenth-century elegance which best suited the kind of ambience he would want to foster. He took a twenty-one-year lease from Samuel Properties at a rent of £12,500 a year, guaranteed by three of his friends, and set about restoring the mansion to its former grandeur. After Howletts, it was to be his second exercise in major restoration and, as it turned out, probably his most remarkable.

The reasons for the rigid preservation order which protected 44 Berkeley Square were not difficult to discover. It was quite simply one of the rarest treasures of metropolitan domestic architecture, the finest private house left in London. Built by William Kent in 1740-2, it was 'one of the masterpieces of the eighteenth century, a Palladian jewel which many consider to be the crowning glory of his career'. Historians jostled one another in their extravagant praise but, while Kent was justly famous for the superb Holkham Hall in Norfolk, for the recently demolished Devonshire House in London, and for much else besides, the fact that he applied his genius to the constraints of a relatively small town house was not widely known. And this was the *only* surviving London house that Kent had built.

In 1740 the area now known as Berkeley Square was the back garden of Devonshire House, fronting on to Piccadilly. Lady Isabella Finch, one of the many daughters of the 7th Earl of Winchelsea, bought a plot of land there and commissioned William Kent, who was then working on Holkham, to build her a house. His instructions were to construct a mansion which befitted the station of an earl's daughter, one which could be used for impressive entertaining but not be too spacious – in other words, a palace hidden behind a terrace. That he achieved this was little short of miraculous.

Fortunately, Lady Isabella, usually known as Lady Bel, was middle-aged, a spinster and likely to remain so. (The whole family were called the 'dark, funereal Finches' by Walpole, and the Earl, nicknamed 'Don Dismal', was a powerful but gloomy Tory politician. The girls were so swarthy in complexion as to make any suitor shrink with foreboding.) This meant that Kent needed only to provide one main bedroom and boudoir, and could exercise his imagination on the more public areas. 'He plainly enjoyed designing this minuscule masterpiece,' wrote Robert Harling, 'and it is easy to believe he had his own way at every turn – the architect's eternal dream.'

The house was, and is still, devastatingly theatrical. The entrance hall is simple enough, with a little cubby hole for the porter, but then, after a few steps, an interior of breathtaking splendour is revealed, suddenly there as if a curtain has gone up on stage. The amazing staircase, which rises through four floors to the full height of the building, is classical in conception and baroque in design, but more than anything else it is of a beauty hardly credible in the space allowed. Walpole said the staircase was 'as beautiful a piece of scenery and, considering the space, of art as can be imagined,' and more recently Robert Harling wrote of 'as spectacular and audacious a piece of architectural bravura as the 18th century can show'. The staircase led up to the grand saloon, once more a unique achievement and the finest room of its period in London. Rising to the height of two floors, with dummy windows seen from the street on the upper level, it was a room made for receptions. The ceilings by Zucchi were still intact when Aspinall first saw the house; indeed, the place was virtually unchanged since 1742, a gem of fossilised elegance. 'Few respectable spinsters of the day can have been housed quite as magnificently as Lady Bel at 44 Berkeley Square,' wrote Christopher Simon Sykes. Fittingly, she was also fond of holding card parties at which London's ladies would gather although they did not exactly call themselves gamblers.

After Lady Bel, the house went to the 1st (and last) Earl of Clermont, William Fortescue, a robust and vigorously healthy man, with calm good manners and an even temper. His conversation was lively and well-informed, his company the most congenial. There was much about him which seemed echoed in the character of John Aspinall, and nothing more than his predilection for gambling. Lord Clermont was known as the 'Father of the Turf', won the Derby with 'Aimwell' in 1785 and was a renowned sportsman. He was also well connected, a close friend of the Prince of Wales and Charles James Fox (gamblers both), while his wife Frances was equally close to Marie Antoinette. It is tempting to think that Fox might have gambled at 44 Berkeley Square; there is no evidence, but it would be far more surprising if he hadn't.

John Aspinall decided that the memory of its former owner should be preserved in the name of the house, and so announced that his club would be known as 'the Clermont'. It is a pity that the name had been invented in the first place; Fortescue lived at Randalstown, County Louth, and when he chose his title he must simply have thought that it sounded grand, for there was no such place as Clermont on any of his estates (he changed the name of his house in Ireland to Clermont, but that was after he had assumed the strange title).

Aspinall again engaged John Fowler to decorate the club, with Philip Jebb as consulting architect, and again gave them *carte blanche* as to cost. (No. 44 is indeed lucky to have been 'created' only twice, and on both occasions by people who did not count pennies.) Fowler is on record as having enjoyed this commission almost more than any other, both because he was not restrained and because he felt possessed by the spirit of the house. He added one shaped plain mirror in a strategic place on the staircase which had the effect of multiplying the stairway into a series of glittering horizontal and vertical views. He kept the splendour of the Grand Saloon on the first floor, but had naturally to accept that lines would be interrupted by gaming-tables, for this was to be the principal room for gambling. For the Club Room John Fowler assembled a group of relaxing armchairs and sofas which any club would envy, and covered both them and the walls in the muddy greens of England, a perfect background to William Kent's glowing marble and gold.

Fowler was given a few months for the task but, when he had finished, the Clermont Club was already without doubt the most beautiful venue for gambling anywhere in Europe. As Harling put it, 'If one must lose a million, this is the place to do so in style.' What Aspinall had done was to resurrect the elegant surroundings which made gambling such a pleasure in the eighteenth century, and rescue the activity from the trough of shamefulness and squalor into which it had sunk as a result of Victorian prudery. Gambling must henceforth be not only enjoyable but proud.

And yet the venture was almost killed at birth by one of those awkward reversals of fate which occur from time to time in John Aspinall's life. One month before he was due to open the Clermont, and when the cost of restoration had mounted to £90,000, he lost all his money on the American stock market and was left almost penniless.

It was perhaps an example of Aspinall's curious application of loyalty that he had invested so much of his funds in a company controlled by one of his friends. Eddie Gilbert had bought control of E. L. Bruce, a large lumber company operating from Tennessee, and Aspinall bought £150,000 worth of stock, half of which was paid up. In the Wall Street crash of May 1962, the price descended from $32 to nil in three days, the shares were suspended, and Aspinall's investment was wiped out. Worse, he now owed £75,000 to the stockbrokers, who visited him in grim and sombre mood to point out that they would be hammered unless he was able to pay up. The debt was sold to a merchant bank and Aspinall spent the next fourteen months paying it off, one instalment per month. The episode presents a vivid illustration of his character, for he did not once consider either of the two consequences one would normally expect to flow from such a disaster: he did not cancel plans to open the Clermont Club (though, as we shall see, he was obliged to relinquish control of the basement), and he did not turn with bitterness or anger upon Eddie Gilbert, the author of his tribulation. The one might be regarded as foolhardy, the other sentimental, but in Aspinall's case both responses were in tune with a personality still rooted in mythical values and boyish enthusiasms.

When he realised that Gilbert was ruined, Aspinall wept. He could not conceive that a man whose wizardry and will he so much admired should be brought low, could not bear that the pedestal should be kicked from under one of his heroes – what he could not conceive or bear he would not accept, and he clung to the firm faith he held in Gilbert's resilience and skill. To do otherwise would have been to admit that his judgment was wanting, and part of Aspinall's success has been due to his persistent refusal ever to envisage such a possibility. It has infuriated the Gaming Board and the Ministry of the Environment for different reasons over the years, but it has nearly always got him what he wanted.

Eddie Gilbert was indicted for unauthorised withdrawal of corporate funds and fled to Brazil. While Aspinall was bound to accept that this meant embezzlement in law, he would not see any moral shame in the actions of a man who, in his view, did everything possible in adversity to save the situation. Immediately, with his wife Jane and Richard Parkes, he boarded a plane for Rio de Janeiro to see what he could do to help. They found Gilbert reduced to penury, living in an hotel, forlorn and miserable because he thought that all his value resided in his rapidly-acquired wealth and that, once denuded, he was nobody.

For a week, Aspinall devoted his energies to the restoration of Eddie Gilbert's self-esteem. Though he was himself now in serious debt, he paid for everything, just as Gilbert had paid when Aspinall had been teetering on the edge of normal life, engaging in an elaborate charade to bolster his friend's reputation. Behaving as if he were among the richest men in the world, Aspinall went to the jeweller H. Stern and bought $3,000 worth of precious stones (he had only £400 to spend), in order that Stern should be impressed and should then heed his advice to use Gilbert's expertise on the stock market. It did not entirely work (Stern invited them all to lunch on his yacht, which turned out to be a picnic on a small boat), but it was worth the effort to save Gilbert from ignominy. Likewise, Jane sold her jewellery (she was by now used to having recourse to this stratagem every now and again) and gave the proceeds to Gilbert. It is significant that Aspinall did not feel moved at any time to suggest Eddie Gilbert should look for employment and renew himself through toil.

Similarly, when later Gilbert was imprisoned in the notorious maximum security prison at Scarborough, New York, called Sing Sing, Aspinall sent money to support Gilbert's wife and flew across the Atlantic to visit the prisoner. With an embarrassing lack of subtlety, he pressed dollar bills of large denominations across the table into the hands of Gilbert, who then had to secrete them through his fly into his underpants. Aspinall appeared to be impervious to the danger, uninhibited by the risk; it was the sort of 'dare' a young boy would welcome, and, on a more mature level, it demonstrated an intense degree of loyalty that would not falter in the face of uncomfortable facts. The only crime he was willing to acknowledge was that Gilbert should be imprisoned.

In the light of these events, it is fairly astonishing that the Clermont Club should have been ready for trading at all in 1962, when its proprietor had just seen much of his fortune disintegrate. The date for the opening was postponed by two months to November, and Pearson, the legendary Hall Porter at White's, was engaged to advise on staffing. This would be, after all, John Aspinall's baptism as an employer, his previous skeleton staff of waiters at his floating games having been taken on *ad hoc*. The Clermont was to be a large organisation requiring secretaries and accountants and a chef and kitchen hands, as well as the usual croupiers. Life would never be quite so relaxed or impromptu as in the old days. Aspinall would be, officially and properly, a man of business.

There was no mystery about the financing of the Clermont. Aspinall had nothing himself, so he raised the money in his customary manner from friends, who were not merely willing but anxious to invest in him. Convinced that there was no one better suited to the running of a smart gaming club, they did not hesitate to buy £1,000 of loan stock each, which entitled them to £100 of shares. In this way, by parting with only 20 per cent of the equity, Aspinall raised £200,000. Big investors included Bernard van Cutsem, Lord Willoughby d'Eresby and Simon Fraser (the three who personally guaranteed the rent of 44 Berkeley Square), and also Jocelyn Hambro and the Duke of Atholl, while scores of small investors made up the total. (Ten years later they would have all their loan stock repaid, plus eight times their investment.) Membership of the club was limited to six hundred persons at 20 guineas a year (£21), and the list of members

presents the best roll-call of rich and exclusive London society of the 1960s that exists. There were five dukes and five
marquesses, nearly twenty earls, one actor (Peter Sellers), one
member of the Royal Family (Prince William of Gloucester),
one writer (Françoise Sagan), two Cabinet Ministers, two
Gettys, two Packers, two Goldsmiths, two Arab princes, two
American ambassadors, and the producer of the James Bond
films, Albert Broccoli.

It had always been Aspinall's intention to use the basement area, with its own entrance down steps at the side, as
a high-class night-club with live music to complement the
gaming club and serve the tastes of the same clientele. But
the crash of Eddie Gilbert's stock meant that even *he* could no
longer indulge his every ambition and had to recognise that
he simply could not afford it. At first he planned to leave it
vacant for a year or two, but then made an arrangement with
his friend Mark Birley to lease him the basement, plus mews
and cellars, for the amazingly paltry sum of £40 a week. With
this Birley created what was quickly to become, without risk
of exaggeration, the best-known and most chic discothèque
in the world, which he named after his wife, Lady Annabel,
sister of the Marquess of Londonderry. Thus the two symbols of extravagant 1960s' hedonism, the Clermont Club and
Annabel's, existed one above the other in the same building.

Aspinall and Birley quarrelled shortly afterwards over the
shared use of part of the basement, including the wine cellar,
and began a *froideur* which was to last for twenty years.
(Birley, a perfect example of the Eton-bred English gentleman with an air of effortless superiority, found it difficult
to forgive the success of Aspinall, whom he would naturally
have regarded as an upstart.) It has to be said, however, that
Aspinall could not have chosen anyone with better taste to
take over the basement, Birley decorating Annabel's with
such exquisite control and such attention to warmth and
cosiness that it rivalled the comfort and elegance of the
club upstairs.

The first two years of the Clermont were something of a
struggle. The club was furnished in a very irregular manner

from Blairman's, a shop in Mount Street where Aspinall
bought much of his furniture. Aspinall told George Levey,
Mr Blairman's young son-in-law, that he would buy all the
furniture he needed, including Regency gaming-tables and
scores of chairs and mirrors, but without paying for them at
once. He proposed to give Levey £200 a month in cheques for
the next three years, in a kind of verbal hire-purchase agreement. Levey assented to the arrangement, for he was by now
used to the man's unorthodox methods. Aspinall had once
turned up in a Rolls-Royce with a brown envelope full of
notes, obviously the day's takings, to pay for a necessary purchase. Besides which, he liked him and applauded his style. If
Aspinall invariably paid late, he never actually let his creditors down, and he looked for their loyalty in return. Once,
during those two years of cliff-hanging, he came rushing into
Blairman's announcing that he desperately needed £2,000
before lunch, otherwise the bank would return one of his
cheques. He would repay the following day, and add £1,000
on top; Levey was his only chance – the alternative was ruin
and humiliation! Though he was nearly sacked for it, Levey
obliged, and Aspinall kept his word. Years later he would
point to the ebullient Mr Levey as The Man Who Saved
The Clermont.

The club soon assumed the reputation of offering the
best food in London. Aspinall took on his old friend from
Oxford, Ian Maxwell-Scott, to manage the restaurant and
cellar, which proved to be a stroke of genius, not only
because Aspinall himself had no head for detail and would
have made a very poor administrator, but also because
Maxwell-Scott's knowledge of wine was exceptional. It soon
became known that the cellar of the Clermont was second
to none, and Maxwell-Scott was responsible, among other
things, for reintroducing Château Petrus to England after
a century's neglect. (It is now among the most scarce and
expensive clarets produced.)

Aspinall's part in the venture was, as always, to entertain.
He would find punters, bring them to the Clermont, flatter
them, amuse them, spoil them. Part of the attraction of the

Clermont was Aspinall himself, although he recognised that he could use other people as 'bait', people whose company was sought by reason of their fame, or name, or strange aura of charm. They would not only inveigle their friends to join, but, more important, would entice the celebrity-hungry and those uncertain herds who needed reassurance that they were mixing with the right people. One such attraction was the 7th Earl of Lucan, a man of enormous presence and beauty, and with a line of illustrious, if occasionally mad, forebears. Lord Lucan looked right, sounded better, and had all the right ideas. People felt more attractive in his company. His parents had been wild left-wing political activists, one of them the Labour Whip in the House of Lords, and Lucan had been obliged to look after himself politically in order to avoid what he deemed corruption. When his mother wanted to take him away from Eton and send him to a mixed com-prehensive school, he had arranged tea for his aunt at the Ritz (he was then about fourteen) and boldly requested that she give him some of the money she intended to leave him in her will, so that he could stay at Eton and pay his own fees. She agreed. This was, of course, behaviour quite in line with the Aspinall philosophy, so one may see why the two men became firm friends.

Years after, Lord Lucan was to be the centre of a consuming mystery, and John Aspinall the one man, perhaps, who might hold a key to it. But for the moment he was content to act as an occasional house-player at the Clermont, without considering himself strictly 'employed'. He was not the idiotic aristocratic fool that some newspapers depicted, because it suited their purpose, but a strange secretive man of some intelligence and odd habits. He signed his name on cheques in a perfectly straight line, preferred unadorned food like smoked salmon, and gave the impression that he hated something intensely, possibly himself.

By 1964, the Clermont Club was the envy of the world for class and sophistication. It was handling the highest stakes in Europe, and John Aspinall was its acknowledged and much-lauded creator. At the same time, much hostility was aroused by the proliferation of gambling clubs in London, which Aspinall regarded as 'chronic', though he was quick to defend the principle of gambling. 'The antipathy towards gambling is based on the Calvinistic teachings of the nonconformist Left which say that pleasure and any profit from pleasure are things to be ashamed of,' he told the *Sunday Express*, and in a letter to the *Sunday Times* he wrote, 'Gambling is an ineradicable and constantly recurring trait in human nature. Whether the stakes are high or low is of relevance to the individual alone, not to any fabricated moral precept. One of the most valuable functions of betting is the corrosive effect it has on such outdated concepts as the sanctity of money and the dignity of labour.'

This is an interesting letter, for it shows clearly enough Aspinall's constant flirtation with paradox, defining truth by the unexpected, upsetting opinions which he liked to consider unreflective with a startling display of surprises. Here was a man making money from the imprudence of others, yet who had less regard for the 'sanctity' of money than the scrupulous savers and careful budgeters who criticised him. Here, too, was a man viewed with distaste by socialists for his lack of concern with the working man, yet who regarded harsh repetitive labour as destructive of the human spirit and inimical to the fun which life may offer. The finest paradox was that most workers, many of whom were betting men themselves, would agree with him.

On the other hand, most working men would be utterly indifferent to, even scornful of, the other side of John Aspinall's life, which was slowly gathering importance and altering his perspectives. For a few years now he had been paying furtive visits alone to the London Zoo where he would gaze upon the famous silverback male gorilla, Guy, locked in his concrete barred prison cell and returning the scowl of a curious public with palpable disdain. Guy was the London Zoo's main attraction, and rare was the visitor who saw him and walked away unaffected. His power, his beauty and his dignity habitually stunned gawpers into reverential silence, and the horrible constraints of his situation aroused a certain woeful pity. Guy seemed philosophic and remote, too grand a personage to complain of his lot, yet betraying through those eloquent eyes the weight of an intolerable boredom.

Aspinall's visits led to an acquaintance with the gorilla keeper, Mr Smith, always known as 'Smithy', who eventually allowed him access behind the scenes. Guy became sufficiently tolerant of Aspinall to permit some small degree of communication and to accept eagerly the exotic fruits which he brought for him, taking the gifts from Aspinall's hand. Smithy said that Guy could spot Aspinall among the crowd outside his bars and his demeanour altered perceptibly when he knew he was about to receive a visit. Guy's influence was more profound than he could realise, and it would eventually benefit his species in a measurable way. John Aspinall formed the romantic, absurd notion that, one day, he would count an adult male gorilla as his friend.

His first step was to buy Kivu, a male gorilla with a sorry past. Like so many caught in the wild, Kivu had in all likelihood seen his family massacred and been treated subsequently with less than ordinary respect. The international dealers were known for their commercial greed and utter indifference to the welfare of animals. Kivu was bought from one of these men for £1,700, and cared for at Howletts with exquisite love by Aspinall's mother-in-law, Mrs Hastings, who let him sleep regularly in her bed and poured pure affection upon him. He responded well for a time, but Kivu's spirit had been broken by his hideous experiences and he survived only a year at Howletts. John Aspinall remains convinced that he died of a broken heart. He is buried just in front of the cottage at the main entrance of the estate.

He then bought a male and a female, Gugis and Shamba, from whom he learnt the foundation of his knowledge of gorilla habits and nature, now acknowledged to be profound. Shamba survives to this day; she has been (in 1987) twenty-seven years at Howletts.

The big gamblers of the Clermont Club had no inkling that their promoter had been a solitary visitor to London

Zoo. They knew about his private collection of animals by hearsay, of course, but they regarded it as a foible, a foolish eccentricity. The clientele of the Clermont was largely composed of the rich Newmarket aristocracy, who traditionally regarded wildlife as merely something to be shot at, and the top echelons of New World businessmen, for whom the excellence of the human species was unassailable, and the rest of the natural world unworthy of much attention. That the proprietor of the Clermont should himself be growing into a conservationist was decidedly dotty. Those few who bothered to think about it assumed he was a dilettante who had found a novel way to show off.

There may well have been some truth in this hasty assessment. Aspinall had created for himself the décor and the manner of a Regency beau out of his time. He had the looks and the wit, the gambling club and the friends drawn from 'society', the contempt for money and the blinding extravagance; he was an extraordinary host and a patron of fine artists and craftsmen;* and he had a mansion in the country with acres of his own. Eighteenth-century gentlemen often boasted a menagerie of exotic beasts for the ladies to gaze upon; they were seen as symbolic of their status and indicative of their ingenuity. Perhaps Aspinall's collection began in this emulative way, as a further element in the structure of his self-invention. If he was seen as eccentric, that would suit him very well indeed, for many a Regency beau was unusual in his enthusiasms.

Added to this, there was an undeniable commercial advantage. On more than one occasion, Aspinall took his tiger 'Tara' to the club, and to see her loping down that elegant staircase was at once beautiful, incongruous and mad. It made the club a constant subject of conversation and was not at all bad for incidental publicity.

There was, of course, much more to it than this, but

---

*He has commissioned works from Spencer Roberts and Leonard Pearman, as well as massive bronze sculptures of gorillas and a rhinoceros by William Timyn.

the neighbours in Kent may be forgiven for not wishing to explore the philosophy behind the cacophony of screeches and grunts emanating from Howletts to disturb their nights. Nor were they at all pleased with the frequency of escapes. Aspinall in 1960 had bears, tigers, cheetahs, gorillas and deer, and he seemed to find it irksome to cope with the matter of security. He was in London at least four days a week, so that the animals were left largely in the care of his wife Jane and his mother-in-law Mrs Hastings, as well as one keeper, Derek Rushmer. They were far more like an extended family than an exhibition. The charm of it was overwhelming. A guest at Howletts would take a stroll after lunch with tigers, children, gorillas, all in complete freedom and friendship. The obverse was the animals' wish to take such strolls when Aspinall was not there.

When the Himalayan bears escaped and were loose on the estate for twelve hours, causing genuine fear to many quiet country folk, the leading neighbour in Bekesbourne decided to do something about it. In the summer of 1960 Mr Mount made an application for an interim injunction to restrain John Victor Aspinall from keeping tigers, cheetahs, bears, apes and deer, on the grounds that he feared for the safety of his children. John Victor Aspinall was so contemptuous of the action that not only did he not appear in court, but he was abroad at the time and could not be contacted by letter or telephone. His lawyers successfully applied for an adjournment for two weeks, during which time there unfortunately occurred another escape. As a result, Aspinall through his lawyers gave an undertaking to the court that he would engage and provide accommodation for a full-time keeper to look after the animals. It was an easy undertaking to give, for neither Mount nor the court knew that such a keeper was already in employment.

Aspinall was making the first steps towards being a responsible zoo-keeper rather than a landowner with a curious private hobby. He came gradually to feel that not only were these animals beautiful and mysterious, but that he, as a member of the exploiting species, owed them a very heavy debt. These decisions were not reached through the careful reading of precise zoological tracts, although naturally his library began to expand with books on animal husbandry and observation of wildlife, books which soon overtook the Zulu collection in extent and later supplanted it in significance. It was on the contrary an unashamedly emotional evolution which took place in direct measure to his deepening ties with the animals. To the amazement of the gambling fraternity, John Aspinall was turning into an advocate of animal welfare. He began to voice his abhorrence of the arrogant assumptions, enshrined in the very language we use, which place all potential good in the heart of *Homo sapiens* and all evil in the behaviour of animals.

Examples abound, and are often enshrined in myth or proverb. Foxes are said to be 'cunning', whereas they are in reality far more stupid than a wolf or dog. A cunning nature is a quality the human does not like to contemplate in himself, so he transfers it to an animal which he regards as an enemy, then proceeds to use it as an excuse for torturing the animal to death. The fox could not possibly aspire to the human quality of 'cunning'. The dove is said to be 'peaceful' because it is white and whiteness is simplistically associated with purity. In fact it is quite an aggressive creature, but to admit as much would be to upset the human order which apportions vice and virtue arbitrarily and treats the living world as if it were bound, in some way, to conform. All the scavengers, including vultures and hyenas, are spoken of in derogatory terms, because their habits are such as we deplore in ourselves, without pausing to reflect that this does not render them deplorable in vultures and hyenas; even naturalists have been known to describe hyenas as 'disgusting' and 'cowardly', which is patent nonsense, and means only that the naturalist is a jot too introspective.

Three of the creatures thus maligned by force of habit are the tiger, the wolf, and the gorilla; these three in particular John Aspinall set out to know and discover for himself. All three are said to be ferocious, and none of them is. I myself have heard judges accuse defendants who have been convicted of murder or violent acts, not merely of having behaved 'like animals', which is a common enough error, but of having no more self-control than a gorilla, which in fact has remarkable self-control.

This degree of ignorance disturbed Aspinall's latent anger as he grew to know his animals better; he felt his friends were being insulted, and would frequently rise to their defence in an explosion of hortatory indignation. As he came to understand the workings of evolution and the intricacies of ethology, so his philosophy deepened, became more subtle and allusive, more committed. He was turning into a proselytiser, one who felt driven to convince his interlocutor that morality was not the monopoly of man, was not even invented by man, but was inherited from his animal forebears, whose parallel descendants, our contemporaries, have inherited similar restraints and preferences.

The tiger, he later wrote, had suffered character assassination which was totally unwarranted; in China it was classed as vermin, a strange term to use of rightful owners of terrain which humans intend to steal. On the wolf, Aspinall was particularly acerbic:

> There are over twenty epithets and expressions in the English language which refer to the wolf – all of them derogatory or pejorative in implication. Our hatred for this animal must stem from the recent pastoral epoch when the great northern forests were rapidly felled and replaced by grassland for cattle and sheep. During the severe winters the wolf . . . became a competitor of ours for beef and mutton. Man declared war on the wolf and in the process attempted a character assassination. It is only in the last twenty years that the true nature of this beautiful pack-hunter has become known . . . The likelihood of the Red Riding-Hood legend is that the grandmother ate the wolf and used its skin as a bed rug.

By observation and experiment, and it should be said also by study, for his proud contention that nobody taught him anything and that he had no degrees in any zoological discipline must not prevent recognition that he was reading widely in this and related subjects, Aspinall was growing into a man with a purpose, and that purpose was fuelled by increasing anger at the stubborn misjudgments which underlay the treatment of animals. Gradually this part of his life assumed crucial importance, against which the business of running a successful casino seemed merely functional. Perhaps he was himself surprised to find that he could be as moved by the spectacle of injustice and as passionately determined to ameliorate it where he could as any radical of the Left. In the first instance, however, it was profoundly felt emotion which drew him to the task. The confirmation of his belief that the terrifying tiger and the fierce, intractable gorilla were nothing of the sort, that their decency could be relied upon, and that he could commune with them on a level which was hitherto inconceivable, touched reserves of tenderness and humility in John Aspinall which, one suspects, are a latent part of human character rarely called upon in lives divorced from contact with other primates. When later he wrote about these first contacts, it was in a way which has to be called moving. The first animal he knew well was the tigress 'Tara', bought from the pet shop at the age of nine weeks:

Tara was a mind-opener for me. We raised her on the bottle and she slept in my bed for the first eighteen months. So sound was her character and so sweet and affectionate her nature that I supposed at first I had an exceptional animal on my hands. Experience subsequently told me that her qualities were typical of her species. To some extent I must have been suborned by the age-old propaganda against the tiger, because I remember being surprised that she never bore malice or resentment . . . the raising of Tara from a cub of two months to an adult swept away many cobwebs. The first to go was the belief that a tiger-cub becomes less reliable and affectionate when it progresses from a milk to a meat diet. The next to disappear was the myth that a tiger will get excited at the smell of fresh blood from an open wound. My experience here was that Tara used to lick a

gash with beneficial effect . . . Another popular story is
that tigers 'revert' to a supposedly pristine state of ferocity
at the threshold of adulthood. This, of course, is far from
the mark, as their natural condition is one of lazy indifference or good nature. My extensive experience of many
tigers has proved that even extreme hunger fails to dispel
their trust and love of man once given and once earned.

Aspinall even challenged the belief that a tigress must not
be disturbed when with her cubs. He visited Tara in her den
when she had her first litter. She purred a greeting, and one of
the cubs approached him. He picked it up. Far from turning
upon him in anger, she promptly collected the other one in
her jaws and dropped it in his lap for inspection. I have myself
seen this happen and know it not to be exaggerated; indeed,
films have been taken which reveal the same. It is difficult to
recall that, twenty years ago, such an occurrence was thought
to be impossible.

To form a relationship with a gorilla is a much slower
process. The gorilla is an aloof, private individual, reluctant
to be disturbed by the insolent proximity of a curious human
unless he chooses the society. After the death of Kivu, Mrs
Hastings raised three more gorillas, of which two, Shamba
and Baby Doll, continue in the colony to this day. It was
to the third, Gugis, the only male so raised, that Aspinall
devoted most of his attention, so learning the precious talent
of mood interpretation. The humour of a gorilla is revealed in
extraordinarily eloquent eyes which, like the human's, may
indicate irritation, disappointment, benevolence, apprehension, enjoyment or love. A degree of trust evolved between
Aspinall and Gugis which continued even when the gorilla
was part of a band of his own species and survived almost
into adulthood. Man and gorilla would play and joust in a
manner which might have seemed extremely dangerous to
the onlooker (and which the female gorillas would watch
with some alarm, occasionally rushing over to protect
Aspinall or deflect Gugis's attention), until one remembered
that the gorilla has the wisdom to recognise his own strength.

Gugis was immensely powerful, but he used his power with remarkable restraint. Films of their play together, when shown in slow-motion, reveal that a swipe from Gugis was actually a mere brush, as he withheld the energy of which he was capable. Again, I may testify to this restraint myself, having frequently played with a younger animal, Djala, and noticed that the bites are not much more than tickles.

Unfortunately, as Gugis grew older, it became apparent that he was emotionally treacherous, pretending to be in one mood while in reality he was in another, and the trust could no longer be taken for granted. Since then, other silverbacks have maintained their tolerance of Aspinall's company even when they are head of a band and are surrounded by a variety of wives, juveniles and infants. But Aspinall's education in the ways of the gorilla began with Gugis, and to that animal he owes the germ of his subsequent influence in the world of animal husbandry.

It should not be imagined for one moment that Aspinall's aim or result was to tame wild creatures. He had no wish to subdue an animal, to render it tractable or docile, but rather wanted to bridge that unnecessary chasm which has for so many millennia separated man from his relations among other primates:

> To cross this bridge and enter the unknown land is a sensation not given to many . . . To those who say how dull must be the company of creatures that have no language or learning, I would answer that the most profound communications are often mute, and that we can learn more from the great mammals than we can possibly teach them.

The idea that one could learn from the observation of animal behaviour was still relatively new, but Aspinall was never attracted by the prospect of accumulating data for their own sake. Rather was it the impulse to glean something of the vast untouched wisdom of animals in the manner of modern ethologists, and to judge what man had lost in long eras of taking himself too seriously. He was stirred by emotional yearning, not scientific curiosity. Even Darwin, twenty

years before *The Origin of Species*, had fallen upon his great
discovery almost by intuition. 'Man in his arrogance thinks
himself a great work, worthy of the interposition of a deity,'
he wrote in his diary. 'More humble and, I believe, true to
consider him created from animals.' Darwin was not the first
to posit evolution; his grandfather, Erasmus Darwin, and
Lamarck had both held that all forms of life evolved gradually
from a common source, not to mention Anaximander in the
sixth century BC. But Darwin was arguably the first to *feel*
its significance, and the reluctance of Victorians to accept his
intuition was due in some part to their inability to feel the
same; it was vulgar to think we were related to such dirty
things as apes and monkeys.

Besides which, it required such a radical translation in
habits of thought to regard other species with anything
approaching respect. Aristotle had declared that life was a
hierarchy, each level existing to serve the one above; thus
plants were for animals and animals for humans, and some
humans were there merely to serve as slaves to the civilised
Greeks. It is well known that the Romans visited the most
appalling horrors upon lions, elephants and bears for their
entertainment, without the smallest moral scruple, though
there were some voices, Plutarch's most notably, raised in
objection. The Church inherited Aristotle's neat and cosy
definitions and refined them. 'Beings that may be treated
simply as means to the perfection of persons,' said St Thomas
Aquinas, 'can have no rights, and to this category the brute
creation belongs.' In such darkness did the human species
remain until late in the nineteenth century.

With Descartes, the prejudices of omnipotent man were
enshrined in the dignity of a philosophical doctrine. He considered that animals were automata, functioning as machines
do. This meant not only that they were soulless, which
the Church already maintained (and still does in Catholic
countries), but also that they could not be hurt. To wrench
a limb from a cat was as harmless (literally) as to snap a twig
from a tree. Malebranche went so far as to kick his dog
around so that he could hear the squeaking of the machine.

1 John Aspinall, aged twelve

2 The Grange, Framfield

3 *(above)* John and Jane Aspinall leaving court after the 'Common Gaming House' case of 1958

4 *(below, left)* 44 Berkeley Square, London, William Kent's only surviving town house, where Aspinall established the Clermont Club in 1962

5 *(below, right)* Howletts

6 Aspinall in 1958 with two of his
first animals, the Himalayan bear,
Esau, and the capuchin monkey,
Dead Loss

7 Damian and Amanda Aspinall

8 Aspinall with his first tiger, Tara, in 1960

It seems to have occurred to no one that if animals were not to be rewarded with everlasting bliss in Heaven, it was more beholden to the humans, who were, to make their lives more comfortable on earth.

There followed the long dismal period of the 'Enlightenment', when Humanists, bestowing upon Man a glory and supremacy quite as lamentable as that inspired by religion, happily subjected living creatures to disgusting disfigurement and torture in the pursuit of knowledge, or sometimes mere curiosity. Examples abound, and one, reported by Addison in the *Spectator*, may suffice:

> A person who was well skilled in dissection opened a bitch, and as she lay in most exquisite tortures offered her one of her young puppies, which she immediately fell a-licking; and for the time seemed insensible to her own pain; on the removal she kept her eye fixed on it and began a wailing sort of cry which seemed to proceed rather from the loss of her young than the sense of her own torment.

To this can be added millions of creatures similarly disgraced in experiments, which, to our shame, continue to the present day; millions reared in dark factories for food; millions torn from wombs for their fur; and millions chased to a slow exhausted death for fun. One may thus well imagine that the disparity between human treatment of our relations in the animal world over thousands of years, and the bold degree of communion which Aspinall was now discovering to be not only possible but natural, normal, might give just cause for gnawing anger. Diners were surprised by Aspinall's decree that the Clermont should not serve paté de foie gras or veal (the only club in London to publish such a decision), but they would have been astonished had they known to what misanthropy this gregarious man was turning. He was beginning to despise the generic snobbery which prevailed even among some ethologists, and refused to make the distinction between 'lower' and 'higher' mammals, which more often than not was a disguise for 'less like us' and 'more like us'. He felt that man and the animals, having come from the same ancestry, were destined for the same future, but that the control of that destiny was in the irresponsible selfish hands of man alone.

The nucleus of the problem lay in our invention of religion. By creating God in our image, we had sanctified ourselves. 'The sanctity of human life is the most dangerous sophistry ever propagated by philosophy,' he said in a speech some years later, 'and it is all too well rooted. Because if it means anything it means the insanctity of species which are *not* human.' The progress of man's inexorable march towards ever more self-indulgence was to him a sad tale of hopeless regress.

Our only chance of reversing direction was to recognise, affectively not intellectually, the importance of our kinship with the rest of life and thus awaken a new responsibility towards all the inhabitants of the planet. Dominion and exploitation should cease and be replaced by respect and humility.

It was perfectly clear to anyone who visited Howletts at this time that Aspinall's dedication to his new cause was genuine and deep. It was also obvious that he spoilt it by bombastic exaggeration. Compromise and accommodation were so foreign to his personality that he was (and remains) blind to their value. He could not see that to pronounce the human race the greatest scourge of the earth in terms so stark might actually sound quite funny, and thus rob the statements of its awful truth. It was this tendency to hyperbole which would be Aspinall's cross in the years to come, when his language made him appear to the impartial less a visionary than an eccentric.

On the other hand, he was always thoroughly honest about his own enjoyment in animal husbandry. He made no attempt to disguise with pious display of virtue his quite obvious personal pleasure. Learning to live with tigers, gorillas and an expanding menagerie of primates was before anything else an enormous joy, a rare privilege. He did it in the first instance for mere selfish reasons, to indulge a pleasure and realise an ambition, and as he learnt more and pondered further, the philosophical implications began to bother him on a secondary level. He was never the kind of ascetic who could sacrifice the rest of his life to the one object of making the world sit up and take note. He was always too much of a hedonist for that, and this, too, made people less willing to accept the seriousness of his endeavour. It seemed that in order to devote oneself to the good of other species one had to deny oneself every happiness given to our own. This was not John Aspinall's style. Secretly, he determined that his contribution would be visible; he would one day be responsible for the salvation of a species.

There was no doubting his passion or his vigour. Yet there were, even then, some questions raised by his partiality for the most glamorous and noble animals. If one is to extend morality beyond the boundary of our own species, it has been suggested, then it should extend so far as to include all creatures, not just the ones thought in human aesthetic judgment to be especially beautiful or impressive. Aspinall freely admitted that he felt 'uplifted' by the animals which increasingly formed the décor of his domestic life; he could not own to similar sensations in the presence of perhaps equally sensitive, equally endangered species which, for whatever reason, did not excite his interest. Oddly enough, Aspinall was guilty of some sentimentality here; he was unwilling to acknowledge that respect for animals had to be impartial and all-embracing. Respect for gorillas must lose some of its power when accompanied by contempt for the fawning domestic dog.

Another consequence of Aspinall's new enthusiasm was to strengthen his belief in élitism and confirm his distaste for social egalitarianism. Darwin had himself been a traditional liberal and Karl Marx had in fact wanted to dedicate his book to him, yet the logical outcome of his evolutionary theories was to throw socialism into disarray. The doctrine that all men were born equal and that differences between them were owed entirely to education or environmental conditions could no longer survive the scrutiny of intelligent men (he thought), for evolution demonstrated that characteristics and differences were congenitally inherited. Hierarchies among people, based upon degrees of power or talent or initiative, were just as inevitable as they were among other animals, for they were passed down in the genes throughout the history of the species.

John Aspinall's close observation of his own animals and their intricate social organisation would uphold his conviction that equality was unbiological and its disciples either mistaken or fraudulent.

6
Gambling for Gorillas

After a somewhat tougher start than anticipated, the Clermont Club continued to gather reputation in almost direct proportion to Aspinall's developing involvement with animals. Never one to be absorbed by details of administration, he was content to delegate management and show himself as the presiding spirit in the evening. It was fortunate that the club made handsome profits, since these were increasingly needed to feed and house the expanding colonies of exotic inhabitants at Howletts. Gamblers' gold was destined for primates' stomachs.

Aspinall prided himself on being an amateur. 'I am lucky that nobody taught me anything. It is a huge advantage to know nothing. A degree in zoology would have sent me along the wrong path.' By subordinating all decisions to the one central aim of giving animals what they like, keeping them, as far as possible, in comfort and happiness, Aspinall was being unscientific, and as his exploits became more widely known, he was looked upon with scorn and rather patient derision. The men with degrees would not countenance the possibility that he might learn by experience and would not forgive his trespassing in their professional pond. He, as usual, enjoyed shocking people in authority, especially if they owed their position to academic toil. He retained a juvenile contempt for 'swots', typical of those who cannot concentrate for long.

It was the habit in zoos to feed animals according to what people thought was good for them, and this generally meant a composite gruel of vitamins and proteins in the desirable proportions. Gorillas are still fed a kind of square grey cake which, apart from being boring, is fairly difficult to munch; in Milwaukee Zoo they used to be fed granulated carrot, which they could only eat by scooping the carrot up and dropping it on to an extended lower lip. Aspinall pioneered the feeding of herbs, plants and fruit to gorillas, simply by offering them and watching to see which they preferred.

Aspinall's point is this: if you should find yourself imprisoned in a grand hotel in the South of France, for example, with all comforts, but given exactly the same food every day, a measured lump of bread and a bowl of soup, then you would suffer from the restrictions placed upon your *enjoyment* of food. Incarceration has already reduced your behavioural opportunities drastically, so that the food you eat becomes *more* important, not less, than it was in freedom. It is the one aspect of your life which may still be enlivened by variety. Gorillas in the wild are used to hundreds of different kinds of food, so it is obviously a deprivation to restrict them to just a few. A deprived gorilla is not a happy gorilla and will not be a breeding gorilla.

In other words, by the selfless application of imagination, one is able to intuit what a gorilla wants. It is only possible if one treats the animal with the most perfect respect, considering his needs and preferences as important as one's own. This Aspinall was prepared to do from the very beginning. His only criterion for the selection of food was the question, do they like it? As a result, the gorillas at Howletts found themselves offered Kiwi fruit, pawpaws, mangoes, spinach, the very finest fresh dates, sugar cane, celery, peaches, nuts, grapes, pomegranates, until the weekly list grew to over 150 different varieties, more or less equivalent to what they would find available in the wild. It was ambitious and indulgent, but it was impossible to deny that it was right. Now, many years later, the policy has proven scientifically valuable as well; in a recent study in San Diego of gorillas which had died in captivity, almost all of them had evidence of tooth decay, in some cases leading directly to death. None of the Howletts gorillas has any tooth decay whatever.

The first gorilla ever to be seen in England was Pongo in the middle of the nineteenth century. He was such a curiosity that his image adorned countless *objets*. He was painted, sculpted, cast in bronze, engraved, written about – a peerless celebrity whose picture still crops up in antique shops. He was fed on cottage pie and died after a few weeks.

A hundred years later, Guy at London Zoo ate (so it was calculated by someone who enjoys this kind of mathematical game) sixteen thousand ice-creams in his lifetime. In old age he retained only fourteen of his teeth.

Aspinall then experimented with the kind of floor-covering his gorillas should use. It was, of course, totally insane to expect them to live their lives on bare, hard concrete. In the forests of Africa they have a 6-inch natural organic litter to play with and rest upon. At Howletts Aspinall tried wheat straw, but found it was too soft and rotted too quickly. Barley straw contained a mite which made the animals itch, so that, too, was rejected. In the end he settled for oat-straw. The director of a European zoo asked him what zoological paper he had read to bring him to this choice; Aspinall retorted by earnestly enquiring what paper had recommended to the Europeans that concrete was the best flooring for gorillas.

Some zoos now use woodwool, but many give nothing at all for bedding. Observation in the jungle shows how gorillas make a nest at night by arranging litter and branches around them before snuggling in. Still, some zoo directors looked askance at Aspinall's 'irresponsible gimmicks'. They objected (and still do object) that straw gives unnecessary extra work for the keepers, a consideration which could never obtrude in an establishment where the animals' requirements are paramount. Their second objection was that straw bedding may be unhygienic. Zoos are frequently fanatical about hygiene. Aspinall held the view that it was better to give gorillas straw, which they like, even if they risk some contamination, on the grounds that they then have the opportunity to develop immunity to the awkward things that live in the straw. It was healthier, he thought, to grow immune than always to remain vulnerable. The attitude is not widely shared in the zoological world.

Even more offensive to the professionals was John Aspinall's insistence that animals and people should mix on a social level and his encouragement of 'bonding'. There was plenty of evidence as to how important was bonding in gorilla society. His gorillas indulged in a certain amount of hugging, tandem-walking (one holding the other from behind, occasionally even in threes), and close face-looking. All this appeared to strengthen their bonds, and Aspinall, by emulating their behaviour, enabled the bonds to cross the species-barrier. On one occasion the consequence of this attachment was given touching expression. Aspinall was walking in the park after lunch with his wife Jane, his son Damian, then four years old, and his band of gorillas, numbering about six. Being young and slow, Damian fell behind the rest and found himself lost and isolated; he began to cry. A female gorilla, Moundou, heard his sobs and turned away from the band to walk back more than 100 yards and look for him. When she found him, Damian climbed on to her back and the two rejoined the family on their afternoon ramble.

The animals naturally increased the burden of family responsibilities. A gorilla once had to be motored up to London to undergo an operation for a hernia in an exclusive Harley Street clinic. He aroused curiosity in the corridors, but could hardly deflect imperturbable British nurses from their duties. The effect was otherwise when workmen came to wallpaper Mrs Hastings's cottage on the Howletts estate. As they went upstairs, she requested they should not make too much noise, as two gorillas were asleep and 'they like their sleep as much as you do'. The men had not heard of the growing population at Howletts and no doubt dismissed her remark as the product of a prematurely senile imagination. As they set about their work, two large heads revealed themselves from beneath heavy blankets, yawning with alarming ostentation. The men fled within seconds, and were never seen again.

A similar panic, rather more understandable, ensued when a man came to deliver sacks of coke. He did not know that a very pleasant tiger, Zemo, was dozing quietly under a laurel bush nearby; or, moreover, that Zemo's favourite game was to pounce upon empty sacks and tear them to shreds, pretending they were prey. He was normally provided with a couple of sacks a day to keep him happy. When the man paused from his labours after unloading five sacks of coke, and lit a cigarette, he suddenly spied a full-grown tiger a few feet away, about to spring. He screamed, and Zemo pounced upon the delicious sacks with fearsome growls. The man was later discovered on his knees reciting the Lord's Prayer.

In the early days of the zoo, there were rather more escapes than were good for Aspinall's reputation with the local population. He was undeniably careless about security, or rather unwilling to concede that those with less knowledge of animal behaviour than he should respond to an escape with fear and hatred. As Hediger wrote, 'escaped beasts of prey are not dangerous absconding criminals, but just wild animals undergoing flight reaction . . . they try first and foremost to put a safe distance between themselves and man'. A wolf once spent five days wandering in the forest while the local press claimed that the neighbourhood was terrorised. Aspinall eventually found her by howling into the night and waiting for her howls in reply. Far from having terrorised the neighbours, none had actually seen her, and she had not eaten for five days and nights.

There was an occasion when local farmers were genuinely frightened, to such an extent that Aspinall has not been forgiven to this day, twenty years later. The gorilla enclosure was mysteriously left unlocked on Christmas Day. Gugis and Shamba decided to take advantage and go for a stroll. Their nostrils were unaccountably seduced by the most delicious smells coming from a farm labourer's cottage not far away. The apes investigated. As the worker and his family prepared

to tuck into their Christmas lunch at a table laden with tur-
key, mince pies, Christmas pudding, fruit and dates, the door
opened and in walked two very large gorillas. As Aspinall
describes the scene, 'The apes had, probably, never even in
the vividness of their dreams seen so sumptuous a repast. The
table groaned with delicacies of which they were inordinately
fond.' They piled in, while the terrified family cowered, and
returned home so laden with booty they had to walk upright.
But no amount of apology or offers of bountiful compensation could placate the unfortunate neighbours.

Aspinall's activities were beginning to attract attention on a
more serious level far beyond the boundaries of Bekesbourne.
One of the first in the zoological world to acknowledge and
applaud his efforts was Professor Dr Ernst Lang of Basle,
in a specialist journal published in Germany. As Dr Lang
was an esteemed authority, who had himself raised a gorilla
and added considerably to knowledge of the ape's ways and
habits, recognition from this quarter was especially welcome.
Aspinall was also courted by the World Wildlife Fund and
invited to lend the weight of his name to their campaign for
a responsible attitude towards the treatment and protection
of wild animals.

The approach placed Aspinall in the kind of position
he had always found uncomfortable. He could not abide
the thought of committees or decisions reached through
consensus and the exchange of ideas. Thoroughly impatient
of debate, his decisions had always been arrived at through
diktat and obedience to his own feelings rather than sustained
analysis of alternatives. He could never have sat on any board
where his enthusiasms might be curtailed by argument. Not
that he was afraid his methods and aims might invite criticism
which would challenge his assurance, for he could rarely be
induced to allow that he might be wrong. His confidence
was unassailable. From childhood, he had always resisted
adherence to regulations imposed by a corporate body and
he was by nature one of the least democratic of men. He
suspected that the World Wildlife Fund might be tainted by
democratic methods and thereby emasculated. An opposite

point of view did not make him thoughtful, it made him impatient.

The World Wildlife Fund invited Aspinall to attend a fund-raising dinner at the Royal Garden Hotel in Kensington and submitted a list of invitees which included a clutch of dukes, earls and knights. Having replied, somewhat ungraciously, that it was 'the sort of dinner I would pay heavily to avoid in the normal course of events,' he agreed to attend but made a special request. 'I would be most grateful if you would sit me next to a person that I know. A lot of people on that list are confirmed blood sports enthusiasts, fish hookers and tigracides, but no doubt you plan to separate them from some conscience money.' To Prince Bernhard of the Netherlands he wrote, 'I am not really one who enjoys social gatherings attended by celebrities.'

In the event, he made an impromptu speech which caused no small sensation, attacking a whole variety of hypocrisies. Glancing purposefully at a number of ladies present, he said, 'The import of rare animal skins to pander to the witless wishes of women is a mounting scandal.' Nevertheless, his potential as an uncompromising advocate of animal welfare was obvious, and he knew then that he would be wise in the future to turn his publicity value to advantage.

Nowhere was his mischievous delight in the shocking implications of his views more clear than in his first television appearance on a discussion programme chaired by Jimmy Savile before a studio audience. The subject under review was whether people or wildlife should take precedence. On the side of people were Peter Jay, sometime UK Ambassador in Washington and peripatetic political commentator, and John Cousins, a union branch secretary whose father, Frank, had recently been a member of the Labour cabinet. For the animals were John Aspinall and Teddy Goldsmith. Goldsmith thundered about the redundant millions of humans in the world and the disastrous progress of medical technique which eliminated many useful natural diseases. A nurse in the audience questioned whether it was not beneficial to conquer malaria and like scourges, to which Goldsmith replied that it did positive harm. The poor nurse was close to tears. Aspinall gave the opinion that 20,000 acres of prime land should be given back to the lynx, bears, wild boars and wolves which once lived in profusion in the English countryside, whatever discomfort that would cause to the people who had since commandeered it. 'We must do it for our own *conscience*,' he said. Peter Jay concluded that he and Goldsmith were no better than fascists in their denial of democratic advance; they were happy to agree. The label of 'fascist' has clung to John Aspinall ever since, and it must be admitted that he has done little to disclaim it. At the end of the debate a democratic vote was taken among the audience, and the Goldsmith/Aspinall case won decisively.

The truth is that he enjoyed being provocative. He also recognised that an outrageous remark could stimulate full-blooded responses, while a sensible and thoughtful one might leave the listener in a lukewarm state of compliance which degenerates quickly into apathy. Aspinall's exploration of the art of Demosthenes was to rely more upon whipping by exhortation than coaxing by persuasion.

When he was not busy winning adherents to his cause, Aspinall was planning protracted journeys into Africa and Asia in search of first-hand knowledge and information on species whose survival was most threatened by the relentless spread of mankind. More often than not, he was accompanied by Teddy Goldsmith. They made an oddly disparate couple. While Goldsmith would study the ecology of the area, the lessons to be learnt from primitive tribes whose understanding of ecological harmony and whose respect for the land and its natural rhythms far exceeded the limited perceptions of civilised Western man, Aspinall was tracking and observing the habits of rare beasts, following herds or watching small family groups. Their interests often took them in opposing directions. Ultimately, the philosophical basis of these interests was in direct conflict, for Goldsmith wanted desperately to awaken an awareness of the ecological facts of life in order to improve life for *Homo sapiens* by regressing to a wiser relationship with the natural world, while Aspinall was increasingly concerned with the well-being of wild animals to the exclusion of everything else. Goldsmith's approach to his subject was analytical, intellectual (though he would shudder at the word), and Aspinall's was intuitive.

Even in Africa, John Aspinall's extrovert nature would not be subdued. With incredible extravagance he would have the finest gastronomic delights, the choicest wines, his favourite chocolates flown in to their remote tent in the jungle. All this required, naturally, a private chartered small aircraft. When a lady in the party felt it was time she had her hair done, he would call in the aircraft to ferry her 200 miles to a *coiffeur*, and once his wife let drop the fantasy that she would love to have a swim, whereupon the pilot was engaged to lift her from the middle of lush remote land to a swimming-pool a couple of hours' journey away. The combination of his vast natural generosity and unbridled flashiness made it bootless to comment on the waste and indulgence of such gestures, but to the zoological world they provided further proof that Aspinall was at bottom a rich playboy with a consuming hobby.

The return to Howletts inevitably meant a further increase in the animal population. He bought more acres to extend the land and engaged more keepers. For the first three years Derek Rushmer had been the sole keeper employed and, since zoos cannot be operated piecemeal, he had barely had a day off. Now the staff began to proliferate. Kurt Paulich looked after the tigers. Richard Johnstone-Scott was in charge of the gorilla band, and George Jacobs came to help Paul Ottley with elephants. As the tigers bred with apparent ease, Nick Marx, Brian Stocks and Bob Wilson were all brought in to assist. They made a motley band, united only by their deep respect for animals. Many were local men whose previous employment could not be held to prepare them in any way for the life of an animal keeper, but it was precisely their lack of theoretic baggage which endeared them to Aspinall. With the exception of the resident veterinary surgeon, not one of the keepers at Howletts was qualified in any way. They had no degrees, had read no zoological papers, had sat for no examinations. Like Aspinall himself, they were amateurs, a word which merits, in his vocabulary, an accolade. They wanted the job because they wanted it, because they felt out of place in any other. Some left Howletts only to come back later, often several times. The unique character of the place has proven irresistible despite manifold hardships.

He also encouraged the keepers to enter the animals' enclosures, like himself, and form close relationships with their charges, a habit which they willingly embraced. This alone made Howletts unique among zoos and further enraged the professionals, who declared that animals would not breed if allowed to 'imprint' on humans by too close an association. The error of this view, until recently thought to be incontestable, would be vividly demonstrated in years to come, as the breeding records at Howletts surpassed the headiest optimism of Aspinall himself. The professionals also warned about the danger inherent in unprotected contact with animals, and predicted that the death of a keeper would one day result.

In 1966 there occurred two events in Aspinall's personal life which did nothing to restrain the onward march of his zoo but which caused some private anguish. His marriage to Jane, the 'Spirit of Park Lane', had been buffeted by instability for some years which had led to distrust. Perhaps the intensity of his commitment to animals hastened the breach; or perhaps the dizzy glamour of her life distorted her priorities. Whatever the case, they were divorced amid some dramatic accusations. The most significant outcome was the judge's decision that, unusually, custody of the children should be given to the father, with the result that Amanda and Damian continued to be brought up at Howletts. Later the same year Aspinall married Belinda Musker, known as 'Min', the granddaughter of Lord Daventry.

Also that year Aspinall's natural father died at the age of seventy. Aspinall had paid regular visits to George McIlree Bruce in an effort to become acquainted with the stranger whose genes he bore. He was not a man outwardly to betray sentiment or reveal private thoughts in a garrulous exchange of confidences, so his feelings for Bruce and the content of their conversations remained secret, apart from some remarks which could be embroidered into a 'story' to be spread for the amusement of friends. Aspinall's deepest reflections were not so to be squandered. That John Aspinall never confides personal anxieties is less due to a gentleman's habitual reticence (which he did not inherit in any case), than a rigid determination not to be reduced by 'understanding'. The idea that he could be explained by the confluence of environmental and educational factors appalled him. Genetic legacy was everything, and with the passing of McIlree Bruce went one of the authors of his personality. He gave an address at his father's funeral, in which he said that Bruce 'will always be remembered by his friends as a great leader, a colourful individualist, one who loved a joke, and a very loyal friend'. These were some of the characteristics which he also liked to see in himself.

The trouble with leadership is that it is constantly frustrated by those who have no wish to be led, and they have always, in Aspinall's life, taken the form of bureaucrats. He has never been able to accept that there are useful bodies created for the protection and guidance of all, staffed by honourable men dedicated to improving whatever situation confronts them. To him, such staff are unimaginative functionaries who delight in thwarting him. For the most part, they assume this role with equanimity; they have become used to it.

A typical instance was Aspinall's struggle to start a breeding colony of *Bos gaurus*, the purest of all the world's cattle, noble and wild and very close to the earliest species of cattle on the earth. It was a worthwhile effort, for the cattle, commonly known as gaur, were near extinction and needed in all conscience to be saved from such an unnecessary ignominious fate. Nor could Aspinall be suspected of bending his energies solely to the salvation of glamorous, exotic creatures, in a kind of ego-extending exercise. To the untutored eye, gaur look much like ordinary domestic cattle, and can have no possible attraction to the public, which is probably why they have been neglected by zoos whose main purpose is to please people. That gaur were not especially beguiling nor as exciting as tigers and gorillas was entirely beside the point.

Aspinall had one lonely specimen, a female, whose unhappy distinction it was to be the only example of her species in the whole of the United Kingdom. In order to import animals, application had to be made to the Ministry of Agriculture, Fisheries and Food, who granted import licences if there were grounds to suppose the importation necessary or important, and further, if assurances could be given that they would not bring with them diseases which might affect domestic stock. On this matter, a number of ruminants and swine were automatically refused entry, and all others had to spend months in quarantine after arrival. After years of trying to find a pair of gaur, Aspinall eventually was offered some from India, and applied to the Ministry for the necessary permit. It was refused. Two years later, in 1968, he applied again, and was again refused. When, finally, he was allowed to have them on condition they be submitted to stringent quarantine regulations, they died in quarantine because no allowances were made for their habits and diet. Aspinall was understandably disappointed. 'I have always had a dream that one day I would look out on to a herd of gaur grazing in a vast paddock,' he wrote. 'I don't hold out any chance for this animal in the wild state.'

Attempts to import gaur continued for the next fourteen years. To discover the outcome we must leap ahead in the narrative. Aspinall wrote to contacts and zoo-keepers all over the world in his efforts, which assumed the dimensions of a messianic quest. He had to succeed at all costs, and never admit defeat at the hands of a mere Ministry. As well as the welfare of the gaur, there came into the struggle some concept of the power of the individual to get his own way; some pride was at risk.

At least it should be possible to permit a mate for the gaur cow – Aspinall wrote to the Ministry in different vein. 'The work I am doing should be done by the government,' he said, 'but the cost has fallen on me so far. I am £30,000 out in my attempt to import gaur but I have not given up. The animal that I have is no use as an exhibit as the public cannot distinguish between gaur and ordinary cattle. For work of this kind, I think a private institution should have every kind of help from the authorities.' That said, he went on to point out that he had been offered a male specimen from the United States, and if he could bring the animal to Howletts, it would now be sufficient to his purposes, for he wanted only that the cow should have company. The request was refused because cattle in the United States were prone to a particularly nasty disease called Blue Tongue, and the Ministry would countenance no risk whatever of introducing such horrors into Kent. The fact that the animal showed no evidence of the disease did not move the men of Whitehall.

There followed a telephone conversation in which Aspinall excoriated a hapless official called Mr Whyllie. 'Pass on my apologies to Mr Whyllie for my frustrated outburst to him on the telephone,' he wrote. 'I have now abandoned the idea in despair.' While accepting the necessity to protect domestic stock, he had in mind issues of far greater significance – the long-term benefits which would derive from increasing the gene pool of the genus *Bos*. 'I am afraid my solitary gaur cow will languish alone for the rest of her life [and] the fate of wild gaur, reduced to a remnant in India and Burma, is sealed.'

The story is interesting for the light it sheds upon difficulties which rumble incessantly behind the scenes in zoo-keeping, and on the chasm of understanding which divides a man concerned with observing regulations passed by Parliament and another moved by contemplation of the destiny of an entire species. To talk to ministry officials about increasing the gene pool of *Bos gaurus* is to shout words to the wind. Their horizons lie in opposite directions.

Some of Aspinall's frustration was alleviated in the writing of 'Random Thoughts on the Human Animal', a brief pamphlet of admitted polemic design printed and privately published in 1967. Quoting from Erricson, Malthus, Marais and Julian Huxley among others, John Aspinall reiterated his conviction that mankind was a parvenu in evolutionary terms, having emerged only in the Pleistocene Age and rising to his present primacy merely in the last five thousand years. His responsibility was vast, and his handling of it deplorable. It was essential, he wrote, that a 'new enlightenment' be forced upon us 'to break down the encrusted carapace of prejudice that has blocked man's intelligence for so long'.

What follows is a quasi-religious, or pantheistic, imprecation to achieve a reunion with Nature, whose delicate balances have been organised over 600 million years. We must learn to respect the ancient wisdoms of Nature, 'to treat her as a mother, not as a slave'. Man's hubris would be his undoing, his complacent tolerance of 'retrogressives and aberrants to breed without restraint' would encourage his headlong plunge towards disaster.

The 'Random Thoughts' end on a note of optimism. In 1967 Aspinall still thought the huge upheaval in attitudes which his recommendations would require was possible. Yet the conflict between his analysis, based upon scientific knowledge, and his political stance, based upon emotion, was irreconcilable. We should develop 'some maturity in our attitude to animals and a more pacific approach to each other,' he wrote. This statement has both clarity and cohesion. While his own respect for animals would deepen and grow more intense as the years proceeded, his pacific approach towards other human societies with political systems which he found disagreeable was still barely discernible twenty years later. Many who would cherish his commitment on the one principle were discouraged by his ambivalence on the other.

The gorilla colony suffered a blow with the unexpected death of Kulu, the largest male gorilla, who, at the age of eleven, was the finest ape in Britain after London Zoo's Guy. He succumbed to strongyloid infection and was dead within a few days, to be followed by two more gorilla deaths. Aspinall confessed to feelings of 'guilt and inadequacy'. Once again, the authorities of the established zoo world nodded sagely. Fatalities were inevitable if insufficient attention was paid to hygiene, for gorillas would encounter bugs in Kent that were unknown in the dense forests of Rwanda; furthermore, they were known to be susceptible to diseases which attack humans and for that reason alone should be kept as far away from people as reasonable. The jolly mix of man and beast at Howletts was, it was said, harmful to the beast.

There was truth in this, as many careful studies, notably by Hediger, had demonstrated. But Aspinall clung to his conviction that his animals should gain strength by developing immunity rather than remain weak from excessive protection. More to the point, his dream of companionship and trust with large primates could never be realised if he and his keepers had to keep a hygienic distance.

He began work on what would be the world's largest gorillarium, with 10,000 square yards of run. Some of the kitchen garden at Howletts had to be sacrificed to make room, but the project was a typical example of Howletts enterprise. Many visitors had already remarked how the animal enclosures were created in harmony with the assets of the parkland, not dumped incongruously in their midst. An ancient tree would serve as focal point in a world created for lemurs or langurs, permitting them to use it without diminishing its beauty. The wolf packs inhabited woodland, the tigers had a water-pool. Natural materials were employed in the building of enclosures, so that the park retained its rural aspect; it merely happened to be home for a variety of unusual creatures. (The one exception had to be the enclosure for elephants, where hideously unbiological concrete was the only material strong enough to hold fences which could withstand the onslaught of those powerful trunks.)

In addition, the enclosures were constructed by Howletts workers and designed by Aspinall himself, in consultation with the keepers, whose opinion was always sought and often prevailed, their experience of the animals' needs being more constant than anyone's. So it was that the new gorillarium took shape according to the views of several men who had watched the gorillas and knew what they wanted. There was no architect. It might be said that the only architects were the gorillas themselves, for their comfort and enjoyment were the only real criteria in the design. Hanging ropes, shoots, slides, things to climb, huge semi-circular objects under the roof to encourage play as well as exercise, covered sleeping quarters, and above all a wide area in which to roam, so that the band could be together when it wanted yet individuals seek privacy when required, made a home for gorillas where boredom was banished and space was a right. It was unlike any other gorilla enclosure in the world. And the owners were perfectly happy to share it from time to time with Aspinall and the keepers.

With the death of Kulu, all Aspinall's hopes for breeding a true colony at Howletts rested on the ample shoulders of Gugis. There had been no gorilla pregnancies at Howletts, but in 1967, when Gugis was eight years old, he started to copulate with Shamba and Mouila. This was cause for rejoicing, as Gugis had shown a reluctance to undertake his masculine duties. Given time, perhaps, a pregnancy would reward their patience. Only one gorilla had ever been born in captivity anywhere in the world, and that was in Lincoln Park Zoo, Chicago, in 1957. From now on, Gugis's libido would be subject to continuous scrutiny.

Min Aspinall was also playing her part at Howletts, rearing three tiger cubs single-handed until they grew too large to handle. They were the three cubs of Zemo, including one, Zorra, who enters the story later. Min raised them with exemplary devotion and care. The tigers were reproducing fast at Howletts, which was not in itself so remarkable, as they were known to be easy breeders and in fact multiplied more readily in circuses even than in zoos, despite the cramped conditions of beast-wagons. What was remarkable was the uniform affability and reliability of the animals. A very high percentage of first births did not survive; it is common enough for cats of various types to eat their first litter of kittens, partly through inexperience, partly through excitability. Also, most males will turn on new young males and drive them out to fresh territory, which in the wild assists their survival. At Howletts it became the norm to rescue a first litter when possible and raise it by hand, and to give a fresh enclosure to the young male and his mate.

Min longed for children of her own, and when she discovered she was pregnant in 1968 she glowed with happiness. A little girl was born later that year and christened Mameena after a character in Rider Haggard; the name was chosen because she had been born during a storm, and 'mameena' is the Zulu word for storm. The happiness did not endure, however. Mameena was born with a congenital and incurable heart disease which afflicts only one in every 600,000, and she died at the age of three months. She was buried at the end of the drive. Min Aspinall was inconsolable. She tried to have another child by Aspinall, with no success. Aspinall said they had 'bred once' but were 'unable to breed again', and that he quite understood why a 'female ape' should want to have children. His choice of words might indicate why his attitude towards women was not always welcomed by them. After that, his marriage, though friendly and spared the unpleasantness which had spoiled the previous marriage to Jane, lost its point and purpose as far as Min was concerned.

Meanwhile, great excitement greeted the urine analysis of Mouila, who was thought to be pregnant with Howletts's first gorilla baby. This hope proved to be unfounded. Though Gugis copulated frequently enough, his exertions were oddly barren.

The American millionaire J. Paul Getty paid a visit to Howletts and left with a rare smile on his sullen face. Later he wrote to Aspinall, 'Your friendship with tigers and wolves was something I had always thought impossible. Your tigers and wolves seem to be as fond of you and as harmless as my alsatians are to me.'

It was increasingly evident that this extraordinary relationship was only made possible by the profits of the Clermont, which along with those of other casinos soared from year to year. By 1968 there were over a thousand gambling clubs in the country, and the forty or fifty biggest ones in the capital had made London the gambling centre of the world, surpassing even Nevada in scale, profitability, and some would add notoriety. We had passed in one giant leap from a country in which all gaming was illegal to one where all gaming was permitted.

There was huge irony in all this, as the Betting and Gaming Act of 1960, introduced with what Lord Stonham icily called 'touching innocence', had been partly designed to hamper Aspinall's activities. It was soon to be recognised as one of the clumsiest pieces of legislation ever passed by Parliament, the results of which were the precise opposite of those intended. To be fair, this was only Parliament's fault up to a point, for the ingenuity of gaming proprietors to undermine a regulation was endless, and nobody enjoyed upsetting rules more than Aspinall.

The gaming houses had certainly done their work on the 1960 Act. They had firstly taken advantage of a small concession in the law which permitted a small charge to be made to cover the cost of gaming facilities provided; they made a very large charge and they made it for every shoe* rather than for every evening. The law did not stipulate how small was small and remained ambiguous about the frequency of the charge. Thousands of pounds were being taken in this way every night. Secondly, the rule that the chances must be equal to all players was circumvented in a novel way. Roulette held a natural advantage to the bank; each of the players was entitled to take the bank in turn; all refused because they could not afford the inflated risk; so the casino took the bank every time. Quintin Hogg (Lord Hailsham) put the matter with admirable clarity. 'When we prohibited games of unequal chance,' he said 'it never crossed our minds that for years the courts would hold that games of unequal chance were not unequal if the inequality passed round the table.'

In 1968 legal pronouncements from two different sources precipitated another long Parliamentary debate. The Law

---

*The 'shoe' is a long wooden box shaped to hold multiple packs of cards. The dealer takes the cards out from the end of the shoe, and repacks new cards at the other end.

Lords finally ruled that profit from roulette was illegal according to the meaning of the Act. And the Master of the Rolls, Lord Denning, laid into the gaming proprietors with his customary Cornish acerbity and ridiculed the way the law had been interpreted by the courts.

On 13 February, the new Gaming Bill was introduced to the House of Commons for second reading by the Home Secretary, James Callaghan, with the soulful words, 'too much has happened during the last six or seven years to make it possible now to achieve what Parliament intended in 1960'. The origin of the new Bill was the failure of the old one. In the House of Lords, Lord Willis was more picturesque. 'It is rather like a man who brings home an Easter egg as a present for his wife,' he said 'only to find that it hatches out into an alligator and eventually snaps his head off. I think that in future Parliament should look very carefully at its eggs.'

As before, none of the legislators imagined he could actually persuade people not to gamble. Quintin Hogg said he was distinctly pessimistic about the ability of Parliament to make people good by Statute, and the Home Secretary allowed that everyone should be able to play as rashly and as often as he liked provided nobody else had a vested commercial interest in inducing him to do so. However, since the 1960 Act had precipitated the very evil it was meant to prevent, and it was no longer possible to revert to the Victorian legislation, some control had to be enforced to protect gamblers from their own worst excesses. The previous Act made no attempt to define what was a 'club', with the result that any group of people could call themselves a club and charge money to play for five minutes. 'It is like the dance of the seven veils,' thought Mr Callaghan. 'As each is stripped away the situation certainly becomes more transparent, but it takes an excessively long time to get to the point, and when you get there what is finally revealed is not necessarily beautiful.'

More dangerous was the invasion of criminals into the casino world, the injection of money of dubious origin and all the tangential squalor which followed – protection rackets and threats of blackmail included. There was no suggestion that Aspinall's Clermont Club, the most sophisticated of them all, had sunk to such depths, though there were plenty of other clubs which were run as a branch of the underworld. On the other hand, the Clermont was guilty of giving substantial credit, which Mr Callaghan called a 'pernicious evil', not only for the personal misery it might cause, which was not the business of Parliament, but for the invitation to crime and vulnerability to blackmail which despair could encourage, which was.

The new Gaming Bill plugged various holes. The most important innovation was the establishment of a Gaming Board, consisting of three members with a full-time staff and inspectorate. The inspectors would have the right of entry to any club without warrant at any reasonable time in order to keep watch on activities within. Licences for casinos would be granted by local magistrates, having regard to evidence from the Gaming Board, from the police, and from local residents, who would have full right to object. The justices would have to be satisfied that there was a genuine need for a gaming club in the area, and that the applicant for a licence was a fit and proper person to run such a club. It was hoped by these two provisions that clubs would be reduced in number to about a quarter of those obtaining in 1968, and that undesirable men would be kept out of the business. Furthermore, Clause 39 instituted a total prohibition on advertising, and Clause 17 forbade credit in any form.

At the Clermont, there was never any worry about John Aspinall persuading the authorities he was a trustworthy and proper person to run a club. In the ensuing years it is interesting that he never raised any objection to the application for licences of other clubs, whereas they all, without exception, objected whenever *he* made such an application. In his mind, to make an objection would be an admission of weakness; he would never fear competition, because he knew well enough that he would do the job better than the rest; that, of course, is why they objected so regularly. On the other hand, there was some concern in Berkeley Square about the clause forbidding credit. Henceforth, everyone would have to pay on the spot, and Aspinall felt this would upset the civilised atmosphere of his club; his attitude was that one could not really do such a thing to old friends!

7
Feasts

For John Aspinall advertising did not imply anything so vulgar as touting for more clients. The Clermont, by 1968, had as many members as it wanted, virtually all drawn from the British aristocracy and those that surrounded them, and most known to each other. The fact that Clermont members were friends already, and could therefore count on not running into strangers at 44 Berkeley Square, gave the house its unique atmosphere among casinos, that of a genuine club rather than a gambling joint where everyone looks shifty and furtive and declines to give his name. On the other hand, Aspinall did not want to take his clients for granted. He wished to make sure they never felt tempted to wander elsewhere. What better than an occasional party to celebrate their good fortune and remind everyone how exclusive and remarkable was the Clermont?

The Aspinall feasts were later to be rendered impossible by legislation which forbade live music or entertainment, but they were such an established feature of the Clermont calendar at this time that a word must be said about them. The feasts were arranged and executed with such panache and wild abundance of pleasure that they must find their way into the social history of twentieth-century London. Not since the impressive parties given by Mrs Vanderbilt at Newport, Rhode Island, in the 1890s had such an extravagance attended a mere dinner, or such care been bestowed upon the creation of special décor. It is no exaggeration to say that Aspinall's feasts were each in their way a work of art, albeit ephemeral.

Of course, one must not forget also that the feasts were followed by gambling at the tables, which the cynical may well think were their primary purpose. No one ever calculated how much was taken by the house after a feast, or whether the outlay swallowed the profit, but they worked on the assumption that they would break even; the beneficiaries were skilled craftsmen, designers and artisans.

Lastly, the feasts had another function, which was simply to gratify the lively whim of John Aspinall. It was he who decided the theme and he who dictated the style. Each banquet was devoted to a hero of the past or a civilisation he especially admired. The important consideration was that *he* should enjoy himself, and if his guests did so as well, so much the better. They were in essence fantastic, dream-like birthday parties given by an imaginative child for himself. Usually, the child wakes up in sorry recognition of the dreary world of his reality. This time, there was no need to wake up, for these were not fantasies; they happened. Aspinall gloried in his ability to make dreams come true. And he appreciated that dreams are never parsimonious; ostentation is their nature, and whimsy their style.

The first was the Feast of Mithridates, given in the Great Room at Berkeley Square on 29 April 1969. Mithridates VI, King of Pontus, was the kind of monarch Aspinall loved to talk about, a figure much larger than life and invested by romantic tradition with accomplishments too numerous to credit. He had formidable intellect, spoke twenty-two languages, was huge in size, overwhelming in strength, obstinate, courageous, subtle, and ruthless. He surrounded himself with men of letters as well as concubines, practised magic and was believed to have so saturated his body with poisons that there was none which could injure him. Mithridates did not hesitate to display his wealth and power, clothing his armies in the most gorgeous raiments and giving banquets the fame of which travelled far beyond his kingdom. So fond was he of food that he gave prizes to the champion eaters among his subjects as well as the best poets, thus oddly combining patronage of over-indulgence with respect for control. The point was he believed in excellence in whatever direction, and his patronage sought to encourage the pursuit of the best.

John Aspinall was also a champion of the principle of patronage, an aspect of his life which was always entirely ignored by the press. He was fortunate in having a young brother-in-law who could rise to the demands he would make. Anthony Little had recently married Aspinall's half-sister, Jennifer Osborne, despite some initial family reluctance. At twenty-one, with long blond hair in the fashion of the day, Little did not look 'serious' enough for marriage. A freelance designer, he had already been heralded as the Aubrey Beardsley of the 1960s, an appellation which naturally aroused Aspers's interest as it complemented his own long-standing admiration for Oscar Wilde. But it was one isolated event which cemented his approval of the new recruit. On a Sunday afternoon at Howletts, Gugis had broken free (yet again) and was heading for the greenhouse, which he would undoubtedly have smashed with much damage to it, and perhaps some to himself. When Anthony Little saw him he simply stood in front of the greenhouse in the path of the marauding gorilla and spread out his arms. Gugis stopped in his tracks and turned. Anthony later admitted that he had never even seen a gorilla before.

Little was commissioned by Aspinall to re-create the gardens of the Palace of Sinope in Lady Bel's former salon at 44 Berkeley Square. What he did was to redesign the room entirely, by building another room inside it with new panelling, drapes and ceiling. Only William Kent's fireplace was left visible. He took three months to prepare for the occasion, with two full-time assistants, and he employed nearly fifty people to make the materials. Nothing was bought; everything was made especially for the evening, including the cushions on which diners were to lounge while eating. It then took two whole days to install the materials and transform the room into an ancient Persian garden, the tables laden with more delicious food than anyone had seen in one place at one time. The effect was breathtaking, beautiful, and absurdly hyperbolic.

Only about seventy guests were invited to this as to all other feasts, gatecrashers being severely discouraged. The only people who did not thoroughly enjoy themselves were the waiters, made to dress up as soldiers in Mithridates' army and looking as if they felt terribly silly. Silliness, however, was an attribute more appropriate to some of the younger guests, the precursors of those vapid individuals who in the 1980s would be called 'Hooray Henries'. It is a strange social phenomenon that the young aristocrats of Britain, educated for a superior role in the hierarchy of the nation, have always shown themselves to be hooligans when there are girls to impress and champagne to quaff. So it was that the Feast of Mithridates degenerated by the end of the evening into a bun-fight, with food hurling across the room; Primrose, Lady Cadogan, was not the only one who failed to duck in time, but hers was the misfortune which passed around the gossips, adding another black mark to Aspinall's public image.

Anthony Little's creations did not endure; they were not intended to. But his designs, and the elaborate yet restrained invitation cards for which he was also responsible, have found their way into the Metropolitan Museum of Modern Art in New York City, where they are displayed as fine examples of twentieth-century English decoration. The collection covers all John Aspinall's feasts: the Banquet of Montezuma, the Banquet of the Diadochi, the Aztec Party, Tiger Tiger Burning Bright, right up to the great Port Lympne Ball of 1984. Little enjoyed the patronage of other rich hedonists, Alastair McAlpine in particular and as frequently, James Goldsmith from time to time, but it is fair to say that Aspinall's parties called upon more lavish invention than others and helped stretch and develop his talents. Anthony later formed the wallpaper company Osborne and Little with his other brother-in-law Sir Peter Osborne, Bt.

Six months after the Mithridates feast, Aspinall gave his Banquet of the Diadochi, on 18 November 1969. The

Diadochi were the squabbling and bloody successors to Alexander the Great, and Aspinall re-created the banquet at which one of them, Seleucus Nicator, entertained three other Middle Eastern kings in lavish Hellenistic style. Guests were greeted on arrival by a collection of dwarfs hired from a Soho agency, whose function it was to insult each person in as nasty a manner as they could muster. They were helped with a bottle of brandy each. On the floor was a 6-inch-thick carpet of leaves and rose petals to walk on, not very popular with the ladies but risibly luxurious. Anthony Little and his assistants had to strip half an acre of leaves from rhododendron bushes in the woods of Hampshire and fill a hundred sacks with fresh green leaves, which then had ten sacks of fresh rose blooms scattered among them. The idea proved so outrageous that it became the norm at every Aspinall party.

Little created the gardens of Seleucus Nicator's palace in Babylon, about 300 BC, with galleries and staircases especially built for the occasion (and glaringly advantageous to fruit-hurlers), and a raised circular floor in the middle on which jugglers, tumblers and fire-eaters performed throughout the banquet. Aspinall wrote the invitation card, mischievously pointing out the extravagant nature of Seleucus, whose possessions were so extensive that 'he had thought nothing of selling India to the adventurer Chandragupta for a mere five hundred elephants'. Aspinall himself took the part of Seleucus. Anthony Little was cast as the architect and decorator Stasicrates 'whose designs were on such a scale of grandeur that even Alexander the Great had once declared that he could not possibly afford them.' Around the walls were glazed brick bas-reliefs depicting the victories of Hercules, Little's finest conceit. They, at least, did not evaporate the following day but were conserved.

On 27 April the following year came the Feast of Asoka, certainly the most original of these parties and singularly appropriate for Aspinall. Asoka, the third Mauryan (Peacock) emperor of India and grandson of the founder Chandragupta, reigned from 264 to 227 BC. He was quite the most powerful sovereign of his time, his dominions the most extensive of anyone in India until the Anglo-Saxon conquest two thousand years later. His capital city was the most populous in the world. Asoka was appalled by the squalor of warfare and forsook conquest for his lifetime, undertaking to persuade instead by a system of ethics; thirty-five of his ethical inscriptions still exist today. They are Buddhist in their gentle respect for life, but, most important, they contain various reference to animals. In the invitation (now a collectors' item), John Aspinall wrote that Asoka 'was the first recorded ruler to include in his edicts measures for the protection of animals. His concept of *Ahimsa*, justice for all animate things, was not only well in advance of his own time but palpably superior to the flimsy, anthropocentric creeds of modern societies.' Asoka's palace was a refuge for wild creatures and birds of many kinds, and his example has passed down through generations of Buddhists. One historian has written, 'If man's fame can be measured by the number of hearts who revere his memory, by the number of lips that have mentioned, and still mention him with honour, Asoka is more famous than Charlemagne or Caesar.'

Asoka's palace was built for the feast with a prefabricated ceiling and tapestries of huge scale and clamorous beauty, which Little designed on felt, over every wall. Live doves and brightly coloured exotic birds festooned the room, and the food was, as ever, lavish and spectacular. The designs for the tapestries may be seen in New York, but the work itself has perished.

Similarly, Little's gorgeous printed fabrics for the Aztec party on 1 December 1970 have entirely disappeared; in their abundance of strong colour and mathematic brilliance of design they were probably Little's masterpiece, at least in this area of his career. His final contribution to his brother-in-law's fanfare of ostentation was to come some years later, at the Port Lympne Ball.

Meanwhile, the zoo at Howletts was growing fast and 1970 saw both some advances which attracted international attention, and many setbacks. The finest achievement thus far was the first successful breeding in Britain of the rare clouded leopard, with three healthy cubs born in the spring. This was one of the first signals that Aspinall's unscientific intuitive methods might be more fruitful than the orthodox approach, and when in time he had offspring from no less than thirteen different species of cat, many reputedly impossible to breed, curiosity from the zoo world overcame the predictable hostility which had endured for years. Twenty-one wild boar and twenty axis deer had also been born at Howletts. Out of a total of 147 individual animals, no fewer than seventy-nine (i.e. over half) had been born on the estate.

There was still some feeling that Aspinall was either not to be taken seriously, or was to be discouraged, both from established zoologists and from Ministry officials. Sir Solly Zuckerman (later Lord Zuckerman), the doyen of zoologists in Britain, had since 1965 been announcing his intention to visit Howletts and observe for himself what was going on there. Aspinall frequently besought him to come, as there remained within him a vestigial need for praise from so high a quarter as well as a more pragmatic hope that Zuckerman's influence could be called upon to avoid some of the frustrating red tape which often seemed to choke initiative in animal husbandry. Zuckerman's response was to suggest Aspinall make a handsome contribution to the funds of the Zoological Society (i.e. the London Zoo) if he wanted to be looked upon favourably. They corresponded sporadically, and Aspinall did buy some animals from the London Zoo to improve his stock and vary its gene pool. But he always knew that Zuckerman was not an enthusiast, and his patience finally gave way when he proclaimed his desire to found a larger zoo park and Zuckerman replied that there were too many already.

'Yes,' wrote Aspinall, 'parks of the wrong sort.' He was not impressed by the so-called safari parks with their general air of circus and amusement arcade, although they were decidedly superior to 'congested conventional urban zoos' (by which, no doubt, he meant to include the very establishment over which Sir Solly presided).

9 Aspinall with Gugis, Baby Doll and Juju

10 Min Aspinall

11 Aspinall with two of the first tigers born at Howletts

12 Aspinall with the wolf, Nushka

13 Invitation cards designed by
Anthony Little for three of
Aspinall's feasts

14 *(above, left)* Gugis

15 *(above, right)* Kisoro, founder of the Howletts gorilla colony

16 *(below)* Aspinall with Zemo

One day it is my ambition that the zoo park will take its place as one of the great breeding centres for threatened species and be acknowledged as such throughout the world. I quite see that this is a difficult task and I had hoped always to have had at least the tacit support of the entrenched zoological establishment of which you are, undoubtedly, the most influential figure. It is quite difficult enough with these new quarantine laws and Ministry restrictions to collect breeding groups of rare animals, but I feel that unless I can enjoy your confidence and support I shall find the going tougher than ever.

Aspinall was already, at this stage, making tentative enquiries about the possibility of going into partnership with Lord Guilford to open a wildlife sanctuary at Waldershare Park, near Dover (the idea came to nothing). Zuckerman told him he was wrong to imagine hostility to his ambitions at the Zoological Society,

but you are slipshod and impatient, and rely upon influence with me . . . I know that you are passionate in your interest in animals. I accept that you are unique in the zoo park world in your interest in conservation. From this point of view I am ready to help you whenever I can. But equally you should remember we are a charitable organisation and, frankly, I don't remember that you have done very much to help us. By our standards you are a rich man. The sort of money you propose putting into the zoo park is beyond our wildest dreams . . . if you want our support, we need yours.

In response to this, Aspinall sent £125 which he had received from the BBC as a fee for filming at Howletts, together with a letter urging Sir Solly to regard him as a pauper compared to the truly rich, 'just one of those strange eccentrics who plough all their money into wild animals'. There appeared to be confusion between the two men as to where priorities lay, and one could not deny the impression that Zuckerman still thought of Aspinall as a dilettante.

The new regulations to which Aspinall referred were prejudiced against Howletts because it was a private establishment not open to the public. The Ministry was far readier to grant import licences for animals which would be placed on show, thus making it clear that its officers placed highest value on an increase in public delight. Nothing could be further from Aspinall's intentions, as they well knew. A typical example of this collision occurred in 1970, when Aspinall bought seven animals from a dealer in Naples, including four horned antelopes and some rare mountain gazelles. His import permit was refused on the grounds that Howletts was not a public zoo. Aspinall offered them to London Zoo, but the offer was declined, and the animals had eventually to go to America to be put on show with no regard for their welfare or their future breeding.

There were times when Aspinall was allowed to import, but he had constantly to be made aware of the favour that was being granted, a favour which was often withheld as if to teach him a lesson. The Ministry of Agriculture, Fisheries and Food wrote sternly reprimanding him for applying for permits after animals were already shipped and on the high seas bound for England. The next time, they said, the permit will be refused and the animals will have to remain on board ship until it sails away. 'We are not prepared to agree to any more importation of ruminating animals or swine on your behalf until you are a bona fide exhibitor.' Manifestly, the day was not far off when Aspinall would have to submit and open Howletts to public view.

In addition, he suffered some reverses with the tiger colony, the chief pride of which was still the extraordinarily good-natured tigress which had started it all, his beloved Tara. She had bred successfully, but was not adept at rearing her cubs, which had to be rescued and reared by Min Aspinall, often in her own bedroom. However attractive this might be, it was obviously not ideal, because unnatural, and Aspinall hoped one day to have his cubs mother-reared and still be welcomed by them and by her; this had not even been tried, let alone achieved, in any zoo in the world. The first attempts along this road were not happy.

Since tigers can only learn by example, an experienced tigress called Daisy was brought over from Florida to mate with the male Mazar, with the intention that Tara would copy her maternal technique. Mazar, who had been Tara's mate for some time, would do nothing but snarl at Daisy through the fence which separated them. Eventually he had to be introduced to her for the experiment to take place. Aspinall and two keepers stood around with brooms and buckets ready to make an infernal noise if necessary, and opened the door between the two enclosures. Mazar went straight in and killed Daisy without a moment's pause for reflection, so fast that it took them all by surprise. They hurled blows upon him to no avail; he would not let go his grip until he had despatched her. From Aspinall's point of view it was a sad but salutary lesson, part of the long business of trial and error which leads to good animal husbandry. One must be prepared to take risks and learn all the time from pain. But in the opinion of the 'entrenched establishment' with which he was increasingly at loggerheads it was a perfect instance of his stubborn irresponsibility.

There was worse in store. Mazar and Tara bred often and successfully and appeared to be a well-adjusted pair. Mazar had some bad-tempered moments which Tara handled with consummate skill, protecting herself from his rages by holing up in her den or taking refuge on a ramp. That he should explode from time to time was by no means unusual, tigers often becoming furious when they wish to copulate and the mate is unreceptive or not in the mood. Watching them mate, which they do quickly and with a lot of growling, it is clear that the degree of violence involved is quite normal, and the female often retreats from the encounter rather battered. The winter of 1970 was particularly wet and Tara's den had become a squelching mess of mud. One morning she was discovered lying there covered in mud and dying. Her windpipe had been pierced, obviously by Mazar's teeth; she must have slipped in the ooze and been unable to protect herself.

Tara's death was a devastating blow for John Aspinall. It was she, more than any other single animal, who had quickened his desire to devote his life and money to the well-being of other species, she who had been the first animal that he genuinely regarded as a close friend. He wept unashamedly when she died, and buried her next to his daughter Mameena at the end of the lime avenue. The revered Dr Ernst Lang of Basle had said Tara was the most beautiful tigress he had ever seen. 'Her kind and loyal nature was bequeathed to most of her descendants.' Also, Mazar himself felt the loss miserably. For three weeks after Tara's death he called for her every night.

There occurred also dangerous moments arising from the proximity of man and animal, the encouragement of which was the whole basis of Aspinall's ambition and which remained one of the principal causes of disapproval from the establishment. The vet, Mr Eric Andrews, once gave Gugis a sack to play with. This ape, as we have seen, could be deceitful, in that his moods were not always easily interpreted. On this occasion, he became so excited with his toy that he went for Mr Andrews, digging a huge canine into the vet's arm and piercing an artery. There was a great deal of blood and much loud frenzy from the other gorillas who charged about not knowing what to do. Andrews managed to crawl out through the gorillarium's kitchen window, while Min Aspinall and two keepers came bearing live chickens to control the apes, who are notoriously frightened of anything which makes an unfamiliar noise. Andrews was treated in hospital and suffered no lasting damage.

An even more lucky escape befell Lady O. in a chilling encounter with Nushka, the wolf bitch. Nushka was a thoroughly charming and reliable animal with one strange defect: though totally at home with men, she did not care to be familiar with female humans. One day she determined she would make her prejudice plain. Nushka leapt at Lady O. from the front and grabbed her by the throat. Lady O. was astonishingly calm and stoical, giving no hint of alarm, perhaps because she was not allowed time to reflect upon what was happening. Equally commendable, Nushka exercised that innate self-control which is so often observed in animals and which many now think to be the evolutionary origin of what we call morality. The wolf could have torn the woman's throat out at once. She did not, for aggression was not her purpose. This was an example of ritualised aggression intended to convey a message, the kind one may see with domestic animals on any street corner, or indeed with humans, when it is misunderstood and labelled neurotic. The message is a warning. In Nushka's case, she needed to show the interloper that she did not enjoy her presence and was capable of doing great harm if her right to select her own friends were not respected. When the attack was over, there was not the smallest mark on Lady O.'s neck; Nushka had declined to use her teeth.

Far more serious was the attack on Robin Birley in 1970. Robin was one of the three children of Mark and Lady Annabel Birley. Aspinall had had little contact with Birley since the club was opened in 1962, due to a disagreement over the use of the wine-cellar, but Lady Annabel remained a close friend in spite of it. As a special treat for the children she took all three, Rupert, Robin and India Jane, to Howletts for the day. Robin, the middle one, had just turned twelve.

Aspinall's contention that tigers were remarkably trustworthy when treated decently had been amply supported by his experience so far. It had none the less been observed that they were extremely sensitive to smells and would behave out of character when they sensed strong body odour or perfume, or even alcohol on somebody's breath (as some keepers knew to their cost after a visit to the village pub). Another oddity of their personality was an unaccountable distrust, or fear, of human children. Unlike gorillas, who know exactly what a child is and treat it with delicate care, tigers seem not to understand that these somewhat smaller humans belong to the same race; they are considered alien. The tigers understandably made exception for Aspinall's own children, Amanda and Damian, whom they had known since infancy.

That afternoon, the party first visited some chimpanzees, one of whom was in an excited state, rushing and swinging and screaming in all directions, all of which made Robin a trifle nervous. He was anxious to get out of the chimps' way. When next they walked over to see the tigers, he was already feeling apprehensive, though it would be quite wrong to depict his slight unease as anything close to fear.

They elected to pay a call on Zorra, one of the three cubs born to Mazar and Tara which Min had reared herself. Zorra was now fully grown and pregnant. The group that went in included John and Min Aspinall, Amanda and Damian, the keeper Kurt Paulich, Lady Annabel, Rupert and Robin. India Jane stayed outside because she was too small. It was felt that Robin would be all right, as he was much taller than one would expect for a boy of twelve.

They all stroked Zorra, who was placid and agreeable. Aspinall picked up the tigress's bowl of milk and drank it, a typically exhibitionist gesture calculated to demonstrate the degree of trust and freedom that existed between himself and the animal and to allay any worries on that account. Robin stroked the cat and was surprised how lean, slim and long she was. Aspinall then suggested they all go to her den, to see where she slept. Zorra was not agitated in any way, but rather listless and apparently indifferent to her crowd of companions. She loped alongside Robin and the others.

Suddenly, she had turned and was standing with her paws on Robin's shoulders. He thought it was all part of the game, though decidedly nerve-racking. Within a second or two she had pushed him to the ground and was standing over him with his head in her mouth. Her upper teeth gripped him by the left temple, her lower took hold of his neck below the left jaw, and Robin heard and felt a horrible gnawing sensation as the tigress attempted to squeeze his head between her jaws and he felt his face being crushed. He did not lose consciousness and felt no pain, but he did recall thinking that this was what it was like to die.

The time it has taken to relate the incident is far longer than it took to occur. Perhaps five or six seconds had elapsed, by which time John Aspinall had thrust his hands into Zorra's mouth and by sheer strength prised her jaws apart, while Min held and pulled her tail. The tigress was forced to release her grip. She then pushed Min to the ground and was about to grab her in like fashion by the face, when Min let out a gigantic scream of reproach, which reminded Zorra where authority resided. If Robin had been saved both by Aspinall's quick action and the fact that Zorra had lost some of her teeth and only had one canine left (with all her teeth she might well have killed him), Min was saved by the fact that she had brought Zorra up from a cub.

Robin was walked to the gate, a gaping hole where his mouth had been and the bottom jaw dislodged, hanging by a strand. He was rushed at incredible speed in Min Aspinall's car to Canterbury Hospital, his head resting on his mother's arm in the back seat. Lady Annabel was sure he was near death; she could not believe he might be saved. Immediately on arrival at the hospital, Robin underwent an emergency operation which lasted many hours, undertaken by an amazing National Health team who achieved the impossible. It was to be only the first of numerous operations that he has since endured to repair the damage of that one second's lack of vigilance. Some of his bones were so crushed that one side of his face was never to grow again, and though he recovered remarkably well and was never in danger of permanent impairment of his sight or speech, his face was to become lop-sided and his jaw-line irregular as he grew to maturity, the right side developing normally while the left remained stuck at its adolescent stage.

Robin Birley felt no bitterness or animosity either then or since. Aspinall visited him in hospital as soon as it was permitted and said in effect that it was bad luck he was attacked and that he regretted the incident. Those who saw Aspinall at the Clermont the next day and knew what had happened, or the gist of it, were surprised to find him in such good humour and apparently unmoved. His cheerful attitude seemed to suggest callousness. But that was not to know the man. He was in fact deeply disturbed and shaken, both desperately distressed for Robin and shocked that his dream of mutual trust between animal and man should suffer such a setback. As usual, he was quite unable to reflect these emotions in his demeanour or behaviour but kept them quietly and intensely to himself. Revelation of feeling might be a sign of weakness or doubt (so interpreted by himself not by others) and was therefore protected beneath a thick layer of what passed for self-assurance.

As for Robin, he was grateful to be spared an avalanche of pity. Had everyone felt excessively sorry for him and shown it, he would by degrees have begun to feel sorry for himself, and probably to assign blame for his condition. His restoration to good health would not have been so easy had self-pity and bitterness been given the opportunity to corrode his personality. He put the episode down to fate and wiped from his mind any incipient temptation to apportion fault. He believes that Aspinall's attitude towards him helped him avoid these dangers.

Lady Annabel did not think about damage to the personality, but only that her son's life had been saved. She wrote to Aspinall thanking him and Min for their presence of mind in acting so quickly to rescue him. For two years she chastised herself for taking her son into the enclosure, and sank into sullen guilt. There was no question of suing Aspinall for negligence; had it been suggested, Robin would have fought hard to prevent it. His feeling of loyalty towards John Aspinall and his admiration for his work with animals have not diminished, nor has his own love for animals. He will, however, always be wary of the essential unpredictability of animal behaviour.

Zorra resumed her customary placidity and never again caused a moment's anxiety to her keepers.

It was by no means easy for Aspinall to retain his buoyancy in the face of such a cruel accident to the son of one of his friends. It was essential to his purpose that the principle of the sanctity of human life be exposed for what it was, an invention by one species to perpetuate its exploitation of and indifference to all the others (save those, like dogs and horses, with which that species had evolved a symbiotic relationship). Only when we are made to recognise that all other forms of life have evolved painstakingly for their own advantage and not uniquely to serve ours, and that we have arrogated to ourselves the right to dispose their fate to such an outrageous degree that we risk making ourselves the only species of primate left on the planet, only then can it seem that injury to one human being among many millions is as nothing compared to the protection of the last few remnants of an entire species. But that does not make the plight of an adolescent boy whose face has been torn asunder any easier to bear. It may have been brave of John Aspinall to continue with his dream; it may have been obstinate and irresponsible; or it may have been visionary. Still worse accidents would occur in the future to tempt him from his goal, and he was to need all the resilience of this vision to withstand them.

Aspinall received some encouragement in the following months. Dr Lang came from Basle to take a first-hand look at what was being attempted at Howletts and afterwards wrote a fulsome letter of praise (and some mild remonstrance directed at Lady O. for giving gorillas treats in the form of smoked salmon sandwiches). It was indeed sweet to receive appreciation from a man who knew what he was talking about after much facile sniping from ignorant journalists. The World Wildlife Fund again approached Aspinall and sought his participation in a '1001' Club of people the world over who were passionate in the cause of conservation, a scheme initiated by the then President, Prince Bernhard of the Netherlands. Aspinall sent money but declined to have anything to do with a committee, despite a personal letter from HRH The Duke of Edinburgh urging him to take a more active role. However, at least he was being taken seriously.

Then, too, he was rewarded with births in his Przewalski's horse herd. These noble rare horses are now extinct in the wild. They come from Central Asia, more specifically Mongolia, where they were first seen by a Westerner towards the end of the last century. His name was N.M. Przewalski, and his discovery fired the imagination of collectors and zoos in Europe. The Duke of Bedford ordered some from the great zoo-man Carl Hagenbeck, whose captured animals were dispersed widely. Zoos did not then understand much about breeding, so that populations dwindled until in 1958 there were only about fifty specimens in the world. A stud book was then established to keep track of their survival rate internationally. Aspinall's Przewalskis were the first to breed in Britain for more than thirty years.

The first honey badger birth ever witnessed in the world took place at Howletts in 1971. I was present when the tiny infant was spotted and can attest to the genuine excitement which spread through the entire estate over a rare but fierce and secretive little creature who would only suffer humans at a distance. John Aspinall was as ebullient as a child at Christmas.

His most robust ambition was still to help save the great Lowland gorilla by establishing a breeding colony at Howletts. Disappointments had merely stiffened his resolve. He had lost three of his embryonic gorilla band (Kulu, Moundou and Dingi) due to an invasion of the strongyloids parasite which had been falsely diagnosed; it was following this that he engaged Mr Andrews and determined that thereafter he would always have a full-time veterinary surgeon living at Howletts. The big male, Gugis, seemed unable to procreate despite regular attempts with three females. The females gave every indication that they did not trust him fully, which may have had something to do with it. They displayed their opinion of him whenever Aspinall went in to play. If Gugis behaved without due regard for the human's comparative weakness, one of the females would thump him on the back (the only one to dare such insolence) until he desisted, and the others never roamed far from Aspinall's side, obviously out of concern for his protection. Eventually, Gugis grew too large and powerful for any risks to be taken with his moods, and Aspinall stopped going in with him. Visitors would watch Gugis from safety and could not fail to observe his ferocious displays of irritation. He would fix a stranger with a prolonged stare, then hurl himself against the wall in a 'bluff charge', his body hair rising and his lips curled back. There was no mistaking that these exhibitions were meant to chase off intruders.

With Kulu dead and Gugis apparently impotent, Aspinall chose to begin again and call upon those reserves of patience which his detractors continued to insist he lacked. He took Min to Holland to inspect the stock of a well-known Dutch dealer, whom we shall call 'Jan', and returned with an infant pair close to starvation which he named Djoum and Mushie. Animal dealers are a notoriously unpleasant group of men. They rarely like animals and are entirely indifferent to the ideal of conservation. They see their function as, baldly, to make money, and in this they have succeeded all too well. For every one gorilla which finds its way into a zoo, possibly five or six have been butchered in order to get him there. If caught by African natives, he may well then be eaten, so that his sale to a European dealer is a marginally preferable fate. On one of his African visits, Aspinall saw a cooking-pot in which several small gorilla hands were floating, and the image haunted him ever after.

Apropos of this, there was an occasion when an American film crew came to Howletts for a television feature. One of them was a black girl, at the sight of whom the gorillas all became curiously agitated. The young lady innocently asked why they were behaving as if they were afraid.

'Because they don't like you,' Aspinall replied.

'Have you taught your gorillas to be racist, then?'

There was of course no intelligent response to such a question, but Aspinall told her that for generations of gorillas the black man is a mortal enemy, and that their apprehension in his presence is now genetically inherited. She was not placated.

Those who wish to protect animals in the wild are understandably horrified by the decimation which must occur in order to send specimens to European zoos, and Aspinall came in for as much criticism as anyone else in so far as he helped perpetuate the traffic by being a willing purchaser. Nevertheless, the traffic would continue whether he bought or not, the gorillas would journey towards extinction at the hands of native poachers and predators, and he at least would not countenance imprisoning a solitary animal merely for exhibition. He upheld his resolve to found a self-perpetuating colony and looked forward to the day when he would not need to buy pitiful individuals from unscrupulous dealers.

Djoum and Mushie were indeed pitiful. They were suffering from malnutrition and the trauma of their capture, which together marked their eloquently expressive faces with terror and hopelessness. In most such cases, the infants die of a broken heart, which for once is not a phrase unduly anthropomorphic. Gorillas are an intensely family-oriented species, and it is no exaggeration to say that an individual which has been isolated from its group at an early age and robbed of warmth of familiar ties quite simply gives up. To offer the necessary affection to such an animal, to restore its confidence and spirit, is a Herculean task requiring patience and selflessness beyond the capacity of most.

It was Min Aspinall, only recently bereaved by the loss of her own daughter, who saved the gorillas' lives. Throughout the months of their quarantine she stayed with them, night and day, in the room set aside for them at the top of the house. She slept with them, gave them sustenance and attention, rarely left their company. It was essential that she take on the task alone, because gorilla babies and infants are far more demanding than their human counterparts. A human baby can be passed around from adult to adult quite happily, and several may share in caring for it, but this would be confusing and damaging to a young gorilla. Quite recently an American zoo found itself with the same problem, of having to nurture an infant gorilla to health and maturity. The zoo director gave the infant at least three different 'mothers', girl students from the local university who took it in turns to sit with the gorilla. His purpose in so doing was to give each girl an opportunity to earn a few dollars and the unusual privilege of playing mother to a baby gorilla. It was an absurdly stupid decision to make, showing as it did far more concern for the

girls' welfare and happiness than for the gorilla's, but the attitude is not uncommon. Even among professional zoo people
it appears almost impossible to break the habit of regarding
the human animal as the first to be satisfied. To subordinate
every consideration to the *personal* happiness of an individual
from another species requires a conceptual shift so mighty
that most are incapable of it.

For Min Aspinall the salvation of Djoum and Mushie was
a private joy, calling upon all the maternal gifts so tragically
thwarted by the death of Mameena. Those months exhausted
her, but they were triumphant. Sixteen years later, Djoum
is the patriarch of the famous band, a huge silverback male
with nobility, power and tolerance. Aspinall is fond of saying
that Djoum is one of the great successes of his life, which is
undeniably true since he is the only silverback in the world
who counts at least three humans as friends and still retains his
hierarchical position within the gorilla band; there is nothing
'tame' about Djoum, but much that is moving. However,
Min's contribution to him in these earliest months (and to
Mushie, who also survives) were crucial. It also demonstrated
that when an animal 'imprints' upon a human to that extent
it may still survive with its status within its own species
unaffected. There have been many other instances since.

Aspinall's emotional commitments to the animals now far
exceeded his attachment to the Clermont, where he spent less
and less time from 1970 onwards, leaving the onus of running
the club to Ian Maxwell-Scott and Daniel Meinertzhagen
(who had started working for him as a house-player at
£10 a night eight years earlier). News of his involvement
with animals, and its serious implications, began to spread
beyond his immediate circle and to attract the attention of
more than mere frivolous journalism. The respected Atticus
column in the *Sunday Times* devoted nearly an entire page to
an examination of his work, and when his old friend Teddy
Goldsmith launched his magazine the *Ecologist* he invited
Aspinall to contribute a cover article on his experience
with the gorilla colony. Entitled 'Living with Gorillas', this
duly appeared in the fifth issue of the magazine and enabled

Aspinall to describe the observations made and the lessons learnt. It also, naturally, afforded him the chance to bruit his own philosophy and declare his purpose.

He first reiterated his belief that mankind's progress has been at the expense of the earth's capital resources and should therefore more properly be termed 'regress', and that 'it will probably take the planet millions of years to recover from the human experience'. Oddly enough, he does not seem to have noticed that this was the opinion of a radical, not of the reactionary that he always claimed to be. (A later Chairman of the Conservative Party in Britain would make blatant the opposite view. 'Evolution meant getting rid of the dinosaurs and replacing them with some more efficient and up-to-date animals,' said Norman Tebbit in the *Spectator*. 'Any socialist would have been dedicated to protecting the dinosaurs in the name of compassion or conservation or something. The dinosaurs would never have been allowed to go. So God can't be a socialist.')

Aspinall went on to explain the point of his mission. 'It was my wish,' he wrote, 'that Howletts might prove to be a sanctuary of some beleaguered mammals and so enable them to survive the ecological blizzards of our own epoch.' In this one could discern a mixture of genuine anger that the great mammals should be reduced to an imminent possibility of total extinction through human greed and thoughtlessness, and a personal desire to be their protector and benefactor. The element of self-indulgence, of 'showmanship' almost, led some to deride his lofty aims and see in them a kind of distorted selfishness. Aspers, they implied, had discovered the ultimate fetish of the exhibitionist. This uncharitable view failed to take account of the obvious – that to achieve anything at all in the field of conservation required passionate commitment of a kind only found among people prepared to inject their own personality into the task. Doctors Lang and Lorenz were also eccentric, self-indulgent, emotional in their approach, yet they achieved far more than the dessicated scientist whose commitment was to facts only, not to feeling. Howletts could never have become the success that it did without John Aspinall's selfishness and single-mindedness. If he derived some pleasure from the vision of himself as an overlord, a feudal magnate on whose bounty depended scores of animals, then it was undeniably the animals that benefited from his vanity. Besides which, this dependence further showed how very much more important were his deepest feelings than his occasional politicking; after all, he was on the side of the losers, the underdogs, those who could not fend for themselves, there being no larger collection of losers in the world than the threatened mammals.

In a vivid passage, Aspinall described the social behaviour of his gorillas and their protectiveness towards him:

> Gorillas have developed an extraordinary capacity to neutralise any over-weening, intrafamiliar exertion of power. An infant or juvenile that is threatened by a large male or female is immediately assisted by the remainder of the clan – whatever the cause. This re-active response is, I am glad to say, extended to include their human friends. I used to wrestle with Gugis until 18 months ago and Shamba on these occasions never left my side. Whenever Gugis stepped out of line she admonished him with a series of threatening coughs, and if his horse-play became too violent or if I cried in pain the whole clan would drive him away with a cacophony of barks and screams.

And he further revealed, unashamedly, the emotional basis of his dialogue with the mighty Gugis: 'Since he was 10 months old we have enjoyed a profound relationship. I cannot doubt his love for me, any more than I can question my love for him.'

More than anything now, Aspinall wanted to retire from business and devote himself entirely to the zoo. At forty-five, he had accumulated several million pounds through astute investment, particularly in one of the companies owned by his friend Jimmy Goldsmith, and judged that he would have enough to sustain the zoo, the costs of which had risen to something over £300,000 a year. He was still actively looking for another property where he could establish a larger wildlife sanctuary. Moreover, his disenchantment after ten years at the Clermont was beginning to depress him. His relations with the Gaming Board had been on the whole cordial, but the law's insistence that clients not be accorded credit, together with the regulations forbidding alcohol at the tables, did not accord well with the expansiveness of a proprietor such as Aspinall. Had he continued, he might well have eventually been tempted to join in the games himself – it was no fun just being a manager – and the need to be surreptitious would have niggled annoyingly. There was also the fact that the profile of London's gamblers was undergoing a radical change. No longer was it a question of a few people who all knew one another, but a whole army of foreigners and casual members, most of whom had been 'fish-netted' by other clubs because Aspinall's preference for staying at Howletts had made him dilatory in the matter of attracting new clients. The success of his gambling endeavours had always been due to his knack of turning punters into friends; now he could not summon the energy to bother.

In 1972 the remaining few years' lease on the Clermont Club was sold to Victor Lownes, who ran the Playboy Club in London. It was the *Daily Express* which first broke the news, in a report uncharacteristically amusing for a popular newspaper. 'Aspinall has worked the Clermont up in the last decade to become the final resort for the discreetly classic gambler,' the anonymous reporter wrote, 'without a heart, without soul, probably before the evening without a wife and by the following dawn without any property.'

The sale of the lease did not affect the continuation of Annabel's in the basement, or the absolute ban on any alterations to the highly-prized building. There was some last-minute squabbling about whether the purchase price should include the wine-cellar, which Aspinall was quite happy to see go, but which Maxwell-Scott, who knew better than anyone the extraordinary value of the wines he had collected, was able to rescue. Aspinall also retained most of the furniture.

Lownes was understandably jubilant. He recovered his outlay in the profits of only three nights' trading. In the United States Hugh Hefner, the ultimate owner of Playboy, could scarcely believe his good fortune. Sue Hunt, Aspinall's secretary, had discovered under a sofa an album of photographs taken ten years before, when the Clermont had just opened, and this was sent to America. Within an hour of its receipt, the deal had been signed.

The price of little more than half a million pounds was absurdly low; Aspinall was anxious to have done with it and spend the rest of his life with the animals.

8

The Arrival of Kisoro

Min Aspinall never entirely recovered from the shocking loss of her daughter Mameena, nor from her husband's wilfully stoical acceptance of it. Though her attempts to carry another child had proven fruitless her desire for motherhood was no less fierce. Moreover, the long and devoted experience of rearing Djoum and Mushie had worn her out while constantly reminding her that she was herself childless. She and John Aspinall therefore mutually and amicably decided to divorce, both remarrying within the year. Min's second marriage was to provide her with three children, including twins.

Shortly after the divorce, Aspinall sent Min a handwritten poem of some twenty lines which was, on the surface, entirely out of character. It said little about him or her and was wholly given to a lament on the tragedy of their little daughter. It is not reproduced here owing to its very private nature, but the poem is obviously so intensely felt and so totally free of contrivance that it must be mentioned as an indication of that part of Aspinall's character which, by his own volition, lay hidden even from his closest friends. It is the work of a deeply sensitive man alive to the simple joys of fatherhood and equally able to suffer from the sudden catastrophe of bereavement. More important, the poem is in no measure self-regarding. Aspinall's words dwell upon the pity of Mameena's stolen life and especially on the grim grief of the mother, and show that he shared that grief in the profound reaches of his being. It is a simple demonstration of feeling, and no one who reads it could doubt either that he was able to understand Min's awful sense of loss, or that he was vulnerable himself. The piece is painfully moving.

This poem on Mameena needs to be noticed because it argues against the prevailing opinion of John Aspinall held even by those who professed to know him. He was said to have a cold centre, a core of steel, which was excused by his friends on the grounds that all gamblers must be harsh and unfeeling and that he certainly could not have engineered a success which involved taking money from the foolhardy as well as the rich unless he was devoid of sentiment. Men who take money from gamblers had perforce to be brutally heartless. For all his *bonhomie* and gregarious pleasure in having folk around him, and notwithstanding even his own frequently expressed contention that his success had been built upon his ability to get on well with people, he was said to lack essential warmth. Moreover, it was remarkably easy to progress from this to the erroneous belief that he was able to consort with wild animals mainly because he was utterly incapable of real relationships with other human beings.

Aspinall's keen awareness of his second wife's desolation, as shown in the poem, belies such a facile assessment. A childhood deprived of the normal emotional props had made it important that he fend for himself from an early age and that he avoid the danger of being wounded by indifference. He had in consequence kept his humanity concealed, and even felt the need to confirm his detractors' views by boasting of his steely core. That this entertaining and most convivial of men should be thought heartless was indeed a paradox, and one which he encouraged. He enjoyed the idea that he should be talked about. The real man was, however, a boy who wept in secret, and it is indicative of his success in creating the personality which he wished to deliver to the world that his second wife did not know until after their divorce how profoundly he felt about their shared loss.

Perhaps, also, it was as a boy that he communed with his gorillas, his tigers, his siamangs, and all the growing richness of his menagerie. He never lost the sense of wonder in their presence, or the feeling of admiration for the way in which they managed their social life. He had to learn how to interpret their responses and their own expressions of anger or dismay or whatever, but at least their emotions, once observed, were straight. His persistent view, despite many setbacks, that most other species were emotionally stable and trustworthy suggested that his experience of the human record in his personal journey had been contrary. In a way, he did give more of himself to the animals, because their moral and emotional development was pristine and had not yet reached the nasty subtleties of the human condition. The shame is that his understanding of those subtleties should be kept largely to himself, for fear it be interpreted as weakness.

What he did not keep to himself was his formidable adherence to the principle of loyalty, based on Zulu, Nordic and pagan legacies, which he elevated above every other consideration. His own devotion to the principle would be called upon more than once in years to come, and he would not hesitate to honour it; conversely, those who, in his eyes, dishonoured the principle for any reason at all would be banished thereafter from his thoughts and his home. There would be some casualties of this harshness, friends discarded without appeal on the grounds that forgiveness was unbiological and therefore to be discounted as a gloss of Judaeo-Christian civilisation. One cannot help noticing, however, that loyalty, being a concept more than a feeling, is easier to adhere to than the demands of emotional ties. Indeed, an excessive respect for loyalty may well take the place of overt emotion, for it is in the end arid and cerebral. Despite appearances, loyalty is not difficult or exacting; it merely requires a mathematical decision with universal application, far simpler than dealing with the infinite nuances of human motive and desire. Loyalty is safer than emotion.

Aspinall's third wife, whom he married in 1972 shortly after the sale of the Clermont, was a Curzon, the daughter of Earl Howe. She had had a trying life for her years. Married to the racing driver Piers Courage, to whom she bore two sons, she had been widowed at the age of twenty-three in the most ghastly manner, Piers having perished on the racing track when his car crashed and burst into flames, burning him alive. Her life immediately crumbled, and remained unfocused until she met John Aspinall who appeared to understand the depth of her distress and to be able to restore her strength of spirit. As it happened, she was to be the ideal wife, content to run the house and support Aspinall's unorthodox life, and still, like Jane and Min, share in the care of animals. Though she never completely lost her residual anxiety about them, she was able to raise two tiger cubs to the point where they, now fully grown, accept her as a friend and happily rub against her in greeting; they have even been known to knock her to the ground in their enthusiasm, and for an aristocratic lady brought up in gentler style to take this in her stride is not an accomplishment to be despised. She has also successfully raised two gorillas, one male, one female.

John and Sarah (Sally) Aspinall had one son, whom they called Bassa Wulfhere, respectively after the grandfather of Alfred the Great and an army of wolves. The names were chosen in accordance with Aspinall's growing belief that Englishmen should bear the names of their forefathers, not those of Roman or Jewish derivation.

Freedom from the Clermont was exhilarating for John Aspinall. He threw himself energetically into plans for his zoos, certain as he was that he was now retired and could devote his life to the animals. He continued his search for new property, and was negotiating for a time with Lord Massereene and Ferrard to use his 300-acre estate surrounding the impressive Chilham Castle in Kent. 'Jock' Massereene (whose full name was John Clotworthy Talbot Foster Whyte-Melville Skeffington) was nervous that the villagers of Chilham might prove obstructive, and Aspinall determined to seduce them with his lavish hospitality. A vast party was given in a marquee at Howletts to which the whole of Chilham was invited. The gesture, for once, was ill-chosen and did not achieve the desired result, the villagers recoiling from the prospect of having their peace disturbed by a May-fair set in permanence. Planning permission was later refused in the light of local objections and Aspinall was obliged to look elsewhere. It was, in the end, a fortunate decision, for what he eventually found was far better suited to his purpose than Chilham.

Public interest in the work at Howletts increased substantially in 1972. Two television programmes included interviews with Aspinall as well as film of him with the animals, and Roy Deverell produced the first of his three films on Aspinall, called *All Things Wild and Wonderful*. To some extent this attention was inspired by the sudden world-wide realisation, encouraged by an international campaign launched by the World Wildlife Fund, that some strains of tiger were on the very edge of extinction. Although there had been warnings from many quarters for some years, they had been largely dismissed as the gloomy imaginings of cranks. The world woke up to reality when it was very nearly too late.

The situation was indeed dire. Of fifty thousand tigers in India in 1930, only 1,850 remained. The Siberian tiger (*Panthera tigris altaica*) was reduced to little over a hundred individuals, while the Chinese variety (*Panthera tigris amoyensis*) was being systematically exterminated by government decree and was described as 'very rare'. There were thirty Sumatran tigers left, about fifteen Caspian tigers in Iran, between five and ten Javan tigers, and for the Balinese tiger (*Panthera tigris balica*) time had run out; it was 'definitely extinct' according to local experts. The Indo-Chinese race (*Panthera tigris corbetti*) may have survived in numbers over a thousand, but it was difficult to be precise as they had been decimated by wars in Vietnam and Cambodia, innocent victims of human internecine squabbles.*

The World Wildlife Fund's campaign was extraordinarily successful, alerting governments and peoples worldwide to the unnecessary loss of these strains. Public opinion was

---

*The Javan and Caspian tigers have both since become extinct.

solidly behind the sentiment and somewhat abashed to discover the situation was so serious. Tigers were being erased from the globe because men still derived peculiar pleasure in shooting them, nowadays from helicopters; or because women felt enhanced by their skins (Aspinall wrote an angry letter to the newspapers describing women who wore rare pelts as 'devoid of pity'); or because so much land was being stolen and forests cut down to accommodate ever-growing hordes of humans that there was nowhere left for the tiger to go.

Public opinion alone would not have been sufficient to arrest the disappearance of the tiger. Governments the world over acted promptly, led by the Soviet Union which forthwith banned the hunting of tigers and the export of their skins. India, Pakistan, Bangladesh, Nepal and Bhutan passed laws with similar effect, and India especially, due to the personal interest of Mrs Gandhi who had inherited from her father, Pandit Nehru, a deep respect for wildlife, took swift and dramatic action. Mrs Gandhi established a 'Tiger Task Force' whose purpose was the immediate establishment of special reserves for India's surviving tigers. In addition, twenty-three western nations agreed to forbid the import of the skins of tigers and other endangered cats.

John Aspinall's contribution to the movement was typically individual. Together with Teddy Goldsmith and the *Ecologist* he hired the cavernous Royal Albert Hall in London at the surprisingly low cost of £800 for three hours and advertised a great 'Save the Tiger' rally in *The Times*, *Time Out* and *What's On*. The meeting took place at 3 p.m. on Sunday, 23 April, and was addressed by a number of speakers, Goldsmith and Aspinall among them.

Aspinall's speech was naturally embroidered with much oratorical flourish, especially evident in his opening remarks, before he turned to the subject of the tiger itself, in which he rehearsed some of his more extravagant views. The fact that they were expressed with some stridency did not diminish their essential truth; Aspinall always believed that exaggeration did not smother the point but rather brought it home to the heart instead of the intellect.

'Wildlife throughout the planet is fighting its last great battle,' he began. Wilful extermination of an entire species was a far greater crime than homicide or even genocide, and the 'tattered and perforated conscience' of our own species carried the burden of guilt and shame. We were witnessing the destruction of evolutionary progress, which left to itself provided for the maximum variety of life forms in a given area without resultant habitat deterioration or depletion of non-renewable resources. We tore off the outer skin of the earth's crust to force it to yield its nutrients, not knowing how we would replace it; we imprisoned and tortured innocent creatures in concentration camps until we were ready to butcher them. When Linnaeus named mankind *Homo sapiens*, 'man the wise', he made a classic blunder. From now on, said Aspinall, the human species should be called *Homo rapiens spoliator*, 'man the plunderer and destroyer'. 'Man is ingenious, man is clever, man is a brilliant improviser, but wisdom has he not. Wisdom is in what you don't do as much as in what you do. Wisdom has a negative beauty. Wise mammals, Nature's fully evolved overlords, are masters of restraint.'

He went on to equate the murder of defenceless creatures not with virility and manliness but with deviant behaviour, and condemned big-game hunters for 'buying the cheapest brand of self-esteem known'.

There followed a passage in the speech which came as a surprise from one so reactionary in the political sphere. 'I have come to believe that extremism in defence of the biosphere is no crime.' Aspinall did not go on to credit radical movements such as the Animal Liberation Front which also thought extremism justifiable for such a cause and did all in their power to disrupt the vicious activities which went on in the food factories and experimental laboratories. These were often regarded as left-wing militants or communists funded by the Soviet Union. Aspinall's idea of extremism was to raise the alarm, not besiege the fort, while his actions in furtherance of the cause remained quietly constructive at Howletts. Anyone who planned to recruit him into the ranks of midnight hippies bent on releasing animals from their 'concentration camps' would have been rudely disappointed.

John Aspinall was warmly applauded, his oratory having successfully planted a seed of disquiet. Press coverage of the occasion was widespread though not noticeably intelligent. The *Daily Express* wrote, for example, 'After nearly a life-time observing the petty greeds of the human species at the gaming tables, it is not surprising to learn that [Aspinall] regards Homo Sapiens as an inferior breed.' It was not to be expected, of course, that journalists should understand the import of what Aspinall was saying, though he was dismayed that they should not wish to try. More upsetting was the size of the audience, some eight hundred in a vast hall which could hold ten times as many; they appeared to occupy only a few rows. It was from this day that he began the long slide into pessimism, that he was made to realise that apathy in the face of the destruction of other species was insurmountable. Before the Albert Hall rally he had imagined apathy could be punctured by passionate advocacy. Afterwards, he began to acknowledge that his work on behalf of other animals might itself be doomed to extinction; he no longer saw himself as fighting a losing battle – the battle was already lost.

To redress the balance, his Siberian tigress later that year produced a cub, the first ever to be born in Britain and a cause for serious rejoicing; after all, the Siberian race was one of those which had been virtually squeezed out of existence, with only a few score individuals remaining in the world. With luck, the race might continue in Kent even if its chances in the Far East should prove illusory.

Later that year there came a severe setback which attracted far more publicity than the Albert Hall speech and helped to depict John Aspinall in the public mind as a dangerous man. Whenever he was abroad it was his custom to leave Howletts in the hands of his young half-brother James Osborne, who had the freedom to invite people to stay for the weekend. He had been a small boy when Aspinall had first started to protect animals and had during his adolescent years taken the proximity of wild species very much for granted, as had Aspinall's own children Amanda, now fourteen, and Damian, eleven. In 1969 James Osborne had been in charge of Howletts while John and Min Aspinall were visiting the dealer Jan in Holland, and had asked some friends to stay, including Murray-Thriepland and a pretty model called Merilyn Lamb, nineteen years old. At that time, James Osborne was twenty-three, and groomed to be Manager of Howletts zoo. The tiger colony had grown to thirty-five animals, many of which James knew personally, although four Siberian tigers, recent arrivals from Canada, were strangers to him.

On the way down to Kent from London, there was much discussion in the car about the unusual relationship that existed between Aspinall and wild animals, resulting in their astonishing reliability. Guests were not expected to be apprehensive; this was not at all like other zoos; James himself was on terms of trust with many of the animals.

After lunch James took his visitors to see the tiger enclosure. Tigers loped up to the fence to purr in greeting and rub themselves against the mesh. James put his finger through and tickled a tiger's nose, to its evident delight. Desultory chat went on the while, until there was sudden and dreadful pandemonium. Merilyn Lamb had stuck her finger through the wire, a tiger had grabbed it and dragged her arm inside, whereupon four tigers rushed upon the arm and savaged it. By the time she was rescued, seconds later, two of her fingers had been chewed off, and so much of her lower arm and biceps lacerated that she had to undergo an emergency operation at Canterbury Hospital lasting eight hours. A wicked irony of this tragedy was that Merilyn Lamb had not very long before played a small part in a film in which she was a model who suffered mauling from a tiger.

Miss Lamb sued both John Aspinall and James Osborne for damages, and the case came before Mr Justice ('Joe') Cantley in the High Court in December 1972. There was not a single newspaper which did not give the case a prominent position; for the first time Aspinall's zoo was on public trial.

The burden of Miss Lamb's case, as presented by her counsel Mr Edward Laughton-Scott QC, was that she was lulled into a false sense of security by Mr Osborne and encouraged to think that all the animals were safe, and that in consequence both he and Mr Aspinall were liable for her injuries which had effectively terminated her modelling career. Counsels for the defendants, Mr Richard Rougier QC, and Mr Robert Johnson, did not dispute the injuries but contested liability.

At one point Miss Lamb went into the Judge's private rooms to show him her right arm, on which half a dozen operations had been performed over two years in an attempt to save it. Passing judgment some days later, Mr Justice Cantley said the arm was little better than an artificial limb. 'Cosmetically it is a disaster to be concealed as much as possible. It is grotesque.'

Laughton-Scott said that not only was Miss Lamb led to believe it was safe to put her finger into the tiger's cage, but also it would have been cowardly had she not done so. Another of the weekend guests had been told that if he did not go in with the tigers he must expect to be sent home. It was against this background of immature jocularity that the accident occurred. The tangential purpose of the suit, namely to belittle Aspinall's philosophy, was made apparent by Mr Laughton-Scott on the first day. 'The only question of gambling in this case,' he said 'is the extent to which he is prepared to gamble with other people's safety.' That the case had nothing whatever to do with gambling, and that Aspinall was out of the country at the time, were not considerations which could be allowed to interfere with an opportunity for cheap insult.

Miss Lamb (who had since the incident become Mrs John Trehearne) wept in the witness-box as she told the court what had happened when she put her forefinger through the wire mesh. Cross-examining, Mr Rougier asked if she knew that tigers were generally held to be fierce in popular belief, and whether she thought all the tigers at

Howletts were tame. 'Yes, I was told they were by Mr Osborne.'

'What Mr Osborne meant was that all the animals reared by Mr Aspinall himself were tame.'

'No, he meant all the tigers.'

'Is not the truth of the matter that there was an element of dare in this? You would be one up on the other guests and be able to say that you had stroked the tigers?'

'No, not at all.'

Cross-examining for James Osborne, Mr Johnson also suggested that Merilyn Lamb had been fascinated by the element of risk involved and brought disaster upon herself, which she denied.

Mr James Chipperfield, of the famous circus family, was called to give his expert opinion on the nature of tigers. He said that forty-seven years' experience had taught him never to trust a lion or tiger (the very point of view, incidentally, which Aspinall's work was bent on dispelling). He made the crucial point that whereas he could be with a tiger inside its enclosure, he would not consider it safe to put his hand into the same enclosure from the outside, and would dismiss any keeper he saw so doing. This was not a position with which Aspinall would disagree.

When Aspinall himself appeared in the witness-box he was quick to counter the notion, put to him by Miss Lamb's counsel, that tigers were quite exceptionally dangerous. Yes, a tiger could kill a man with one blow, but then so could a horse with one kick. 'I would not be alive today if I did not trust tigers. I trust them completely. But they are different from us. They have different habits. You have to know them and understand them, then you can trust them as you would trust your wife or child.' It was nevertheless an arduous and lengthy process to make friends with a tiger.

At the request of Mr Rougier, he demonstrated for the judge three soft calls which were habitually made by a young tiger to express different moods and which were easily understood by another tiger or by a human being who knew those signals. He then told the judge that of his twenty best friends more than half were wild animals. He denied that this implied he was callous or indifferent to the lives of humans. 'I have a great respect for tigers and a great respect for human beings.' On the other hand, he admitted, in a phrase which made headlines everywhere the following day, that he would sacrifice the life of his own daughter if it meant saving an animal species from extinction. Of course, the proposition was hypothetical and in no way suggested a lack of love for his daughter, but he told the court, 'I think everyone would accept that no one human life is worth a whole animal species which has survived two hundred million years of evolution.'

In truth, this was a philosophical statement of faith which had little to do with the suit for damages under consideration, but counsel wanted to establish the eccentricity of the defendant's attitude when compared with the common view, and Aspinall was not disposed to disabuse him. It was not, however, his eccentricity which was on trial.

More to the point, he said that he would not dream of putting his hand into a tiger's cage when visiting a zoo whose population he did not personally know, and that for young friends of his brother to do so in emulation of his affectionate relationship with tigers was 'insupportable folly'. He had absolute confidence in his brother not to take risks and he was 'extremely upset' that such a beautiful young lady as Miss Lamb should have been injured. No visitor had ever put his or her hand through the wire mesh before. He deplored the practice of other zoos where an animal which had savaged a human was automatically killed. Tigers were 'sound stable citizens' and 'if an animal savages anybody it is usually the fault of the human being'.

Questioned about the accident which had disfigured Robin Birley, Aspinall was asked if his experience on that occasion had let him down. 'Yes, it did. I admit it,' he replied. 'I realised afterwards it was because I had overlooked the fact that the tiger was in a late stage of pregnancy.'

The next to give evidence was James Osborne, who freely admitted that he had been showing off to his guests when fondling the tiger through the mesh; he was proud of his brother's achievement and wanted to demonstrate it to other people. The tiger had taken his fingers in its mouth in a non-aggressive manner. He had withdrawn his hand and shown the others the teeth-marks which it bore, then stroked the tiger again. He had not seen Miss Lamb put her hand through the wire and it had not occurred to him that she would do so.

Evidence having been completed, Mr Justice Cantley reserved his judgment for a later date. The press was certain to report judgment at some length, as it had become clear there was a feeling abroad that Aspinall's arrogant style, his insolent certainty should be punished. It was the first time his unorthodox philosophy had been brought under scrutiny and his absence of doubt or humility was deemed unattractive. A man who dared question that human life was not necessarily a superior value deserved chastisement.

Judgment came two weeks afterwards, on 19 December. Mr Justice Cantley held that John Aspinall was not to blame for the accident. On the other hand, James Osborne was held responsible because he had not indicated that four of the tigers were strangers to him when he had previously shown photographs of some hand-reared tigers playing with children at Howletts, and he ought to have known that his guests might copy his actions with regard to the tigers. He praised Mr Osborne's courage in admitting he had been showing off, and likewise commended Miss Lamb's 'high courage' in managing to lead an active life despite her horrible injuries. She, however, was one-third to blame for the accident since there was an indication she still maintained some apprehension concerning the tigers, in which case she should not have ventured near them. Damages were in consequence reduced from what they might have been, and James Osborne was ordered to pay £10,600 plus all Miss Lamb's costs.

The case was a salutary one for John Aspinall. His chosen vocation must needs henceforth be indulged with greater circumspection, for he was much more shaken and worried by the event than his demeanour in court had indicated; and he was aware as never before that those who would support the grand purpose behind this vocation were indeed a pitifully small number. He would have a long struggle ahead.

Another blow from a different quarter had come in the summer of 1972 when Aspinall casually read in the local newspaper that Messrs Robert Brett & Sons Ltd intended to establish a pit for gravel extraction right next door to Howletts. What became known as the 'Gravel Pit Dispute' thus began with a furious letter from John Aspinall to the Bridge-Blean Rural District Council objecting to the plan in the strongest terms. The Brett firm would devote no less than 73 acres to the extraction of sand and gravel, for which a huge processing plant would need to be constructed. Fifty-five vehicle journeys per day would be made to and from the site. It would be a devastating attack upon the peace of the animal sanctuary.

Through his solicitors Herbert, Smith, Aspinall made a closely argued thirteen-point objection to the proposal, hammering especially on the themes of noise, traffic and ugliness. Kent County Council were astonished that such a seemingly innocuous venture should stir up great passions; they received 120 letters of objection. (Andrew Nitch-Smith of the firm of solicitors, who knew his client very well, wrote to Aspinall, 'I dare say you can claim credit for 118 of these!') Overwhelmed by the vision of Kent countryside being turned into a vast industrial nightmare, and not a little swayed by the very interesting point that the gravel pit scheme would pollute the Little Stour, the only pure water chalk stream in the south-east of England and one of only six or seven in the world, Kent County Council refused planning permission. They may even have been slightly intimidated by the power and influence Howletts seemed able to wield. But the day was far from won for Aspinall. Robert Brett & Sons appealed against the decision, as a result of which Kent County Council were obliged to set up a Public Enquiry, to be held in Bekesbourne Village Hall. This duly took place on 18 September 1973.

The spectacle of impressive London counsel descending upon a tiny village hall to argue for and against a gravel pit was reminiscent of Gilbert & Sullivan. The Rt Hon. Sir Derek Walker-Smith QC MP appeared for Aspinall, with Robert Carnwath as his junior. He had a difficult task to perform, for, as he said, one could not easily prove damage to the animals at Howletts until the species were extinct, by which time it would be too late. To show that they needed tranquillity in order to breed and survive he had to rely upon expert opinion.

The enquiry was then treated to a clutch of letters from zoo directors the world over, alerted by Aspinall to the threat which hung over Howletts. Jiri Wolf, the Przewalski's Wild Horse studbook keeper at Prague Zoo, from whom Aspinall had bought the original breeding animals of his herd, wrote, 'We delivered them to Howletts convinced that there they will find the best conditions for breeding. In the whole world there are only two hundred of these most precious horses and they are entrusted only to experts with the best references . . . These animals are a cultural heritage of the past and we have a duty to save them for future generations.'

Warren Iliffe, director of the zoo at Portland, Oregon, wrote to the effect that Mr Aspinall's park represented a vital insurance against the loss of endangered species and that his breeding experience added to the world's knowledge. 'They may be the only specimens we have for reintroduction into the wild when safe preserves are established,' he wrote. Dr Oeming, from Edmonton, Alberta, said that if Howletts was forced to close, 'the loss would be a world loss, and one which could not be retrieved'. For Herman Ruhe, Howletts was 'one of the few true places of refuge for the rare animal species which are threatened by extinction in their native homelands'. Dr Lang also wrote from Basle, expressing his alarm at the project which would be 'a smack in the face for anyone who has given the problem of nature conservation serious thought'. Dr Kurt Benirschke, director of the San Diego Zoo, universally regarded as one of the finest in the world, rose to elegant hyperbole; the destruction of Howletts, he said, would be worse than demolishing the Louvre.

In his peroration, Sir Derek Walker-Smith attempted to divert emphasis from these far-flung esoteric opinions, to which he rightly judged the Bekesbourne villagers would more than likely be indifferent, and to depict instead before their imaginations the most vivid personal disaster. 'Where there is tranquillity there would be activity,' he said. 'Where there is seclusion there would be intrusion; where there is quiet there would be noise; where there is peace of rural nature there would be bustle and the turbulence of industrial operations.'

Despite this the prevailing mood did not augur well for Howletts, yet the gravel pit proposal was killed in the end for the sake of Bekesbourne, not to protect wild animals from disturbance. The Secretary of State for the Environment, with whom the ultimate decision lay, was at that time the Rt Hon. Geoffrey Rippon QC MP. Rippon dismissed the appeal brought by Robert Brett & Sons on the grounds that the damage to the environment would outweigh any commercial advantages which might accrue; they would have to look elsewhere to dig their gravel pit.

Although the dispute ended favourably for Aspinall, it would not be fair to suggest that he won the case, which turned out to his advantage almost in spite of the parade of zoological advice. On the other hand, the villagers were not slow to acknowledge that no one else could have done it for them. Only Aspinall could afford the £16,000 costs, all of which he bore himself. A village enquiry of this kind is generally a much tamer, milder, knitting-needle affair, and as no local farmer could have afforded to take the matter any further, it is almost certain the gravel pit would have gone ahead for want of any purposeful opposition, against a background of impotent grumbling. Aspinall received some kindly letters from neighbours thanking him for having 'saved the valley'.

What mattered to him, however, was that he had saved the animals from interference. His overriding concern, amounting almost to an obsession, still was to breed gorillas successfully, and the prize continued to elude him. Male gorillas reach sexual maturity between nine and ten years, when the hair on their backs begins to turn silver. Females have a monthly menstrual cycle, averaging thirty-one days between periods. At Howletts there were several sexually receptive females, who presented themselves regularly to Gugis, aged fifteen, without result. Gugis was able to copulate whenever called upon, but it was by now sadly apparent that he was for some reason infertile. As for Djoum, he was still too young. It was beginning to look as if Aspinall's ambition might be thwarted, and, in so far as it concerned the well-being of the species, that ambition was now definitely questionable. As more and more gorillas were taken from the wild their fragile numbers were depleted, a process which could only be justified if their birth rate in captivity were able to compensate. As Dian Fossey was to write some years later after her long sojourn in the Virunga Mountains of Africa, 'I cannot concur with those who advocate saving gorillas from extinction by killing and capturing more free-living individuals only to exhibit them in confinement.' (Incidentally, Dian Fossey continued to despise zoos with a passion, until she visited Howletts in 1984 and subsequently declared it to be the only zoo in the world for which she would make an exception. She was murdered by poachers in Rwanda the following year.)

It appeared that time was running out for the gorilla, only seconds (on the evolutionary time-scale) after its peace was invaded by man. The lowland gorilla (*Gorilla gorilla gorilla*) had been known to science only since 1847, and was described by Wilson, Savage, du Chaillu and others as ferocious and naturally prone to attack. The highland gorilla (*Gorilla gorilla beringei*) was an even more recent discovery, first seen in 1902. The distinctions between the two are so slight as to be virtually invisible even to an anthropologist, and the one is now recognised to be a sub-species of the other. There are between thirty and fifty thousand lowland gorillas remaining in the wild, and under two hundred of the highland variety, intimately known only to such intrepids as Carl Akeley (who persuaded King Albert of the Belgians to create a national park in the Virunga Mountains for their protection), George Schaller and Dian Fossey. All the gorillas in captivity, including the Howletts groups, are lowland.

Thus the largest of the apes, and the one most capable of communion with the human, was both the last to be discovered and likely to be the first to disappear. To contribute towards this disappearance rather than arrest it was, for someone who felt like John Aspinall, a fearsome, a devastating responsibility. Only if his animals could breed would he be able to help them. He came close to despair and seriously considered surrender.

As a final gesture, he made an appeal in the *International Zoo News* (which he owned and published himself, incidentally). A few weeks later there came a letter from Lincoln Park Zoo in Chicago announcing that they had an eleven-year-old male, Kisoro, who had bred already and whom they would be happy to lend to Howletts as they were themselves getting rather short of space. Aspinall, quite literally, jumped for joy; he was transported with excitement. He sent an immediate telegram: 'Everyone at Howletts is thrilled with the possibility of having Kisoro as a guest, and will certainly treat him with as much respect and loving care as the arrival of the President himself.'

It was already known that Lincoln Park had, at that time, the best gorilla collection in the world. Kisoro had been with them since the age of three and had fathered two children. There was no reason to doubt that he would father more. The fact that Lincoln Park was ready to send him on loan to Kent reflected the new zoo philosophy which was beginning to emerge, that it no longer mattered which zoo had the most or best of any species, but that the species should breed and flourish. Competition, for the benefit of individual zoo directors and municipal committees, was being replaced by international co-operation, for the benefit of the animals. This was a philosophy which Aspinall applauded wholeheartedly.

In response to the insistence of Dr Lester Fisher, director of Lincoln Park, that Kisoro should travel with every comfort and in the company of the resident veterinary surgeon, Aspinall wrote, 'I am very moved that an institution as important and as large as your own takes the actual care of a great animal so conscientiously – a welcome relief from the attitude of most zoos who regard their rarities merely as exhibits or prestige symbols.' He added the characteristically barbed remark, 'We have to quarantine primates for six months after they arrive – a ridiculous law since it does not apply to humans.'

Preparations over the next few months were intense and detailed. Commissioner Franklin Schmick came ahead from Chicago to inspect Howletts, and reported back that he was impressed by the 'truly fine collection' he saw, speaking not as an expert. Aspinall suggested that, in his view, it was essential Kisoro travel not only with the vet but also with his 'buddy', the gorilla keeper; he, naturally, would be responsible for all expenses.

Kisoro was eventually booked to travel on Pan American flight 168 from Chicago to London on 21 October 1973. He had to be sedated and placed in a crate, specially built to the precise dimensions of 60 inches by 60 inches, by 36 inches wide. The airline company had further to undertake to keep the temperature constant and suitable for gorillas, and promise that Kisoro would be last on the flight and first off on arrival. The vet, Dr Erich Maschgan, and the head primate keeper, James Higgins, were booked to accompany him. It was a major event which attracted a great deal of interest in the Chicago press, though the British newspapers, unimpressed by the fact that at 4,000 miles this was the longest journey ever undertaken by a gorilla, ignored it. After a Pan American delay of twenty-four hours, Kisoro,

Maschgan and Higgins landed at Heathrow on 22 October and were met by Aspinall and staff. They proceeded immediately to Howletts, where quarantine regulations were to be observed *in situ*.

Initially, Kisoro was placed in an enclosure adjacent to the two females who would be allocated to him, Mouila and Juju, so as to be introduced to them gradually. Mouila adjusted to the newcomer with serene calm indifference, but Juju showed every sign of nervousness, not to say terror. Whenever Kisoro displayed to her, thumping his chest and yawning, Juju just sat and screamed.

Kisoro experienced no difficulty in settling in and was eating like a horse in the first week. No doubt the enormous variety of exotic fruit which Aspinall provided, to be peeled and enjoyed at leisure and even concealed beneath the straw floor-covering, convinced him that the journey was worthwhile.

As soon as the period of quarantine was over, the great silverback was properly introduced to his two females in the same enclosure. Juju screamed and panicked for no reason at all, it seemed, her behaviour infecting Mouila to such an extent that both females turned upon the luckless gorilla and attacked him. Kisoro was majestic under siege, Aspinall reported to Fisher: 'He fended them off by waving his arms at them, similar to an immensely powerful wrestler being attacked by two beautiful women – all he wanted to do was defend himself and get out of the way.' He added that Kisoro was obviously missing Higgins, the keeper who had by now returned to Chicago.

To Jeremy Mallinson, director of the famous Durrell zoo in Jersey, Aspinall wrote that Kisoro had the temperament of a statesman, because although Mouila and Juju were terrified, 'he uses considerable restraint during the over-reaction of the two girls and never seems to cuff or bite them seriously.'

Kisoro quickly established his position as patriarch and the females settled down readily enough to allow him to mate without objection. Within weeks he was mating regularly with four females in his group and hopes of starting a colony at last were well-founded. There would still, however, be some time to wait.

The degree of co-operation between Aspinall and the Lincoln Park Zoo was to flourish and prove beneficial in the long run. It was an important development, first because it demonstrated that Aspinall's enterprise was not merely the personal 'dream' which he had for so long fostered, but was recognised as valuable in zoological circles, secondly because it was symptomatic of the new spirit of responsibility obtaining in the zoo fraternity. For thousands of years animals had been exhibited with little regard for more than the satisfaction of human curiosity; for hundreds they had been used as voiceless objects for experimentation or the advance of 'learning'. The time had at last come when their well-being and their continuance were paramount. It must be remembered that when Lincoln Park sent Kisoro, and the many other animals that were to cross the Atlantic in the ensuing months, Howletts was still a private establishment, not open to the public. Kisoro was sent to procreate a diminishing species, not to divert the curious. Aspinall was relieved to have animals from reputable sources and to rely less on the unscrupulous animal dealers whose attitudes and behaviour were offensive to everything he held dear.

At almost the same time, Andrews having left Howletts largely because he did not share, or did not understand, the peculiar purpose of the enterprise, Aspinall advertised for a full-time veterinary surgeon in the *Veterinary Record*, the journal of the British Veterinary Association. It was answered by Tom Begg, who had previously worked at the zoo in Jersey and who had never heard of Howletts. He went to meet Aspinall at 1 Lyall Street in Belgravia (which was then and is still Aspinall's London home), and after a brief interview was employed on the spot. Begg has remained at Howletts ever since. Descended from a long line of Scottish veterinary surgeons, Begg is typical of the kind of man who has worked with animals all his life without ever finding a position which enables him to treat them with the respect he feels, and who found that position at Howletts. Another such is Harry Teyn, senior elephant keeper. His story may serve as an example to help explain the dedication of many of the Howletts keepers who resist the temptation to progress to other zoos where they might earn substantially more and might even find themselves honoured with a title of some sort, in order to remain where they belong and where they feel the animals need them.

Harry was born in Leiden, Holland, the son of a social worker. When he was very young, the family moved to Middelburg, a small town in a rural part of the country, where Harry quickly became fascinated in everything that lived in the foliage. From the age of three he collected and observed rabbits, frogs, toads, worms, beetles, in fairly blatant compensation for the lack of affection at home. The Teyn family was neither stable nor happy, and when Harry's parents separated, the three children were sent off to an orphanage. As soon as it was discovered they were not genuine orphans, they were sent back home (Harry very reluctantly) to their mother, who was not at all pleased. ('She threw a fit,' says Harry, graphically.) At the age of twelve, Harry packed his bags and left home. He stayed in various hostels for a couple of years, then trained to be a bricklayer. But his past had made him so intractable and rebellious that he was taken into psychiatric care. With splendid percipience, the psychiatrist recommended that young Harry should find work with a circus or a zoo. He was then fourteen. The circus did not appeal to him, with its tricks and its indignity, but the zoo idea attracted. Harry now says he was lucky to find what he wanted to do.

Rhenen Zoo took the boy on and found him a foster home, where he was treated with unfamiliar kindness. He worked first with small cats, then with elephants, but the persistent rebellious streak caused his undoing after five years and he was sacked. There followed a short period at Amersfoort private zoo, and eighteen months' National Service during which Teyn trained as a sniper and rose to the rank of corporal. He emerged more mature, less troublesome, and immediately sought to work again with animals. He joined the Dutch animal dealer 'Jan' whose unscrupulous exploitation of wildlife he found repellent and whose treatment of the beasts was shameful. One gorilla in particular was so skinny and neglected that Harry asked Jan (who was amused) if he could take him home and try to rescue him. He stopped by a doctor's surgery and sat in the waiting-room with the gorilla on his lap. The animal was then examined properly and thoroughly, with the diagnosis that it had fluid on the lungs, enteritis and pneumonia. It was almost certain to die. Harry took the animal home and nursed it for a week before it surrendered. 'That really broke my bloody heart,' he says. Afterwards, Harry cared for twenty-three gorillas that passed through the dealer's hands without a single fatality. He saved money, in effect, for the man he despised, as the dealer only thought of animals in terms of cash in disguise and their good health made them more valuable.

After a year, John Aspinall and his second wife Min came over from England in search of gorillas, and Jan attempted to sell a lowland gorilla to them as a mountain gorilla. Aspinall was doubtful. He asked the young assistant what he thought, and Harry boldly agreed with him (to the fury of Jan, of course). Aspinall asked Harry to take them back to the airport, and gave him £10 with the request he buy some decent fruit for the gorillas. Harry was astonished; their gorillas habitually ate only bread and forage.

On his return, an almighty row ensued between Harry and Jan, resulting in Harry's dismissal. After a brief period of idleness, watching deer and birds, and sudden marriage to a Dutch girl, he wrote to Aspinall and asked for work. That was in 1969.

Initially, Harry Teyn was placed with gorillas, then antelopes, other hoof-stock, black leopards, and wolves. He relished the work and gracefully conceded that Aspinall was the first man he had ever come across who thought about animals as he did. Six years later he left, to 'better' himself, a decision he now derides as the worst of his life.

He went to a wildlife park in Scotland but quickly left when he found methods intolerable. Animals were slaughtered for money. His wife left him but he soon met his present wife, Karen and took her back to Holland. Harry now had no income, a pregnant wife and a featureless future. He swallowed his pride and wrote to Aspinall again, who without hesitation invited him to return. When he arrived at Port Lympne, the black leopards ran over to greet him and treated him as if he had never been away. Eventually he was placed in charge of his own section at Howletts, the elephants, and given a house. In 1980 he left again and went to Edinburgh Zoo for three years, by this time with two children as well as a wife to support. Harry lived on unemployment benefit for six months, controlling the temptation to plead for rescue from Aspinall again as he did not want to 'make a convenience of him', but penury overcame him and he was again taken on at Howletts. Since that day, he has been senior keeper with the African elephants and knows where his destiny lies. Harry Teyn, a superb elephant man, is an example of the kind of 'misfit' who frequently finds a home where other men might only find a job.

John Aspinall himself was certainly enjoying his retirement. He did not look back upon the sale of the Clermont Club, which everyone regarded as his creation, with regret, despite the commonly held view that he had let it go for a risible sum. He had between £2 and £3 million invested, largely in Jimmy Goldsmith's companies, and together with the proceeds of the Clermont sale, he judged that he would have enough to devote the rest of his life to the sole benefit of wild animals. Even the additional property he was looking for would not be an unnecessary drain on resources, for it would be large enough to open to the public without restricting the animals' privacy and space and would in time be able to pay for itself; he even envisaged the day when the new wild life sanctuary would help support Howletts. He was by now employing half a dozen gardeners and a dozen keepers, as well as carpenters and maintenance men, for a fair proportion of whom he also provided accommodation. It was an ambitious, lordly undertaking, reminiscent of the responsibilities of an eighteenth-century landowner for his brigade of tenants, and virtually unique in the twentieth century as something undertaken from scratch rather than inherited, but the role suited John Aspinall and he was happy. He could now see clearly the comfort of his family and the future of the sanctuary to which he was deeply committed.

Then there came a fearful shock. The sudden rise in oil prices, whose injurious effects were felt worldwide, also had calamitous consequences for Aspinall. Put very simply, the Wall Street crash swept away, with the finality of a single stroke of the broom, all his investments. The news came through one afternoon at tea in Lady O.'s cottage. 'That's it,' he said, as he put down the telephone. 'It's all gone.' Not for the first time in his life, Aspinall found himself penniless. 'I lost everything,' he says. 'My money melted like snow in summer. I was bust.'

History, of a kind, was repeating itself. Aspinall's earlier financial collapse could be attributed directly to his stubborn loyalty towards a friend, Eddie Gilbert, to whose investment skills he had entrusted his funds. Now it was the advice of his closest friend Jimmy Goldsmith which accidentally brought calamity upon him. By tying his investments to Goldsmith's he had left himself no room for escape. As he had always invested with borrowed money, and as interest rates shot up to 17 per cent, the value of his stocks was wiped out at the same time as he could no longer afford to buy more to replace them. The cost of feeding his animals represented a massive haemorrhage on his ability to continue paying interest.

He now claims he always knew it would happen one day. Fortunes are made and lost, and in the milieu he had chosen they occur rather more dramatically than elsewhere. He now found himself without a club, without an income, without any capital, and with huge responsibilities which he was determined not to relinquish. Least of all would he ever contemplate squeezing the resources necessary for the upkeep of the zoo. The animals would never be allowed to suffer, and it is remarkable that in the four dark years which followed not one animal was sold, not one keeper was sacked.

Aspinall's fortitude at this time was little short of astonishing. Both those who knew and admired him, and those
who found his self-assurance and political attitudes harshly
unattractive, alike paid tribute to his resilience. He was not
heard to complain, to bemoan his lot, to sink into pessimism.
He simply did what needed to be done, and remained a
cheerful, ebullient companion.

What needed to be done was indeed drastic. He mortgaged
his house at 1 Lyall Street for a substantial sum; he was even
willing to sell it, and would have done so had not the prospective purchaser backed down. He mortgaged other properties
which kept him going for a few months. He returned to
gambling at other clubs, winning more than £160,000 at
blackjack over a period of one month, which was enough to
feed the animals and pay the staff for some time. When the
revenue from these initiatives dried up, he sold all his wine,
then gradually sold his books and his pictures. Lady Sarah
sold her jewellery.

A routine was established whereby James Osborne drove
up to London every week with a car-load of *objets*, ornaments
or prints, to be delivered to Goldsmith's bankers in return for
£3,000, the weekly bill for grain, fruit and wages. Goldsmith
thought it would be helpful for Aspinall to understand the
moral obloquy of financial suffering – that he must part with
something to drive the message home. Within a short time,
the mansion at Howletts was visibly depleted as a result of
this policy. On his return Osborne divided the £3,000 into
brown envelopes. There were even times when Aspinall
would gamble with it in an attempt to increase it before
the division was made. As by law the casino had to keep the
cheque, he had until the following Tuesday (when it would
be presented) to gamble. Once, when the staff were late
receiving their wages, their spokesman was angry. Aspinall
pointed out that he was being deprived as well as they, albeit
to a lesser degree, and they agreed to wait.

Before long, money was owed to fruit and grain dealers
and other suppliers all over Kent, but the zoo managed
generally to pay up just before any threatening letter arrived.

'Every week is a miracle,' Aspinall used to say. Parting with
his own treasures was bitter, since he was not an indiscrimi-
nate collector, but a man for whom every piece meant
something. He seems actually glad that some items went to
adorn Jimmy Goldsmith's house.

In the midst of all this, at unquestionably the worst
possible time, the property he had been hoping to discover
for his wildlife sanctuary fell into his lap. His old friend from
Oxford days, Alan Clark, who lived nearby at Saltwood
Castle, telephoned to tell him that a neglected estate of 275
acres, some twenty miles away, was up for sale in twenty-
seven lots. Clark was interested in two of them. The estate
was Port Lympne, the beautiful Cape Dutch style mansion
which had once belonged to Philip Sassoon, and where,
between the two world wars, the brilliant and influential
had been entertained in lavish style for the month of August
every year, Sassoon preferring to stay in London during the
other eleven months. More to the point, the fields and
woodland were totally unsuited to agriculture, and therefore very well suited to animal husbandry, and the whole
estate was an idyllic suntrap, facing south across the English
channel. Aspinall went to see it once, and made a bid for
all twenty-seven lots the same day. The cost was £360,000.

9
Port Lympne

Nobody had ever really lived at Port Lympne. In the days of its prime, Sir Philip Sassoon had employed twenty-four gardeners to toil all year round in order to make the exquisite gardens perfect for three weeks in August; the rest of the year Port Lympne had simply waited. By the time John Aspinall came upon it in 1973, it was utterly forlorn and sleepy; just three employees prevented it from slipping into the ground. Mr Holyoak, the caretaker, was paid £10 a week. The one surviving gardener, Mr Bardon, worked three days a week for £7.50, which had to be paid by postal order as he had no bank account; he lived on his old age pension. And Mr Leadbetter mowed the lawns fortnightly at £20 a time. Yet the house, which seemed to have been forgotten on a hillside in Kent, was once regarded as one of the most historic built in England in the twentieth century.

The architect for Port Lympne was Sir Herbert Baker, whose finest work this was said to be. Construction began just before the First World War, and was completed shortly after the cessation of hostilities, whereupon Sir Herbert went off to India to help Sir Edwin Lutyens design the imperial city of New Delhi. At Port Lympne he had been able to indulge the desire for perfection, every architect's dream, without restriction on cost. Two-and-a-half-inch French bricks were used exclusively, and the entire roof was covered in old Kent tiles. Window-frames were made from English oak and rafters from stained Oregon pine. The bronzework was designed by Bainbridge Reynolds, and for the interiors Sir Philip Sassoon commissioned young artists to paint original murals. These were Rex Whistler, Glyn Philpot and Michel Sert.

The floor of the entrance hall, which continued right through the house to the west terrace, was an intricate mosaic of black and white marble in varying concentric curves; each piece, and there are thousands, was different from the rest. This inspired idea was matched by the hugely impressive Moorish courtyard in the centre of the house, with fifty-two white marble columns, green marble floor and five fountains. The windows were made from thick Tuscan alabaster to reflect an opaque glow over the courtyard.

Port Lympne was indubitably a folly, but a folly lent dignity by exquisite taste. Almost immediately, it was a famous centre of luxurious entertainment. Sassoon had a wide acquaintance collected during a lifetime at the epi-centre of events. He had been private secretary to Lord Haig, and an under-secretary of air, as well as MP for Hythe (which at least indicated he knew the local area well and did not pounce upon it from afar). He had been a baronet from the age of twenty-four, inheriting from his father and grandfather, and, supremely, he was known as one of the art connoisseurs of his time. An invitation to Port Lympne was something of an honour to be cherished.

When the Treaty of Paris was being negotiated in 1921, Clemenceau and the French Prime Minister, Aristide Briand, were guests at Port Lympne for five weekends; a special telephone link with the Elysée Palace in Paris was installed in the octagonal library. For the next eighteen years a constant stream of the celebrated and the accomplished (occasionally both) came to enjoy the lavish hospitality which brought the house alive during the summer months. They included Winston Churchill, Lloyd George, Stanley Baldwin, Lord Beaverbrook; the Prince of Wales and Mrs Simpson; Emerald Cunard and Sybil Colefax; Douglas Fairbanks, Mary

Pickford, Charlie Chaplin ; Lawrence of Arabia; and virtually every prominent politician and influential aristocrat of the day.

Then, in 1939, Sir Philip Sassoon died and Port Lympne descended into a kind of coma. During the Second World War it served as barracks to Czech pilots, who, with other matters to contend with, paid little heed to the beauty of the place and did no small damage. It was later bought by a Colonel Waite in the 1950s, who did further damage by way of 'improvements', then turned his back, leaving the house to suffer neglect for nearly twenty-five years.

The most obvious casualty was, of course, the garden, once Sassoon's most personal triumph and glory, for he designed it himself. Though many of the plants had died, and others grown out of control, the ragstone terracing had held up well, and the imposing staircase of York stone, ascending through 116 steps, was intact. The garden of cascading parterres, all facing south in a steep declivity, was in urgent need of attention.

In May 1973, John Aspinall called in the help of Russell Page, who had previously worked on the grounds at Howletts. It would be difficult to imagine a better adviser, for Page had not only known the Port Lympne gardens well throughout the 1930s, and could remember its now submerged details, but he had written an article on it in the *Listener* in 1934. Page surprised Aspinall by declaring that in his opinion, with careful unhurried work, the gardens could be made even more beautiful than before, as mature as Sir Philip Sassoon had imagined they should become after his death. It was as if the intervening thirty-four years were merely a distressing interlude. Even the landscape gardeners who were contracted on Page's instructions, Hillier & Sons of Winchester, had originally worked for Sassoon.

Aspinall immediately set five gardeners to work, with one mason to concentrate on restoring the terraces; this was very soon increased to seven gardeners and two masons. Their task was indeed daunting. The great border beneath the western terrace, 135 yards long, with each bed 18 feet wide,

had to be dug over by hand twice, then plied with 200 tons
of elephant dung (a commodity fortunately in ample supply
– the elephants were among the first animals to take up residence in Port Lympne). It was later planted with 2,500 herbs
and shrubs. The eastern terraces had to be dug out from
beneath 30 feet of scrub and briar. Nine hundred and sixty
phlox were ordered, in eight varieties, for the phlox garden,
and untold numbers of annuals for the distinctive striped and
chess-board gardens. This would all take years to achieve,
and the undertaking was typical of Aspinall's attitudes and
tastes. No effort must be spared, no economies made, the
result must be overwhelming *and* beautiful. To this end,
it was far better to move forward slowly, with the help
of skilled artisans, than to rush headlong into mediocrity.
Above all, it was symbolic that Aspinall felt a real responsibility towards Sir Philip Sassoon and his vision, a kind of
distant posthumous loyalty.

He was fortunate in being surrounded by heady eagerness.
He wrote to Russell Page that the chief gardener, Hills, was
'a marvel of enthusiasm and seems to welcome more and
more work'. Hillier & Sons had to be discouraged from
despatching botanical rarities which they found exciting,
Page pointing out that Sir Philip had preferred simple
two-colour schemes.

Inside the house a similar energy prevailed. Although most
of Michel Sert's murals had perished, experts from the Tate
Gallery in London were able to restore Rex Whistler's Tent
Room to a condition close to the original. It took them over
a year, and the outcome was to add an important room to the
half-dozen left in the country which can be wholly ascribed
to Whistler. Glyn Philpot's whimsical Egyptian frieze in
the dining-room was likewise restored, while the amazing
Moorish courtyard was in such good condition beneath the
dirt that marble masons brought it back to its original state
in only three months.

In the meantime, one could not forget the purpose of
the entire enterprise, which was to provide a home for
the expanding family of animals. Almost immediately, the

elephants, rhinoceroses and some hoof-stock, including the Przewalski's horses, were moved from Howletts to Port Lympne, where they visibly enjoyed the large spaces and extra freedom. In the long term, however, Port Lympne would have to be opened to the public, because Aspinall would not have enough money to sustain the project alone, even if his fortunes improved. The zoo park would have to be placed 'on the map' if only to make ends meet. Still, he would not compromise on the essential, that animals be left in peace and not made to parade if they did not feel like it.

It had taken several years to find the ideal place, and care would have to be taken that plans were not thwarted by local interference. The earlier plan to enter into a partnership with Lord Massereene and Ferrard in order to establish a zoo park at Lord Massereene's home, Chilham Castle, had foundered on the strength of villagers' objections. Kent County Council had refused planning permission in the face of 557 signatures threatening rebellion and the ill-conceived argument that wolves would interrupt sleep. This time intentions would have to be very carefully explained. In fact, Aspinall need not have worried, for Shepway District Council was a much less pusillanimous body. They considered the plans for Port Lympne Zoo Park, applauded the restoration of an important house, and passed assent by a margin of thirty-six votes to six. The date was set for the opening one year hence.

There remained the overriding problem of cost. It was still true that John Aspinall had lost his entire investment portfolio with the Stock Market slump of 1973-4, when shares had tumbled by up to 75 per cent. It was still true he had no casino and no source of income, nor any near prospect of having either. His assets were dwindling weekly. And in the midst of all this – the most severe setback of his life – Aspinall plunged into a project which would have made even a rich man hesitate. The initial purchase of Port Lympne had been covered with a loan from Barclay's Bank, but that would not last forever and the repayment terms were predictably punitive. Somehow or other a great deal of money would need to be found in order to finance grandiose operations already under way. Carts did not always follow horses in the schemes of a natural gambler.

More or less out of the blue, rescue was promised in the guise of a majestic Arab prince.

Lady Sarah Aspinall's brother-in-law Geoffrey Keating was a large, lumbering man with no grace but considerable wit. Though he had many rough qualities, his repartee thickened to rudeness and arrogance with alcoholic encouragement, and his friends' tolerance was constantly stretched. Keating, who enjoyed life in high society and was capable of turning up to dinner, uninvited, in a helicopter, had for some years been an agent of British Petroleum, in the course of which duties he had made many useful acquaintances. His fluent tongue, gregarious habits, and urge to improve himself socially made him the ideal 'contact man'. As such, he was remorselessly used by Arab potentates, most of whom he knew personally long before the oil boom of 1973 had made them rich beyond the ambitions of Croesus. In those earlier days Keating had flattered them, reverenced them, run errands for them, and had so far been repaid with royal disdain and a clutch of promises.

Now that Aspers' zoos were in a bad way and might yet collapse, an opportunity presented itself which Keating seized upon with some excitement. An Arab potentate was known to be interested in the larger mammals and wanted a zoo of his own. According to Keating, he thought about little else but wildlife. Keating got word to him that the most enlightened zoo in the world was in financial trouble and might welcome His Highness as a partner. The approach was very well received. Yes, His Highness would like to see Howletts and meet Mr Aspinall. Arrangements were set in motion.

The wealthy Arab prince was spending part of the late summer in England. He and his retinue would be pleased to motor over to Howletts on a Sunday in September 1974, where they would take tea and discuss Mr Aspinall's proposals.

Preparations for this important visit were intense. Aspinall had been advised by Keating that the prince was inordinately fond of very sweet things, so the cook and Beryl (who had been the children's nanny and had stayed on with the family) spent two whole days making piles of patisseries laden and stuffed with sugar. Keating also said that at least six Rolls-Royces would bring the party and that Aspers should wait for a sign from him, Keating, before going forward, otherwise he might offer obeisance to the wrong Arab.

He need not have worried. When the six gleaming cars turned into the drive, flags flickering, and debouched eighteen men in sparkling white robes and head-dress, it was immediately obvious which was the prince. Aspinall bowed in greeting and presented Lady Sarah and Lady O. to His Highness, whereupon the whole party went for a leisurely walk around the grounds of Howletts and the zoo. Aspinall naturally put on a fine performance, going in with the wolves, tigers and gorillas, and playing impressively with them all. The tour was an enormous success, the prince telling Aspinall through his interpreter (who was also Commander of his personal bodyguard), 'Allah has blessed you'.

This went down very well with Aspinall, who responded in like manner, telling the prince that the great primates were all 'children of Allah' and that those who protected them were doing work which Allah would applaud. This bizarre exchange took place as they walked back to the house across the clean lawn, startling the deer with their flowing robes which flapped in the breeze. The potentate nodded sagely.

The tea was indeed amazing, and the prince clearly enjoyed it. He was even sufficiently well-disposed to grant the extraordinary request that Lady O. be allowed to sit with them (women were habitually banned from The Presence during a meal), which was just as well, as Lady O.'s response to a refusal could not be safely predicted. Even the lesser men in the retinue were expected to stand, and the bodyguard spent the entire tea poised neatly behind his master's chair.

Conversation proceeded more happily than Aspinall had any right to hope. Through the interpreter, His Highness asked how much it cost to run the zoo, to which Aspinall replied, £400,000 a year. That, of course, was allowing for the occasional day when the public was admitted, adding to the revenue. 'If His Highness were your partner, he would not want the public to be allowed in. How much without public?'

'Double,' said Aspinall, with some exaggeration. He added that he did not choose to admit the public, who were useless as far as the animals were concerned, and would much rather be in a position to exclude them. This was met with much approval and nodding, interrupted by the occasional (perhaps ritual) spitting. Aspinall then went on to talk about Port Lympne, which did not have time to see.

He said it would cost £2.7 million to launch Port Lympne properly, and if His Highness would like to be a partner in this exciting enterprise for the benefit of the children of Allah, he would contribute exactly half, that is £1,350,000. (Aspinall inflated the sum by £100,000, being the amount he suspected he might have to bribe someone in order to see the deal through to a conclusion.) The prince immediately agreed to this, and added that he would personally pay all the running costs. This was a totally unexpected bonus which brought from Aspinall a torrent of appropriately obsequious phrases, that His Highness was a most generous man, that he was the most illustrious prince of Araby sent by Allah for the salvation of his children, and so on. The Arab took his hand and patted it, saying that he should bring his family to the Middle East and stay as his personal guests, which would give them both a better opportunity to discuss the matter. They shook hands on what gave every sign of being a gentleman's agreement. Aspinall wrote hurriedly to Russell Page with the news. 'He was madly impressed,' he said. 'You had better think about an Arab border and get designing a mosque-pavilion.'

The next few weeks were spent preparing the trip east and constructing the necessary financial machinery to cope. As usual, Aspinall was not himself able to do much in this direction, grand ideas being his forte rather than the detailed implementation of them, so he appealed to Jimmy Goldsmith for help. Jimmy knew just the man for the job. A young chartered accountant from Ipswich, Mike Leathers, had recently applied to join Goldsmith's company, Cavenham Foods, specifically to set up its banking subsidiary, Anglo-Continental. Jimmy forthwith sent Mike Leathers to Aspinall to establish a corporate structure for both zoos ready for the prince's lawyers to inspect. Until then the whole zoological enterprise had been for fifteen years a purely private venture by one man employing others to make his dream come true. Henceforth it would have to be a limited company with directors and boards of management. At the very least, it would save a fortune in unnecessary personal taxes paid by Aspinall himself.

In December, Aspinall and Lady Sarah went to the Middle East laden with gifts, including a rare edition of the classic *Birds of Arabia* by Richard Meinertzhagen, a beautiful Japanese bronze tiger (the best item from his own collection), a film of Howletts and the animals, aerial photographs of both zoos, and an album of photographs depicting every animal Aspinall had. Lady Sarah took an exquisite ruby brooch for the prince's favourite wife. Finally, a pair of live tigers and a set of powerful binoculars completed the bounty. There was real purpose in these gifts, which Aspinall could ill afford at this time. He imagined that valuable presents would demonstrate his own worth as a minor feudal prince in his own right, that they would distinguish him from a vulgar businessman. Just as the Zulu chieftains had done, and as feudal English lords before them, Aspinall showed respect by giving beautiful treasures from among his own possessions, in recognition of a joint appreciation of art and joint knowledge of rank. Intuitively, he knew the form better than someone who had not been imbued with the wisdom inherited from beyond the species. Or so he thought. As it happened, the whole sorry episode demonstrated nothing so much as Aspinall's naïvety and fantastical perceptions of the real world.

They spent five days alone at a luxury hotel, waiting for a summons to the Palace. Of course, they knew full well, didn't they, that the prince was besieged by people who wanted money, particularly now that the oil revenues were flooding in daily as never before. They understood. But they were getting a trifle bored. Aspinall wrote to Russell Page, 'I am hoping to come back with the prince as my partner, which means the coffers will be open and the public excluded.' Then the summons came, and Aspinall took wife and gifts to his liege lord, the one offered for admiration, the others for more permanent delight.

Once again, the meeting went uncommonly well, with smiles and nods and handshakes. The film of Howletts was particularly popular, and the binoculars greatly appreciated, though the Japanese *objet* and the rare book were merely glanced at. Geoffrey Keating was present, and made the interview more awkward than it need have been by whispering signals to Aspinall to remind His Highness that he, Keating, had long ago been promised a house. With land. And a swimming-pool. Aspinall obligingly repeated these demands, which were acceded to. Indications were made that there should be no delay in proceeding with the arrangements outlined by Mr Aspinall, and that he would shortly hear from His Highness's lawyers in London with a draft agreement.

John Aspinall was understandably elated by the interview, which appeared to confirm his most extravagant hopes. Nevertheless, he was sufficiently alert to the atmosphere of sycophancy around the prince to anticipate that some of the courtiers might wish to have him put in his place. The night before he returned to England, he had a meeting with the prince's London business representative, who he knew would be a crucial link in any chain between himself and the prince. This powerful representative promised that he would do all he could to help promote the arrangement, and that, by the way, he would quite like some tigers himself.

Back in London, Aspinall waited 'in gentlemanly fashion' as he now says, for ten days before calling the prince's lawyers to ascertain what progress had been made. They expressed surprise, and entire ignorance of any partnership plan. But they would investigate. Later, they reported back that there were no instructions received from His Highness, or from anyone else for that matter, but a little 'gossip' had reached them, referring to Aspinall's visit. That was all. This was indeed cause for dejection.

Aspinall spent the next days frantically trying to get word through to the Middle East without success. It was clear to him, or so he thought, that the deal had been scuppered by jealous intrigue, that courtiers were actively preventing any advance merely because they did not want action to be taken which had not been directly recommended by themselves, otherwise their privileged position in the royal circle might be undermined. In a letter to the Rt Hon. Harold Lever MP PC, Aspinall was not in the least circumspect in voicing his suspicions and his irritation. The prince had agreed verbally, he said, 'but I cannot get past his representative here, who refuses to relay the instructions for want of a colossal bribe which unfortunately I cannot pay him.' (At the same time, he told Lever that he intended to repay the £8,000 he had borrowed from him with eight post-dated cheques for £1,000, an interesting sidelight on the pressures which beset him at this time and the piecemeal way in which he was having to continue from week to week. Lever was not the only friend who had lent him small sums of money.)

It gradually became all too clear that the prince was not, after all, to be his partner. He smarted with a sense of betrayal for months afterwards, and he never forgave the prince. That his representative should obstruct the deal for his own ends was perfectly understandable, though hardly attractive. But that a potentate, a man whom Aspinall would feel naturally impelled to trust because of his position as a leader, a man who set standards within his race, that such a man should break his solemn word, twice secured with a handshake, was utterly unforgivable. It is no exaggeration to say it was, to John Aspinall, even incomprehensible.

The prince had an annual income of well over £100 million, tax-free. Had the arrangement been honoured, it would have cost him the matter of only a few days' income, a paltry bargain to keep, one might have thought. Aspinall's view was that, while one may understand that a promise must occasionally be broken owing to circumstances, this particular promise was a peccadillo to one such as the prince, and that made his dishonour all the more black. In many ways, Aspinall continued to see the world with romantic optimism.

It was now up to Mike Leathers to approach the funding of the zoos from an entirely different direction. He had to start with a clean slate. He determined that the purchase of Port Lympne and the running costs of the zoos should be kept separate, the former to be covered by a loan, the latter by soliciting subscriptions for shares in the company which would henceforth administer the zoos, from friends scattered over the world. In the first instance, to cope with the purchase of Port Lympne, it was obviously sensible to raise money from Jimmy Goldsmith.

The initial mortgage arranged with Barclays fell through as it became apparent that Aspinall would not allow his animals to suffer in order to provide collateral; they would eat it before he handed it over to a bank. Goldsmith was by now a very rich man as well as a very old friend. The affection between the two was genuine and durable, with the result that Aspinall was perhaps the only man in the world with whom Goldsmith would keep in touch by means of a long telephone call, several times a week, from whatever corner of the globe happened at that moment to harbour his restless energy. He is often depicted as a curiously steel-plated ally. Goldsmith will do all he can to stand by a friend and see that he does not go under. He will arrange matters to keep him afloat by use of his influence and direction, by setting up the necessary machinery, but it will then be up to the friend to turn his fortunes round so that he can discharge his debts in time. Goldsmith meanwhile will guarantee them. It is businesslike, efficient and professional, and starkly opposite to the philosophy of Aspinall himself, who will give whatever he has, hardly expecting it to be returned. The one is a cerebral attitude, the other emotional.

Goldsmith raised the money for the outright purchase of Port Lympne, with an additional sum for the restoration work, through the banking subsidiary of his company, Anglo-Continental; Mike Leathers was on the management team in the financial accounting section.

At the same time, Leathers established the company known as Howletts and Port Lympne Estates, with a limited liability of £220,000, which owned all the properties, except the London house at Lyall Street, on which a mortgage was raised. At the same time the decision was taken, somewhat reluctantly, that both zoos would have to be open to the public.

Legally, John Aspinall was stripped of everything he had as an individual. He wrote to friends all over the world soliciting their support, and invited them to buy shares; almost all of them rallied without hesitation. While this indicates that a great many people believed in Aspinall, it was nevertheless the one moment in his life when Aspinall was almost tempted, but not quite, to cease believing in himself. One of the replies he received in answer to his summons gives some impression of his spirits. It is from Claus von Bülow, in whose flat he had given his first party in 1959. After greetings from 'Sunny and I' (Sunny was von Bülow's wife, whose descent into a drug-induced coma was the cause of several court hearings many years later), von Bülow says,

> Never in the many vagaries of your finances in 20 years have I known you to sound so depressed . . . The best things in life come with the longest shots . . . In a year you may be the only solvent one among us. Do not even think on the lines of the last paragraph of your letter. It makes *me* happy to try and help.

One cheerful event seemed to augur well for the future, if only in a symbolic way. Aspinall discovered that Sir Winston Churchill, who had stayed frequently at Port Lympne as the guest of Sassoon, had once painted a view of the front along the south terrace. Writing to Churchill's daughter Mary Soames, he asked if by good fortune the painting might still be with the family. Yes, indeed it was. More than that, Lady Soames would be happy for Aspinall to have the painting on permanent loan so that it could hang in the revitalised house.

As an added pleasure, it was a fine and warm picture, not just the indulgence of a famous man. Aspinall looked forward to the day when Port Lympne would look as enticing in reality as it did in Churchill's artistic vision.

It was not easy to predict how long this would take. With uncomfortable irony, the gambling world was enjoying its most spectacular expansion in profits with the sudden invasion of colossally wealthy Arab punters trying to find ways of enjoying their vast oil income. London was awash with Arab guests who took over whole districts, buying expensive houses rather than staying in hotels; some of them ended their day at the Clermont Club, where the 'drop' increased dramatically as a result. John Aspinall could not have sold the Clermont at a worse moment; had he retained it and resisted the impulse to retire, the financial leap-frogging, retrenchment and sacrifices which characterised the following six years would not have been necessary. Aspinall, however, was a man of resilience and determination who would not allow setbacks to thwart his aims. The same could not be said of his gambling friends.

Ian Maxwell-Scott had for some years been working at the Clermont day and night, almost without pause, and the pressures had told. In the last few months before the club was sold, his drinking had assumed alarming proportions, threatening his ability to run affairs efficiently, and his gambling losses loomed over him like a building about to collapse over his head. Aspinall would not even consider asking him to resign; he was an old friend, and one does not hurt old friends. Instead, he looked after Maxwell-Scott, without ostentation, and lightened his work. Another 'house' punter and old friend was Dan Meinertzhagen (incidentally the great-nephew of the Meinertzhagen whose classic *Birds of Arabia* was given to the prince), who similarly found himself without a rein when the club was sold. It was as if Aspinall had been their source of control, the club their refuge as well as their responsibility, and without either they lost all reticence and crumpled. Maxwell-Scott proceeded to inch close to ruin, like a soul deprived. But by far the most dramatic casualty was Lord Lucan, who had over the years become an *habitué* at the Clermont and had found there the popularity and comfort which his private life denied him.

Lord Lucan's marriage had for some time been a source of pain. Lady Lucan was generally regarded an unstable woman, easily given to hysterics, suspicious and resentful. Some of her friends were known to have recommended she undergo urgent medical attention, which she always resisted. The strain upon the marriage became too acute for either of them to bear, and they separated.

There followed a protracted, bitter quarrel over the custody of their two children, which was eventually fought in open court at great expense and to Lord Lucan's deep embarrassment. He retained the aristocratic distaste for public hearings of private matters. Moreover, if there was one constancy in his erratic life, it was his complete devotion to the children and his conviction that his selfless attention to their welfare was infinitely preferable to their exposure to (in his view) the harsh neuroses of a demented woman. He fully expected the court to see this as clearly as he saw it himself. He made no allowance for the court's opinion that his irresponsible gambling might make him a miserable parent quite as dangerous for the children's future as an unstable mother. After a tremendous long fight, Lucan lost his case and the boy and girl were delivered to the custody of Lady Lucan, while he retained the right to visit.

Lucan never recovered from this decision. He smarted with anger at what he deemed to be the court's, any court's, unjustified bias in favour of wives, who must necessarily make the better parent despite any evidence to the contrary, and he could not bear the insult to his own self-regard any more than the separation from his children. He also, pathetically, imagined his estranged wife to be exulting in her triumph. For the next two years, Lord Lucan gradually disintegrated; he was consumed by concentration on a single idea.

He was still a member of the Clermont under its new ownership and management, but his special place there as a favoured and flattered senior figure had evaporated; the club no longer gave him the solace his torment demanded. On 7 November 1974, Lucan arranged to have supper there with some friends and booked a table for 11 p.m. At 8.45 p.m. he drove past, then changed both his clothes and his car and went to his wife's house at 46 Lower Belgrave Street, off Eaton Square. It was a Thursday, the usual night off for the children's nanny, and he expected therefore that his wife would be alone once the children were in bed.

Lord Lucan did not appear for supper at the Clermont. He was next seen by Ian Maxwell-Scott's wife, Susie, when he turned up at her house in the country, 45 miles from London, just before midnight. Maxwell-Scott had not come home yet, so Susie was obliged to deal with him alone. He was considerably dishevelled in appearance and had blood on his trousers. He wrote three letters and stayed until 1.15 a.m. Mrs Maxwell-Scott reported his visit to the police thirty-six hours later. Meanwhile, the car he had borrowed, a Ford Corsair, was parked in Newhaven, on the south coast, between 6 and 8 a.m.

What had happened the previous evening at 46 Lower Belgrave Street seemed fairly clear. The children's nanny, Sandra Rivett, had not taken Thursday off at all. She had broken her usual routine and taken Wednesday off instead. She was therefore in the house. Someone came into the house and murdered Sandra Rivett when she went to the basement to see what was going on. She was allegedly battered with a length of lead piping. The light was not on, and it was later supposed that Lord Lucan was the intruder and that he had intended to kill his wife, but had slaughtered Miss Rivett in error. When Lady Lucan came downstairs to investigate, the intruder leapt at her, struck her and grabbed her by the throat. Then his fury abated and he went upstairs to the bathroom, thus giving Lady Lucan an opportunity to escape. She fled to the Plumbers' Arms, the pub opposite, in a state of panic, and the police were called. It was 9.50 p.m.

Lady Lucan was taken to St George's Hospital at Hyde Park Corner. Lord Lucan meanwhile telephoned his mother, the Dowager Countess, and told her there had been a 'terrible catastrophe' and would she please come to the house as quickly as she could. He then left. One of the letters he wrote was to his brother-in-law, William Shand-Kydd, in which he said that his wife was certain to blame him for what had happened; she would pretend he had been the intruder. Detective Sergeant Graham Forsyth found the body of Sandra Rivett, still warm, loosely hidden in a canvas mail-bag in the breakfast-room. The children were upstairs in bed. The Dowager Lady Lucan arrived as bidden. Forsyth was still at the house when the missing earl telephoned to speak to his mother just after midnight.

It is the following morning, 8 November, that John Aspinall comes into the story. After emergency telephone consultation with some of those closest to Lucan, Aspinall summoned them all to his house in Lyall Street for a scratch lunch at which they would decide what to do. Only men were invited. They included Charles Benson, an old friend of Lucan's from Eton schooldays; Dominick Elwes, son of the portrait-painter and Court Jester of the gambling set; Bill Shand-Kydd; Dan Meinertzhagen; Stephen Raphael; and Aspinall himself. The meeting was hastily arranged, with no staff present, and they had to raid the refrigerator for food. It was a simple meal of cold salmon and white wine.

They all later declared that their purpose was to advise each other how best they could help Lucan if he were to call any one of them, in accordance with the demands of the law. They were simply airing opinions in the face of crisis. No record was ever made of the conversation at this crucial luncheon.

Meanwhile, a warrant was issued for the arrest of Richard John Bingham, 7th Earl of Lucan, on suspicion of murder. To this day, Detective Chief Superintendent Ronald Hardy still holds a valid warrant for the arrest, which, according to his last public pronouncement on the subject, he one day intends to serve. Mr Hardy believes Lord Lucan is missing, not dead, and that he has most likely taken refuge in South Africa.

Others take the view that, having abandoned the car in Newhaven, he drowned himself in the English Channel, first taking precautions to ensure his body should never be found. His guilt is assumed by almost everyone. At the inquest on Sandra Rivett, Lady Lucan identified her husband as the assailant who attacked her, as he had said she would. It also transpired, on the evidence of Susie Maxwell-Scott at least, that Lady Lucan had frequently accused her husband of planning to hire a professional assassin to kill her, and that he had thought her mad. She claimed that all her husband's friends conspired to make her appear to behave irrationally so that she could be proven insane. It was certainly true that Lord Lucan wanted his wife committed as a lunatic.

Counsel for the Dowager Countess, Mr Michael Eastham QC, ventured the dangerous notion that Lady Lucan's intense hatred for her husband might lead her to tell lies out of a taste for vengeance. He was bound by 'the inescapable and unpleasant duty of suggesting that what she is saying she knows to be untrue'. At this point the coroner interrupted him and forbade him to go any further.

Lord Lucan was committed for trial in his absence. Lady Lucan sold her story to an evening newspaper; presumably written for her by a jobbing journalist, it made dreary and daft reading. She later spent a short time in a hospital for the mentally ill.

Nigel Dempster claimed in the *Daily Mail* ten years later that Lucan had planned the murder and made two practice runs, driving to the south coast where his speedboat was kept. He planned to dump his wife's body in the Channel, instead of which he dumped his own. Shortly before the murder, he had borrowed £5,000 from a friend, and had taken up training in Hyde Park to improve his general fitness, a most uncharacteristic gesture. Certainly, Sandra Rivett's body had been bundled into a mail-bag as if in preparation for transportation somewhere.

This is not the place to rehearse again the more detailed accounts of what is now a well-known story. But it is helpful to examine how far John Aspinall was involved, if at all apart from the mysterious luncheon of 8 November, and what light this involvement throws upon his character, or at least upon how that character was perceived by others. It has for long been an item of unpublished gossip in newspaper circles that, of course, Lucan went from Susie Maxwell-Scott's in the early hours of the morning to Howletts, where he poured out all the circumstances to Aspinall and implored him to put an end to the whole ghastly mess by feeding him to the tigers. Such a solution might sound plausible to some, but it is no more than fanciful nonsense.

Had Lucan made such a request, Aspinall might well have wanted to honour it. He is emphatically not the kind of man to counsel caution, not to invite one to pull oneself together and face the consequences of one's actions, nor to offer comfort in distress. His understanding of friendship is archaic, classical and simple: a friend does what is bidden by the deep ties of loyalty without question, without seeking to enquire why. He does not demand explanations, nor does he offer advice unless it is sought. He obliges. He makes his actions the instrument for fulfilling the friend's wishes. What he himself may feel or think is utterly immaterial, and irrelevant to the principle at stake. Moreover, Aspinall knows better than most people that a secret is not a secret if it is shared by two individuals. For him, however, to betray a confidence would be unthinkable. Lucan must have intuited this quality in Aspinall over the years of their acquaintance; Aspinall may even have voiced it. In his situation, he was well aware that if he told Aspinall the truth about how he intended to die and asked him to keep it secret, it would go with him to the grave. Not his mother, not his wife, still less a police officer, would be able to shake it from him. Even had he wanted to break the confidence (for Aspinall has his moments of private doubt like anyone and is by no means always as confident as he appears), he would not do so for entirely selfish reasons: he would not want to be seen betraying one of his own most cherished principles, and could not bear the fall in self-esteem which would ensue from this. There are those, however, who believe that Aspinall is quite incapable of keeping a secret even when he knows he should – (an assessment he firmly disputes). His love of a good story (they say) overrides every consideration, and it is doubtful if he could have kept this one to himself. A good raconteur does not turn his back on his best material.

There are several objections to the theory anyway. First, Aspinall is a very lazy man and would not have been anxious to get out of bed at two or three in the morning. A frivolous point, perhaps, but not when one knows how deeply the man sleeps; like one of his animals, he sleeps as nature decrees, untroubled by dreams or neurotic imaginings inherited from waking hours. Secondly, tigers would only eat a human if they were starving. As they eat only once a week anyway, and sleep even more deeply than Aspinall, it does not seem likely that they could be persuaded to overturn all their habits in one night to assist a murderer on the run. Thirdly, Lucan's car was found at Newhaven a few hours later. Someone would have had to drive it there. Aspinall does not, cannot drive, and would have had to engage the services of an accomplice to get rid of the car, which would entirely compromise the virtue of secrecy. That same accomplice, or another, would have had to drive Aspinall to London in time for breakfast at Lyall Street, where he was located at 8 a.m. And why leave the car at Newhaven, when Dover, Folkestone or Deal would have been on a more direct route?

This last objection is the only one which applies to yet another theory, that Lucan did go to Howletts, had a conversation, and later drove himself to Newhaven whence he accomplished his suicide. He may have chosen Newhaven precisely because it was not the obvious destination from Howletts, as Dover would have been.

There is another possibility which does not seem to have been bruited in Fleet Street, though it has occurred to more than one police officer. According to this, someone laid a plot with Lord Lucan to get rid of the dreadful wife who was making life such hell, hired a killer (just as she often suspected her husband would), and told him to do his job on Thursday, when the nanny would be away. As we know, she wasn't, but the hired killer could not imagine that the woman coming down the stairs was anyone but the lady he had been told it would be, and since he did not know Lady Lucan or Sandra Rivett by constant acquaintance, he would not be aware of any mistake. He did the job and left. Lord Lucan turned up as planned, expecting to find the deed accomplished, and was horrified as soon as he realised the terrible mistake. He also knew that his wife would accuse him; in fact, she would be quite right to, for he was the only man she saw in the house. There was no way out. All this accords with the various statements Lucan made, on the telephone to his mother, in the letter to Shand Kydd, and verbally to Susie Maxwell-Scott.

If this were true, then the assassin would have had to be disposed of somehow, probably by another assassin, with an endless spiral in view; or perhaps paid off very handsomely indeed, which would have been perfectly easy in those circles. Something like this was clearly in the minds of investigating officers when they went to interview Aspinall. It was later revealed that they had, somewhat foolishly, prepared themselves by learning what the upper classes and rich gamblers drank, and had practised their intake of cocktails and their suave manner in private. Of course they miscalculated and seemed thirty years out of date, like actors in a Marx Brothers film. Whether this be fair or not, it was true that police officers came upon a charming, co-operative, but totally uninformative interviewee in John Aspinall. They were perplexed and floundering, angry dogs bumping into one another; or chess players whose every move is mated. They had never come upon anyone as resolute as this, and though they could get nowhere, neither could they rid themselves of the feeling that there was something worth investigating. As for Aspinall, he reverted to his rebellious schooldays at Rugby, enjoying every minute of discomfiting those in authority, and doing it superbly.

For three weeks the French police watched the house of Digby Neave outside Paris, inconspicuously they thought, and Claus von Bülow wrote with the news that 'two New York detectives came here last night to see whether I was hiding Lucky'.

The Lucan saga demonstrates what people thought John Aspinall was capable of, and helped to draw the lines of his public *persona* more clearly. That he had been working hard on rescuing a great country house, a public monument, from ruin throughout the previous year, that he had done so against all the odds and within sight of bankruptcy, that he had continued to place the welfare of his animals above every other consideration, none of this was of interest to the public or the newspapers. What mattered was that he was ruthless in the application of his principles and may have harboured a suspected murderer.

He was certainly not surprised that Lucan might have killed his wife. The missing earl had confessed to him some weeks earlier that he would like to, and had even gone so far as to tell Lady O. (whom he regarded as a substitute mother) that he intended to. She had replied to the effect that he must do whatever he thought was right.

In all this, only one conclusion is safe; Aspinall behaved throughout the investigation like one of his great Zulu heroes, discreet, honourable, firm and unyielding. The rest he would consider to be nobody's business but Lucan's. When asked by Ludovic Kennedy on television what he would do if Lucan were now to walk into the room, he replied, 'Embrace him'.

It was now nearly two years since Kisoro had arrived from Chicago, bearing hopes for a breakthrough which could change the history of breeding gorillas in captivity. He had proved disappointingly slothful in making his attentions felt, but at the beginning of 1975 it looked very likely that one of his females, Juju, was at last pregnant. She was from that moment understandably the object of intense curiosity.

Gorillas had long been regarded as one of those species (like giant turtles and boa constrictors) which may be kept in captivity, but never persuaded to breed. With almost incredible stupidity, the zoo directors who had thus decided that gorillas were 'impossible' did not perceive that the conditions they imposed upon their prisoners might have something to do with it. One of the great authorities on the principles of zoo-keeping, Dr Hediger, wrote that there was only one criterion for assessing suitable biological conditions, and that was success in breeding:

> To the zoo biologist this is like arithmetical proof to the mathematician. When breeding does not occur, something is wrong with the methods of keeping the animals; if breeding does occur, it is a guarantee that the conditions are essentially right, since regular breeding presupposes, at least among the higher animals, a certain measure of well-being in the parents.

This being so, gorillas had not bred because they did not want to, because their lives were miserable, because there was no biological point in making baby gorillas.

Considering the large numbers of these apes which had been captured since the middle of the nineteenth century and held in zoos all over the world, it is astonishing, not to say shameful, that none was ever born until, in 1956, a baby appeared in the zoo at Columbus, Ohio, taking everyone almost completely by surprise. This was the first ever birth of a gorilla in captivity. Still the lesson was not learnt. George Schaller, who had made a study of the species in the wild, wrote that 'the treatment of apes in zoos has been and often still is scandalous':

> The creatures sit alone behind bars, like prisoners in solitary confinement. Even today infant gorillas and other apes continue to be purchased at exorbitant prices only to pine away for lack of proper attention . . . young apes need the same kind and amount of attention given human infants. Zoos which cannot or will not provide their charges with

such care should not be permitted to keep them . . . If nothing else, man should show some ethical and moral responsibility towards creatures which resemble him so closely in body and mind.

A year after the Ohio infant, a female gorilla in Basle, Switzerland, known as Achilla, conceived but suffered a miscarriage. One had to wait three years for a successful birth there, in 1959 only the second in the world, and then watch with some anxiety as Achilla demonstrated quite clearly that she had not the faintest idea what to do; the infant opened its mouth in search for the nipple, but she did nothing to assist. She clasped her baby affectionately none the less. It was the first intimation that gorillas must learn the skills of motherhood from their peers; Achilla had simply not been taught. The infant was rescued and reared by the zoo's director, Dr Lang, who described the experience in a delightful book, pioneering the detailed observation of a gorilla as it grows to maturity, called *Goma the Gorilla Baby*. Achilla was pregnant again the following year, and she actually raised her new baby, Jambo, without assistance from Dr Lang, providing another record for Basle. Dr Schaller was quick to underline the difference: 'Jambo was the first infant to be raised with its mother in captivity, showing that a zoo which treats its animals well, both physically and emotionally, can succeed in breeding and raising even the most delicate of creatures.'

That supreme populariser of ethology, Konrad Lorenz, made substantially the same point:

Anthropoid apes are the only captive animals which can derive serious bodily harm from their mental suffering. Anthropoid apes can become literally bored to death, particularly when they are kept alone in too small cages . . . It is no exaggeration when I say that real success in the keeping of anthropoid apes was only achieved when it was realised how to prevent the mental sufferings caused by confinement.

It had long been established that male gorillas were so adversely affected by captivity that their genital organs sometimes failed to develop adequately. Perhaps there were certain oestrogenous plants in the wild of which man knew nothing.

Aspinall had already made a start by providing vastly more space in living and sleeping quarters, by obviating the danger of boredom, by seriously embracing ethical responsibility towards the animals, and by having his keepers as well as himself treat their charges well 'both physically and emotionally'; he was bestowing upon his animals a kind of love of which none of their brethren in zoos had the smallest experience. This was his besetting sin in the eyes of the scientists, who echoed Hediger in his conviction that 'in captivity nearly every normal relation between one animal and another is spoilt by the constant presence of man, with consequent failure to breed'. In encouraging such close friendships between animals and men, Aspinall was the worst enemy to his own designs. It was this attitude that he was hoping to prove wrong. Lincoln Park, which had some success in breeding gorillas before the 1970s, had taken the risk in sending Kisoro to him in full awareness of the unorthodoxy of his methods. He was not entirely without allies. But he was still without results.

Finally, Juju gave birth on 2 April 1975, to a baby they named Kijo.* Lester Fisher of Lincoln Park Zoo in Chicago sent a jubilant telegram which could not have been more personal had Aspinall been the father. 'I am as pleased and proud as you are,' it said. For John Aspinall, it was one of the most exciting moments of his life, which brought forth an exhibition of joy quite different in nature from the satisfaction derived from the challenge of Port Lympne, the pleasures of gaming, even the pride in his own children. He was simply exhilarated. To Fisher he wrote, 'It is difficult for me to express in words our gratitude to you all for the brave decision that you made to send Kisoro to us. [He is] the first gorilla to have sired progeny on both sides of the Atlantic.'

---

*Kijo is now a full-grown silverback, with two females pregnant to him.

At first, Juju held her baby upside-down, but she soon got used to him and, with some gentle encouragement from Aspinall and the keepers, she became an excellent mother. Hardly had they recovered from the excitement of this event than another baby was born, on 30 April, to Shamba, again sired by Kisoro. 'Our debt to you widens with every passing month,' Aspinall wrote to Fisher. Shamba was, alas, not such a model parent. She showed no interest whatever in her offspring, even five hours after its birth, so the baby had to be rescued and was hand-reared by the keeper, Richard Johnstone-Scott. This infant was known as Kimba.

On 11 July, a third female, known as Baby Doll, gave birth; this infant was unfortunately weak from the beginning, having inherited a uterine infection from his mother, who in turn paid him little attention. Lady Sarah Aspinall took this baby into the house and looked after him day and night for six weeks, feeding him every two hours, even throughout the night. Every possible attempt was made to save the child, even so far as injecting him with penicillin and giving him regular blood transfusions from his mother's blood. But the baby eventually, after six weeks and two days, succumbed to his infection, and died in the doctor's arms, with Aspinall and Lady Sarah present. It was their first loss.

'The death of Kisabu cast a pall over everyone who had come to know him,' Aspinall later wrote, 'It seemed amazing that even in six weeks a gorilla baby could generate so much love and affection.'

Then Mouila gave birth to Koundu on 6 October. Copying Juju (with whom she was living in a band which included father, wives and infants), she soon learnt to hold the tiny infant the right way up and patted it approvingly. No one had known she was pregnant, and it was Aspinall who found the child when he was visiting the whole family. At first she was a model mother, but after nine weeks she neglected Koundu dangerously, for no obvious reason, and Lady Sarah took him in. There was clearly much to learn from close observation now that there was at Howletts a thriving and growing family.

Kisoro was by this time a champion breeder, with six progeny (four at Howletts, two in Chicago), five of whom were living. Within the space of six months, and after waiting nearly ten years, Howletts progressed from having no home-bred infants to having three. John Aspinall's dream at last looked possible. As he was not slow to tell anyone who asked (and many who did not), his ambition was nothing less than to nurture the largest and happiest colony of breeding gorillas in the world.

10
The Best of Friends

In a remote château at Coucy-les-Eppes in France, a lonely female gorilla, three years old, awaited her fate. Her name was Sidonie and she belonged to Monsieur Claude Tek, recently deceased, whose widow hardly knew what to do with her. When Monsieur Tek's will was opened, however, it was found that Sidonie's future had been attended to. Monsieur Tek stipulated very precisely that she should be offered to Howletts Zoo Park in the south of England, this being the only place deemed fit by him for a homeless gorilla.

Apart from being rather pleased that his experiments had already achieved such trusting approbation abroad, Aspinall was delighted to be able to add to the group, and moreover to afford his daughter Amanda, now sixteen, the chance to forge a personal relationship with one of the animals from the beginning. Sidonie would be given to Amanda's charge until such time as she could be integrated into the established group, and, if Aspinall's ambitions could be realised, his daughter would inherit his interest and continue his work. Amanda, more beautiful even than her mother, was destined in her father's eyes to become a Wild Life Princess. But the choice would have to be hers; he could only encourage.*
Even had she shown no interest, however, it is impossible

---

*Amanda did in fact care for Sidonie for a number of years but had to withdraw from the relationship when Sidonie became too dependent.

to imagine that Aspinall would have denied a refuge to
Sidonie. He accepted immediately.

A crucial part of Aspinall's long-term plan was to establish
a cohesive group or 'band' of gorillas, echoing their natural
habits. Most gorillas in captivity were kept singly or in pairs,
largely out of ignorance, whereas the gorilla is a supremely
social animal which needs to be part of a group of anything
between ten and twenty individuals. Sidonie would take her
place alongside the other four breeding females in the growing Howletts colony, which Aspinall was determined should
be as close to the gorilla norm as possible. In this regard, as
in some others, his work was pioneering.

Early cursory observations of gorilla behaviour, interpreted for the most part in human terms or at least within
the parameters of human post-Freudian understanding, suggested that gorillas stayed loyal to their group because the
males had continuous access to willing females. This was
fundamentally mistaken. In the first place, a male shows no
interest in copulation unless a receptive female entices him,
and then the matter is dealt with in a careless, perfunctory
manner; secondly, groups remain stable and appear happy
even if there are no *receptive* females among their number
for months on end. So sex was not the bond. George Schaller
observed that gorillas have very strong attachments, in the
wild state, to members of their own group, and he concluded
that they felt more secure and content among intimate friends
and relations than with strangers. Just like people, in fact. The
cement which binds them is simple: 'Gorillas always gave
me the impression that they stay together because they like
and know one another.' Aspinall had already noticed among
his group what he called 'an almost passionate unity', not so
much against a foe as for the pleasure of privacy.

Following Schaller, Dian Fossey made even closer observations during the long years she lived with gorillas in
the forest. Groups, she concluded, were admirably stable,
cohesive social units whose composition might be altered by
births, deaths, or movements of individuals in and out of the
group. A typical group would comprise one silverback male,

who was the undisputed leader, sexually mature females, over eight years old and bonded to the silverback for life; one or two junior males, blackbacks, between eight and thirteen years; and anywhere from three to six infants and babies. The composition might vary, but the silverback leader was essential – no group could survive without him.

At Howletts there was the silverback male, Gugis, who had sadly proved infertile; the borrowed silverback, Kisoro; two adolescents, two juveniles and two newly-born babies. The females included four breeders, two juveniles, and one newly-born baby, Kimba, the most important birth so far since the future of the generation to come would depend upon her (females caught in the wild were very rare). Kisoro was proving so productive that there was certainly room for another female by his side; the younger females would eventually belong to a new group to be headed by Djoum, the promising male now eight years old and on the threshold of maturity.

If the social unit was slightly larger than in a corresponding human group (though it would not appear at all unfamiliar to eskimos and some tribes even more remote from civilised man), the three surviving infants were remarkably close to their human counterparts. At birth they had been tiny, weighing 4-5 pounds, so weak that they were not able to cling to their mothers' fur without assistance from them, their movements ungainly and as yet not co-ordinated, and with a vacant expression exactly like that of a human infant. At the age of one month, they were able to follow with their eyes the movements of other members of the group. They would remain close to and dependent upon their mothers until they were about three years old, after which they would travel about within the group under their own steam, as it were, and be boisterous and playful. Their development, then, was about twice as fast as that of a human infant and, like the human, they would maintain strong social ties with the mother even after they had learnt to fend for themselves.

A hierarchy was gradually established among the Howletts band, which made for further stability and harmony.

'Contrary to popular belief,' wrote Schaller, 'a dominance hierarchy does not cause strife and dissension but promotes peace within the group, for it relegates each member to a certain status and position: every animal knows exactly where it stands in relation to every other animal.' The silverback male was naturally dominant over everyone, and correspondingly benevolent and good-humoured, one might almost say polite. The females had their own rank order, influenced by the order in which they had been acquired by the male, and they dominated the juveniles who dominated in turn the infants emerging into childhood. Disputes sometimes arose between females, especially when personality interfered with the rank order strictly laid down, at which point the silverback would intervene (when he could be bothered), to separate the combatants. He would suffer no impudence, but was remarkably patient with the young.

George Schaller described a typical gorilla band in the wild, based on hundreds of careful slow observations, which is worth quoting in full for the pleasing warm harmony it depicts:

> The leading silverback males of groups are dictators who by virtue of their size and position always get their way. But these males also are tolerant and gentle, and this is especially evident during the periods of rest. The females and youngsters in the group genuinely seem to like their leader, not because he is dominant, but because they enjoy his company. Sometimes a female rested her head in his silver saddle or leaned heavily against his side. As many as five youngsters occasionally congregated by the male, sitting by his legs or in his lap, climbing up on his rump, and generally making a nuisance of themselves. The male ignored them completely, unless their behaviour became too uninhibited. Then a mere glance was sufficient to discipline them.

This pattern of behaviour was now to be seen daily in the grounds of a house in Kent, five miles from Canterbury, almost certainly for the first time since gorillas had been wrested from their habitat to live as guests of a human host. The only obvious difference was that the host, John Aspinall, and his keepers, joined the party in its quiet rumination, sitting with the silverback and frolicking with the youngsters. Aspinall was now adept at interpreting the meaning of that pregnant glance and was careful not to overstay his welcome. For an hour or two, he was not the host but the guest.

A few months after the birth of Kisoro's various children the Lucan affair was exhumed to deflect Aspinall from his zoological retirement and parade him once more before the public in his less noble guise. The occasion was an article in the colour magazine of the *Sunday Times* by James Fox, illustrated with a number of old holiday snapshots in Acapulco depicting Lucan, Lady Annabel Birley, Jimmy Goldsmith *et alii* and insinuating that a rich gang were somehow in league for mysterious purposes. One of the illustrations was the reproduction of a drawing by Dominick Elwes which showed Lucan at a table in the Clermont Club with John Aspinall, Sir James Goldsmith, and three others. Elwes had been one of the holiday party in Acapulco. His apparent collusion with journalists marked him out as a possible traitor, and some of the friends exploded into various degrees of fury.

Dominick Elwes was one of the most entertaining men of his generation. Son of the portrait painter Simon Elwes, he had all the advantages of talent, markedly handsome features, and above all, wit. His contemporary, Kenneth Tynan, paid him the most eloquent of compliments when he said that 'like a true alchemist, he turned all our dross into gold . . . people of quite remarkable ordinariness are permanently judged in my mind because of the skill with which they were sketched by this superb verbal cartoonist.' Elwes's extraordinarily vivid, mercurial, effervescent conversation, packed with anecdote, learning and the most accurate mimicry, made him a companion designed to raise the spirits. When he dined at Aspinall's table, it was he who dominated discourse and, for once, Aspinall took second place. They frequently worked as cue for each other. Even that most brilliant raconteur Peter

Ustinov is reported to have said that Dominick Elwes was the only person to whom he would defer in conversation.

Years before, he had featured in a dramatic elopement, pursued by the press, and had known a small degree of fame; he promised well. A friend of Aspinall of long standing, he had been instrumental in rescuing Howletts from its Victorian clutter and spotting the Palladian purity beneath. Now he had three growing sons and considerable expenses. It was his misfortune to enjoy entertaining the very rich without the money to enable him to be accepted by them as an equal. His talk was his passport. He relied upon it to secure his membership of the set he aspired to. His conversation literally sometimes bought him his breakfast, as he was constantly poor and increasingly resentful that his sure talents as an artist were not sufficiently lucrative to permit him to pay his own way with the high-spenders. These therefore supported him with their patronage, commissioning paintings, and meanwhile considered him their resident entertainer. There was something proprietorial in their attitude towards Elwes, which was not always attractive.

It was Tynan again who said that Dominick Elwes set too much store by the favourable opinion of people, which was doubtless true. Unlike Aspinall or Goldsmith, he needed to be liked and approved, he had not the confidence to be indifferent to private judgments of him. Tynan went on to say that many of the people whose approval Elwes so desperately sought were manifestly inferior to himself. It is unlikely that he would have shared this view. He was subject to fits of depression when he would be so morose and miserable as to wish to put an end to himself, but these were due largely to his sense of having failed to make his name. In March 1975 he wrote to John Aspinall, 'I look back on my life with nothing but unhappiness; only the incredibly funny times, more often than not with you, have made it bearable.' There were some who thought he was weighed down with the burden of Catholic guilt.

Elwes gave his Clermont picture to James Fox knowing that it would be published. The *Sunday Times* paid £200 for the reproduction rights, which Elwes sorely needed at the time. It was the biggest error of his life.

He ought perhaps to have known better, for he was well aware that the code of loyalty professed by his friends could be ruthless in its application. He knew how Robin Douglas-Home had been ostracised a few years earlier for a similar transgression. Douglas-Home was another typical Aspinall acolyte – aristocratic and amusing – and he also had been so hard-up that he had accepted £50 a week from Aspinall to play the piano at the Clermont Club. For a man who was cousin to a Prime Minister (Sir Alec Douglas-Home) and to a successful playwright (William Douglas-Home), as well as being in line to the earldom of Home (his son will be the next Earl), it seems scarcely credible that money worries should have driven him to subservience and despair, but then the practice of primogeniture in Britain, which passes an entire inheritance to the eldest son and nothing to the others, though efficient, can be harsh.

Douglas-Home had sold to the *Daily Express* a photograph he had taken of Aspinall in his swimming-pool at Howletts, with his tigress Tara in mid-air as she dived in to join him. Aspinall had invited him down for the weekend on the strict understanding that no photographs should be sold to the newspapers, a condition he readily accepted. He was paid a mere £50 for the outright sale, but the cost to the well-being of such a depressive was severe. Aspinall, who thought his betrayal 'base', had fired him on the spot, a blow which accelerated his decline and confirmed his misanthropy. Not long afterwards he committed suicide. (Irony is never more seductive than when it is vicious: the photograph which ruined Douglas-Home is now the most famous single image of Aspinall and his animals and has been reproduced the world over.)

The pattern of events was ominous. As soon as the row over the *Sunday Times* exploded, Elwes wrote frantic letters to everyone concerned, letters of apology, letters of recrimination, letters of self-defence. He wrote abjectly to Lady Annabel, whose photograph with Lord Lucan had appeared on the cover, and to her son Robin Birley. He threatened to sue James Fox; he blamed the police for releasing photographs from Lucan's private album in their possession; he blamed Victoria Brooke, another friend, for selling pictures. In fact, he had never taken a photograph in his life and did not own a camera, so he could hardly have been accused of betrayal. There was only his painting, which was innocent enough, to indicate his having consorted with the enemy. Still, it was a foolish move, and he soon realised what he had risked. His letters show how frightened he was of losing his 'position'.

This is not the place to rehearse yet again the details of Elwes's sad ostracism; they have been published often enough and continue to cause pain to his family. It is sufficient to say that he felt himself, with some cause, to be the object of refined vindictiveness, and that his reasonable explanations were met with obtuse stubbornness. Now, too late, it has been established beyond refutation that the photographs published in the *Sunday Times* were supplied by another party and that Dominick had nothing whatever to do with the transaction. More to our point, it is significant that Aspinall took his side, interceding vigorously on his behalf. Dominick, he said, was foolish, but everyone knew his character and should not be astonished by a new manifestation of it. You cannot feel betrayed by someone you had long since learnt was indiscreet. He anticipated that memory of Dominick's 'error' would eventually fade, and meanwhile he did what he could to mitigate the anger and speak up for his friend.

Yet it was obvious that the society Dominick craved, the only one he felt at home in, would henceforth be denied him. In September, three months after the newspaper article, he killed himself. The suicide note he left is said to have been bitter but, since the coroner wisely refused to release it, no one has seen it, and the reports of its contents are cruelly speculative.

On a wet November day a Memorial Service was held at the Jesuit Church (more properly the Church of Our Lady of the Immaculate Conception) in Farm Street, Mayfair, at which two addresses were delivered, one by Kenneth Tynan, the other by John Aspinall.

As one would expect of an accomplished writer, Tynan's speech was expressed in dignified and well-chosen English, quietly spoken but with a hint of angry sarcasm hovering behind almost every word. 'He loved the world of wealth and ceremony far more than it deserved,' he said. 'Certain rich people elected him their Court Jester and he happily embraced the role. But they never really accepted him because in the final analysis he did not have quite enough money.'

Aspinall, as one of those 'certain rich people' obliquely attacked by Tynan, went to the pulpit to give his oration. He always enjoyed a stage. Leaning over the pulpit, grabbing the lectern with both hands, throwing his voice at all four walls, he delivered what someone later called a 'tribal' speech, reverberating with quotations from Oscar Wilde, Cicero and Anglo-Saxon literature, with Churchillian orotundity, and (some thought) breathtaking insensitivity. Aspers was once more showing off, knowing full well that his approach would shock the congregation and cause nervous shuffling of feet or shame-concealing coughs. No attempt was made to commiserate or lament; rather was it a performance to glorify the deceased's qualities. Dominick, he said, had been like a bard in an Anglo-Saxon court, describing the events of the day to the assembled lords in entertaining fashion. 'He unlocked the word-hoard.' He had been from a long line of Saxons who yearned for posthumous fame, and he would have it, in the immortality of the genes. Genetic inheritance was mentioned four times (Aspinall was certainly not counting, for the address was spontaneous), and Dominick's failure to make money was ascribed to 'a genetic flaw'. It was, despite all, a magnificent exhibition, which brought Elwes to life in a rich parade of verbal portraiture. All who had known him were entranced.

Well, almost all. As Aspinall came out of the church he was approached by Tremayne Rodd, a godson of Dominick's mother, who swiftly punched him on the jaw and ran away down the street shouting, 'That's what I think of your bloody speech, Aspinall.' Rodd thought the address was tasteless, but his reaction to it was more so, especially in front of Elwes's children.

The victim was neither angry nor, it seemed, surprised. 'I am used to this sort of thing in dealing with wild animals,' he said. However, press photographers were delighted and the attack was front-page news in the morning papers. Tynan declared that it was a pity that what was intended as a tribute to Dominick should be remembered as the occasion for an upper-class punch-up. It turned out to be only the beginning of an even better story, the most celebrated public brawl in England for half a century, that between Sir James Goldsmith and Richard Ingrams, editor of the fearless satirical magazine *Private Eye*. Ingrams picked up the news and asked Patrick Marnham to use it as the basis for an article. The full-page essay, entitled *All's Well That Ends Elwes* contained one serious error in suggesting that Goldsmith had been present at Aspinall's lunch the day after Lord Lucan disappeared. That was enough. Goldsmith sued, and so began a mighty struggle of titans, a kind of *perpetuum mobile* of litigation, which continued for years and is part of publishing history.*

Dominick Elwes's family did not appreciate the fury of Tremayne Rodd. Timothy Elwes said so in the clearest fashion in a statement:

My family and I wish to dissociate ourselves from the cowardly gesture gratuitously made on our behalf, after the memorial service for my brother Dominick. My brother had specifically requested John Aspinall, one of his greatest friends, to make an address at his memorial service. The speech would have delighted Dominick, who knew full well that John's would be no conventional panegyric. We

---

*Goldsmith sued *Private Eye* for three civil libels in the summer of 1976, and later brought a rare case of criminal libel against the magazine. He won his action in civil libel and was accorded a public apology, but he dropped the criminal libel. Goldsmith was the ultimate victor in the long struggle, though *Private Eye* survived the onslaught.

feel sad that such an occasion should have been marred by so deplorable an incident.

Both he and Jeremy Elwes wrote privately to Aspinall reiterating their view. Dominick's aunt had been congratulating him on his having captured the essence of the dead man's character, at the very moment he was punched by Rodd. Nevertheless, the publicity had done considerable damage to Aspinall's reputation at large, as was amply shown by poisonous letters he received calling him 'high-class scum' and 'vermin' of which society should be cleansed. The letters did not matter in themselves, but they demonstrated how easily newspaper reports could create a personality in order to vilify it. Aspinall repaired to his home and his tigers. He did not understand how his unorthodox style could be a stone in his shoe, which was unfortunate since he would need all the public tolerance he could get in the years to come.

Such had been the excitement generated by gorilla births that one might easily overlook other equally impressive breeding achievements at Howletts, steadily mounting over the years. The successful experiment in exporting Kisoro gave Lester Fisher at Lincoln Park the courage to send over a pair of extremely rare snow leopards which faced certain oblivion as a species unless some way could be found to breed them. Aspinall was eager to make the attempt and ready to foot the bills, although mountains of bureaucratic glue had to be unstuck, mainly on the American side, before the animals could make the journey. Saul Kitchener, the head keeper in Chicago, called the bureaucrats 'feeble-minded' and 'dense', language frequently used by the earthy idealists engaged in animal husbandry. The snow leopards arrived in the spring of 1975, and two years later arrived the first snow leopard babies ever to be born in captivity.

Since that day, a total of twelve snow leopards have been born at Howletts, a previously unheard-of accomplishment in England, to add to the first honey-badger in the world, the first Siberian tiger in Britain, the first clouded leopards and the first Przwalski's horses for thirty years, events already catalogued. The tiger colony was expanding rapidly, with over twelve breeding females producing twenty cubs a year. Before long there would be the only two African elephants ever born in Britain, the first fishing cats to be born in Britain, the first Chousingha (four-horned antelope) and the first Calamian deer outside Asia. Howletts also has had the only Javan brown langur births in the UK, and is now, ten years later, embarked upon its most ambitious breeding project, to save the rare Sumatran rhinoceros from extinction.

But this is to anticipate. What was significant was that the world zoological community was taking a very keen interest in the achievements at Howletts under the unconventional direction of its maverick owner, whereas ten years earlier they had scorned his untutored pretension. They were likewise stung by his cavalier attitude towards those among them who did not satisfy his own strict standards. He was asked to lend a female gorilla to Hanover Zoo, for example; this is a not uncommon practice among zoos where breeding potential is regarded as infinitely more important than ownership (as we have already seen with Lincoln Park). Aspinall was naturally well-disposed towards the idea in principle. He went to Hanover and was so disappointed by the conditions he found, the state of the gorillas already there, with their long-hanging arms and poor muscular development, with the scientifically-prepared food they had boringly to eat, and with the architecture of the gorilla-house, that he declined to put one of his animals among them.

As for the tigers, they were now so numerous that it was becoming feasible that some should be sent back to India to breed there and increase the local stock. This, after all, was the whole point of preservation. Guy Mountfort of the World Wildlife Fund wrote seeking support for his plan to reintroduce tigers into the wild, and Aspinall promised a pair from Howletts, which he would send free of charge, even paying the cost of their journey. But he wondered whether they would learn hunting skills and would be effectively protected against human predators. Moreover, he was not sure that Indians were good game wardens. 'I would have to be very sure that my animals would be safe before I parted with them,' he replied.

As it happened, the granddaughter of his first animal Tara, a tigress from Twycross Zoo also named Tara, was sent back to India, where she gradually adapted herself to her new life of total freedom and was only rarely spotted. Despite this the central problem remained – possibly incapable of resolution – namely that whereas gregarious animals such as ungulates or lions may successfully be returned to the wild, the tiger, solitary and nocturnal, faced a difficult task of adaptation. The only way in which a tiger cub can learn how to kill is from its mother, and the teaching process may take up to two years. A zoo-bred tiger would necessarily be deficient in these skills, and might well resort to killing domestic animals or humans in order to survive. The awkward conclusion is that while Indian tigers may thrive and increase in places like Howletts, their numbers will continue to diminish in their natural habitat, where they ought in other words to be, and will one day dribble to extinction, thus presenting those like John Aspinall who passionately want to prevent their disappearance with a nice ethical conundrum. For there are too many tigers born at Howletts, and they must go somewhere; if not to the wild, then to other zoos, which may well be horribly inferior in their care and in their respect for the animal.

Though Aspinall had supported the World Wildlife Fund for many years, he gradually became aware that their approach to conservation was fundamentally different from his own. When Prince Bernhard of the Netherlands resigned his post as International Head of the WWF, Aspinall wrote in provocative vein to Sir Peter Scott: 'When you all decide who is to be the next head of the Fund, I make one special request – that he is not a big game hunter or shooter of beasts and birds for pleasure. [This was] the worst crime that Prince Bernhard committed.' He also accused the Fund of suffering from what he called 'royalitis', excessive hankering after royal patronage and obsequious behaviour when it has been won, to which Sir Peter quite properly replied, 'The main advantage of Princes is that they can talk directly to heads of governments.' Prince Bernhard had been enormously effective in having conservation measures adopted all over the world, through painstaking persistent lobbying. Aspinall would neither have the patience for such work nor find in it any romantic allure.

Nevertheless, his objection to conservationists who enjoy killing was a valid one which mirrored general public consternation at the blatant paradox underlying the commitment of many otherwise estimable men. The Duke of Edinburgh, arguably an even more effective propagandist on behalf of wildlife than his predecessor at the WWF, also slaughters wildlife for the pleasure it gives, though considerably less than when he was a young man. Apologists for shooters and trappers argue the utilitarian point, that some animals must be culled for their own sake, and that others are 'pests', but they do not face the philosophical implications of such arrogance, nor are they interested in its ethical double-think. To Aspinall, it appeared gross hypocrisy.

His other somewhat inconsistent quarrel with the organisation was that it had become too 'political', by which he meant 'left-wing'.

Aspinall continued to support Friends of the Earth, the Fauna Preservation Society, and many like bodies, both financially and morally. But his most fervently engaged support was reserved for individualists like himself, especially Arjan ('Billy') Singh, the legendary solitary forest-dweller who, single-handed, founded the famous Tiger Haven in northern India, and rehabilitated Tara's granddaughter to life in the wild.

Meanwhile, Kisoro continued to impregnate his harem regularly, and baby gorillas at Howletts became the norm, no longer a cause for astonishment. Shamba gave birth to Kambula on 1 June 1976, and Baby Doll had her second son, Kibabu, on 25 May 1977. A month later Shamba was again about to have a baby, unsuspected by the keepers; it was a member of the public who first spotted that a birth was imminent. First a tiny leg showed, Shamba pulled it, then snapped the umbilical cord and the baby was born dead. It was a girl.

Later that year occurred an event in the gorillarium which threw everyone into sedentary gloom. Kimba, the first infant born to Shamba and subsequently raised by Richard Johnstone-Scott when Shamba neglected her, was found hanging from a rope a few weeks before Christmas. She had somehow contrived to get her neck twisted in the rope during play and had strangled herself. Her neck was not broken, for the post-mortem showed she had died from asphyxiation, but this was hardly a consolation. Quite apart from the loss of their only female infant, Kimba's death was a very personal tragedy for Johnstone-Scott, who had been with her every day of her life and had watched her grow and integrate with the group. She was like his own, and his grief was immeasurable. Had anyone doubted the truth which Howletts was dedicated to proclaiming, that there is no necessary gulf between man and the other primates, his doubts would have been dispelled on that glum December day.

Not long afterwards, Aspinall himself suffered a similar personal loss with the unexpected death of Gugis at the age of nineteen, at the very peak of his mighty maturity. He succumbed to pneumonia, undetected because his physical condition had appeared excellent until the last twenty-four hours. Though not the first fatality among the gorillas, this was the most severe to Aspinall personally. The death of his previous silverback, Kulu, ten years earlier had caused him to despair about the future of the colony and to lament the passing of an animal he respected. In the case of Gugis, he had long since surrendered any hope that he might procreate and was relying on Kisoro and, eventually, Djoum to continue the line. Gugis was loved for his own sake. Aspinall had known him since he was a fragile ten-month-old; his own daughter Amanda had grown up alongside the gorilla; he had learnt most of his skills in mood interpretation through hundreds of hours with Gugis, whose moods were particularly volatile and deceptive. Man and gorilla held for one another that conmingling of affection and respect which comes with knowledge of personality and tolerance of all faults. Billy Singh understood the effect the ape's death would have upon Aspinall, and sent his condolences without delay.

Every man or woman who has dealt closely with the great apes has felt a similar inter-specific bond which cannot be derided. George Schaller, David Attenborough, Dian Fossey, all struggled to express the depth of the rapport they felt. Jane Goodall tells of an occasion in the wild when she held a palm nut out and a chimpanzee approached her to investigate. Nervous at first, he looked about him, then took the fruit and at the same time held her hand firmly and gently with his own. Here is her reflection upon this seemingly mundane event:

> At that moment there was no need of any scientific knowledge to understand his communication of reassurance. The soft pressure of his fingers spoke to me not through my intellect but through a more primitive emotional channel: the barrier of untold centuries which has grown up during the separate evolution of man and chimpanzee was, for those few seconds, broken down.

It was precisely this 'barrier of untold centuries' which was being broken daily at Howletts. Is it any wonder, then, that Gugis should be mourned with dignity? Aspinall was by now all too familiar with that far from maudlin attachment which Konrad Lorenz called an 'immediate bond with that unconscious omniscience we call nature. The price which man had to pay for his culture and civilisation was the severing of this bond . . .' Remember, these are not the words of a gibbering romantic, neurotically fond of his pets, but the product of years of careful study and reflection by one of the world's most respected ethologists. This marriage of solid common sense with the heady perception of lost paradise characterised Aspinall's approach and rapidly gained him adherents. Konrad Lorenz certainly took his work very seriously indeed. A man who has once seen into the intimate beauty of nature, he said, cannot then tear himself away from it; he must become either a poet or a naturalist.

If the world did not choose to understand why John Aspinall should lament the death of a lowland gorilla, then the world was deprived. The world, in his view, included most of the 'scientific' naturalists who, unlike Lorenz and Schaller, were arid desiccated souls, impervious to the possibility of communion with their objects of study.

He decided that he would write a book celebrating the animals at Howletts and his life with them. It would be blatantly polemical and would pour passion into every page. Sentiment would not be eschewed, but rather pricked into life, leaving the reader trembling with the sense of wonder. Macmillan agreed to publish. There was also the thought that, with the zoo's finances continuing precariously to depend upon the weekly depletion of the owner's house, a book might make some money. At the very least it could bring in more visitors. But Aspinall never lost sight of his principal purpose. To Nicholas Gould he wrote, 'I am more interested in my own pretensions than profit,' which was just as well, since no book could earn the kind of money he would need to operate two zoos. When asked what advance he would like, he replied, 'Pay me enough to feed the animals for a month.' This was calculated at £7,000.

He wrote the book in longhand (not only does Aspinall not drive a car, but he has never touched a typewriter), usually at weekends and sometimes in the back of the car driving between Port Lympne and Howletts. Twenty titles were considered, the first being *Aspinall's Animals*, before agreement was reached on *The Best of Friends*, with an amazing photograph on the dust-cover showing Aspinall bearing the great Gugis on his back.

By any judgment, even without bias, the book is a remarkable and unusual piece of writing. It is really an extended essay, in the manner of an eighteenth-century *philosophe*, interrupted with flashes of personal feeling and provocative behavioural insights. There are chapters on gorillas, tigers, and other animals including wolves, elephants and rhinoceroses, amusing stories and salutary ones, and a passionately argued epilogue the prose of which rises to the elegance and sophistication of Bertrand Russell, without his paralysing logical inhibitions. The theme and purpose of the book are two-fold, and by now familiar: to enthuse the reader with a love for wild animals; and to make him face the dreadful scourge of human proliferation.

The author is at pains to show how individual are his animals, to identify them and describe their different personalities like so many dramatis personae in an epic play. This is to kidnap the reader's affections before the polemic proper is launched and to dispense with the easy and comfortable notion that animals are a 'problem' to be considered rather than sentient beings whose own future is at stake. 'Gorillas vary as much as humans in disposition and character,' he writes. Again, 'there are bold tigers and timid ones, honest tigers and treacherous ones, predictable and unpredictable, noisy and silent, hot-tempered and good-natured.' He talks about the character of these animals as only one can who has lived with them on intimate terms, and his choice of words is self-consciously literary and impressive, as if struggling to mould a language equal in grandeur to its subject. The gorilla, unlike the chimpanzee, is aloof and distant, with a high emotional threshold; he is not easily excited. 'The thongs of affection that bind the gorilla are hidden in his fur.' The subtle alliteration and metric balance of the sentence give it power and poetry. There are many such. This is the language of a man who is still in awe.

Nor does Aspinall forget that converts to the cause must also be visitors to Howletts. 'I know of no other zoo', he writes, 'where so many gorillas of different ages and sex can mix freely together . . . [Howletts is] one of the poorest zoos in the world, but rich in philosophical commitment, in dedication and in ambition.'

To illustrate the point, *The Best of Friends* is stuffed with the most startling photographs ever to adorn a naturalist tract. They not only gave the book enchantment but also, together with *Echo of the Wild*, the second of three television documentaries made by Roy Deverell on the work of John Aspinall, which appeared the following year, they brought the serious nature of his dedication home to many who knew only of his gambling.

When, however, he turned to his obsessive theme of the destruction of the planet by overweening mankind, repeating the gravamen of his address at the Albert Hall and of a multitude of private conversations, Aspinall's eloquence tended to spiral out of control and leave his readers breathless. He sounded demonic, unbalanced, uncompromising; epithets he would moreover glory in, as the qualities of saintliness, balance and compromise were among those he despised most heartily.

Three aspects of Aspinall's writing conspired to antagonise some readers and vitiate the book's success. First, the unrestrained use of his favourite devices of paradox and surprise led him to suggest that mankind, 'in uncontrolled, cancerous growth', burdened with aberrants and deviants since its natural predators (bubonic plague, malaria, typhus) had been neutralised, ought now to be decimated.

Second, his attempts to draw parallels between the social organisation of some animals and his own political views were, to say the least, provocative. Japanese macaques, for example, are governed by something resembling a perpetual oligarchy. The Java monkeys have a 'king' with four wives; his heir is always the child of one of these wives; there is never rule by usurpation and the ruling family is never deposed – the dynasty continues. Aspinall gleefully claims this demonstrates that inequality of opportunity is the primate slogan, purposefully ignoring those species which can be said to organise themselves into a more 'democratic' system.*

Third, there is a page of self-analysis which guilelessly trumpets the writer's qualities and excuses his faults, admits to a gift for inciting admiration and lays claim to all the virtues needed for a political career save that of being subservient to the suffrage. 'Whatever my faults, humbug and hypocrisy

*Group-living primates are overwhelmingly hierarchical.

are not among them.' Aspinall seems to suggest that if he is not more famous and powerful it is because he is unwilling to lower himself to the standards of the mob. It is a most unfortunate page, which his editors ought to have excised without appeal, for his simple honesty appears on the page the most monstrous self-satisfaction.

Nevertheless, Aspinall received a goodly amount of appreciative 'fan-mail' when his book was published, and he was especially pleased to earn the plaudits of those he admired. Konrad Lorenz, for example, wrote to say he actually *envied* Aspinall's rapport with the great beasts. He went on:

> There is a sort of intuitive understanding, one might say a sort of freemasonry, between people who really know animals, and few professional ethologists know them as well as you do. You have no idea of the joy and utter sympathy with which I have read your book.

Despite the encouragement of a German and an Italian edition, the book did not sell well. It carried too many messages which people did not want to hear. Even worse did it fare in the United States of America, where the absolute sanctity of the human species is revered more than anywhere in the world and its right to infinite advancement encouraged. So appalled were the Americans by the messianic tone that most literary editors refused even to allow the book to be reviewed. In their eyes, Aspinall's cry of repentance on behalf of humankind smacked of communist influence or lunacy. The American publishers, Harper and Row, sustained a significant loss.

The Best of Friends remains an important document for anyone who wishes to understand the nature of John Aspinall's ambition and to see what mattered most to him beneath the extrovert eccentricity. It was written during the precarious period of his relative poverty, when the future of the zoos was a constant worry, yet at its best it attains an uncharacteristic serenity. The book finishes with a credo which the publishers cut by about half:

I believe that a wildlifer must not expect to be rewarded with recognition or worldly approval. His work will be to him his recompense. Only in his own peace of mind and self-esteem will he find solace.

I believe in *Jus animalium*, The Rights of Beasts, and *Jus herbarum*, The Rights of Plants. The right to exist as they have always existed, to live and let live. I believe in the Buddhist concept of *Ahimsa* – justice for all animate things. I believe in the greatest happiness for the greatest number of species of fauna and flora that the Earth can sustain without resultant deterioration of habitat and depletion of natural resources.

I believe in the sanctity of the life systems, not in *the sanctity of human life alone*. The concept of the sanctity of human life is the most damaging sophism that philosophy has ever propagated – it has rooted well. Its corollary – a belief in the insanctity of species other than man – is the cause of that damage. The destruction of this idea is a prerequisite for survival.

I believe that wilderness is Earth's greatest treasure. Wilderness is the bank upon which all cheques are drawn. I believe our debt to nature is total, our willingness to pay anything back on account barely discernible. I believe that unless we recognise this debt and renegotiate it we write our own epitaph.

I believe that there is an outside chance to save the earth and most of its tenants. This outside chance must be grasped with gambler's hands.

I believe that terrible risks must be taken and terrible passions roused before these ends can hope to be accomplished. If a system is facing extreme pressures, then only extreme counter-pressures are relevant, let alone likely to prove effective.

I believe that all who subscribe to these testaments must act now, stand up and be counted. What friends Nature has, Nature needs.

II
Setbacks

The relentless depletion of Howletts continued for six years, proceeds from books, paintings and furniture disappearing down the eager throats of rhinoceros, elephant and tiger. Among much else, Aspinall sold many rare and beautiful books on animals, including Aulebert's *Monkeys*, four books on mammals by Richard Lydekker, and David Giraud Elliot's *Cats* (more properly called *Monograph on the Felidae*), as well as the Oscar Wilde collection (his second). His best picture, a Wilhelm Kuhnert of a tiger, also went, as did a lovely painting of parrots and peacocks by the seventeenth-century Flemish artist Melchior Hondecoeter.

The set of Pugin chairs from Windsor Castle was split up, Jimmy Goldsmith taking some for his house at Ham Common, while Aspinall retained one and another two went to the Temple Newsam Museum in Leeds. These chairs had come to him by accident, having been ordered for sale by a functionary at Windsor in order to clear a store-room some years earlier without due attention to its contents. The chairs are dated 1866 and bear the initials V.R. on the underside. Quite obviously they belonged to Queen Elizabeth II and ought not to have left the castle at all (discreet suggestions to this effect were made when the error came to light), but the sale was perfectly legal. Aspinall's one remaining chair sits in front of his desk in the study at Howletts.

It was evident that such erratic sources of income would eventually dribble to a close and that something more durable would have to take their place if the zoos were to survive. Reluctantly, Aspinall decided that he would return to the gambling world from which he had retired with such hopes in 1972. His reluctance was founded not only upon the need to emerge from relative tranquillity in the country, but also upon the provision of the law which stipulated that the proprietor could not participate in the games. This removed all the enjoyment for a man like Aspinall, and incidentally removed one of the attractions for punters. Nevertheless, his reputation was now paramount. It was privately admitted even by his competitors that there was no one who ran a gaming house quite like John Aspinall, and his reappearance on the scene was a cause for some concern among them.

To the punters, however, the news was entirely welcome, and those who had been members of the Clermont in the earlier days were quick to indicate their support. A number of people lent items to fill out a new club, including the Marquess of Londonderry who raided his vaults at Wynyard to find dozens of silver knives, forks, spoons, which had not been used for half a century. Nor would staff be a problem, as it was well known in the gambling world that to work for Aspinall was to reach the top of one's profession, and that one did not apply for such a job, one waited to be invited. Many of the old Clermont staff would be available. To divert some of the new Arab gamblers away from the twenty-nine established casinos in London, without advertising, would present a difficulty.

Suitable premises were found in an attractive small house at 1 Hans Place, on the corner of Sloane Street, on which Simon Fraser, one of Aspinall's oldest friends, took a lease on his behalf. This satisfied one of the principal conditions which had to be met before application could be made for a gaming licence, that there should already be premises available. The others were that the applicant should be a 'fit and proper' person, capable and diligent, and that he should be able to prove there was an unstimulated demand for a gaming establishment in the area. There was never any problem showing Aspinall's ability, but the demand was more tricky. There were thirty-one permitted areas in the country, London being a special case as the capital. Aspinall would need to demonstrate before magistrates that his proposals were welcome in Knightsbridge; the Gaming Board could present evidence to the contrary, and competitors as well as residents could make objections.

The Gaming Board was also empowered to examine bank accounts and investigate the background of directors. Aspinall could not raise the money alone (it would cost nearly £1 million to set up and open the club) and urgently needed a partner more solvent than he. At the suggestion of Teddy Goldsmith, he and Aspinall flew to Gstaad in Switzerland to persuade Jimmy Goldsmith that he should be Aspinall's partner in the new enterprise. This he agreed to do out of friendship, not because he had a consuming desire to own a gambling house. Never whimsical in financial matters, he wrote explaining the position to Aspinall. 'People who are not intimately involved in business', he began, 'find it difficult to follow figures.' He went on:

> In your case, the most important thing was to keep Howletts and Port Lympne alive, and to do this I have had to arrange loans of approximately £600,000 which bear interest of about £120,000 a year. On top of this, so as to avoid you personally going bust, I have to give guarantees of about £300,000. I have therefore had to take a risk of nearly £1 million, at a running cost of £120,000 p.a. or £10,000 a month, and I think you will agree that not much pressure has been put on you . . . I thought these facts should be recorded so that you could get a better grasp of them.

Despite objections from all and sundry, the licence was awarded and Aspinall's club prepared to open in the summer of 1978. Aspinall himself suspected that the Gaming Board was not at all happy with the decision in his favour. As he tendentiously put it, 'when Sir Lindsay Ring prays, he kneels towards Mecca' (Sir Lindsay Ring was No. 2 to the Chairman, Sir Stanley Raymond, and Mecca was one of the three largest casino chains in the country). Moreover, he was totally frank before the magistrates in declaring that the only reason he wanted a licence was to feed his animals. The Gaming Board regarded this as flippant; the magistrates as refreshing.

Events turned in Aspinall's favour very soon after the club opened. For months the Chief Inspector of the Gaming Board, Jack Lynch, and his team had been collecting evidence of major infringements of the Act by rival clubs, including the alleged acceptance of cheques on non-existent bank accounts and the destruction of cheques. One casino was suspected of having broken the rules with regard to soliciting in outrageous fashion. There were between 100 and 150 big punters in London whom every club wanted to get its hands on. According to one rumour, this particular casino employed a private detective to tour all the rival clubs and take down the registration numbers of cars parked outside. It then persuaded a policeman in Leicester to feed the numbers to the police computer and discover names and addresses of the punters. When Jack Lynch visited its premises, as the Act empowered him to do, and exposed the practice, an enquiry was instigated and the casino lost its licence.

Something akin to farce broke out when the casino appealed and objections to the appeal were made by another club. The proprietor of the first club then set about compiling a dossier on practices common at the second, and leaving this dossier (carelessly) on top of a pile which the Gaming Board inspectors were likely to encounter. The result was a gathering snowball of enquiries, appeals, and convictions which closed some of the best-known casino empires in England. Not least annoying to the casino owners was the relative invulnerability of Aspinall, who to their utter consternation not only ran his club with more style but did so without resorting to murky skulduggery. The Gaming Board could never quite believe it. Within a very short time Little

17 *(above)* Winston Churchill's
    painting of Port Lympne

18 *(right)* Lady Sarah Aspinall

19 *(below)* Port Lympne, designed by Sir Herbert Baker, formerly
    owned by Sir Philip Sassoon

20 *(above)* Lady Sarah and John Aspinall introduce their son, Bassa, to family friend

21 *(below, left)* Sir James Goldsmith

22 *(below, right)* Teddy Goldsmith

23 *(above)* Bassa with Juju and Kijo, the first gorilla to be born at
    Howletts

24 *(below)* Bob Wilson and Brian Stocks

25 Amanda Aspinall, Lady O., Lady Sarah, John and Bassa Aspinall

Aspinall's (so-called because of its Dinky-toy size) was taking 10 per cent of the total drop for the whole country. This was largely due to the successful spread of Aspinall's renown among the new crop of Arab gamblers. The Kuwaitis, in particular, became regular visitors.

Not only that, but the club's reputation for food and congenial atmosphere completely outclassed its competitors. It was generally agreed that Aspinall's absence from the gambling scene for six years might have worked to his advantage, in the sense that it was doubtful whether, had he retained the Clermont Club, he would have avoided all infringements of the Act in the face of such Machiavellian competition.

Aspinall's other reputation, as a breeder of rare mammals, was gathering pace at the same time. The Zoological Society of London (i.e. London Zoo), setting aside its earlier sniffy disdain towards his endeavours, wrote to ask for his help. They had a female gorilla, Lomie, who had failed to mate with their legendary male, Guy, despite her having bred with another male years earlier at Bristol Zoo. They did not know what to do to encourage her, until it was suggested she be sent on loan to Howletts for a trial period of three months. Although he was not then short of breeding females, Aspinall readily agreed. He was confident she would breed in the surroundings he provided. 'The presence of other gorillas seems an important stimulant to mother care,' he wrote. 'We have found that if you isolate a mother with her new-born young she can lose interest.' He guaranteed that any offspring would be shared with London Zoo.

This new confidence was cemented by a visit from the Director of Zoos, Mr Rawlins, who saw for himself what had been achieved in births and in habitat. 'The gorilla enterprise is a magnificent one,' he wrote, 'and I do congratulate you on what has been done. We are honoured and delighted to benefit from all this work by sending Lomie to you.' She travelled from London in a station-wagon.

Lomie integrated well with Djoum and Mumbah, at that time the only two adult male gorillas to be kept *together* in captivity, and was observed to mate frequently. The three months prescribed for the experiment had, however, to be indefinitely protracted, and Lomie had her first baby two years later. Once again, the Zoological Society was near ecstatic in its praise; the curator of mammals, Mr Bertram, noted 'the excellent improvement in her behaviour and mothering abilities, thanks to the environment provided for her at Howletts.' Lomie was an unwitting peacemaker; relations between Aspinall and the London Zoo took a new turn with her adoption into the family.

She is still there today and has had two children, both raised by herself, but her eyes betray the instability and isolation of her earlier years; they are not the eyes of a gorilla who gives her trust wholeheartedly, but of one who keeps most of it in reserve, expecting anxiety to tangle her at any moment.

As for the tigers, they were breeding with such regularity that space would eventually run out, and Howletts would be a victim of its own success. Tigers in the wild require a hunting territory of several square miles. Although they were given much more than a cage at Howletts, they could not enjoy natural conditions, still less so as their numbers increased. Aspinall was at last obliged to give surplus cubs to other zoos, assuring himself as best he could that they would be well cared for. (Today, when over 350 tigers have been bred, it is no longer even possible to obtain such assurances and one is reduced to the feeble hope that half of them may be happy.) Something of Aspinall's attitude towards the tiger is displayed in a letter he wrote to the Australian gambler and publishing tycoon Kerry Packer, to whom he sent a pair of tiger clubs shortly after the opening of Little Aspinall's:

At this age their play-biting is quite nasty and every time one gets one's hand or arm nipped from over-excitement you want to sock them quite hard on the mouth or the side of the head; by six or seven months old they will have learnt not to bite in play and to keep their claws in as well. The only way they learn is by punishment immediately after the event. Such a clout should always be followed by a making-up immediately after, which you do by trying to

imitate their own friendly noise, phut-a-phut phut-a-phut.
I am getting Brian Stocks, the tiger-keeper who raised the
babies, to write to you with a judgment of their characters
– very important that this is taken note of. [They came
from exceptionally reliable stock and stable parents.] Try
and see them for 10 or 15 minutes every day. They are very
tactile animals and love being stroked and kissed . . . Don't
be worried at their biting, at the moment that is natural,
just as children have tantrums and get over-excited, so do
they. These animals have a marvellous character, infinitely
more reliable and stable than that of dogs. When they are
adult, though, they will see you as a powerful male of their
own species; the bond that will ensure your protection
is that of mutual trust and affection, not dominance. At
this stage, dominance is not resented at all, as one would
expect with young.

These instructions sound suspiciously authoritarian, as if
the object were to 'tame' the tiger into obedience, an aim
Aspinall would strenuously deny. At least, they reveal the
at times awkward disparity between intention and method,
for although the tiger must be allowed to behave like a tiger
according to the ancient dictates of his genes, he must also be
tractable to a certain extent in his life with humans; the parent
tiger would exert the same discipline over its young.

As it happened, Kerry Packer was not permitted to keep
this pair, Australian law being firm on the principle that one
could only keep exotic animals if they were the prime source
of one's living. Instead, he gave them to Western Plain Zoo
and donated £20,000 to build a handsome enclosure for them.
Naturally enough, they are called 'John' and 'Sally'.

Both Howletts and Port Lympne by 1979 attracted the
attention of professionals for their apparent ability to reverse
the relative importance of man and animals in the available
space. By virtue of a confusion of purpose, many zoos the
world over were flooded with people coming to look at
animals confined in boxes. Most clung to a nineteenth
century notion of freaks and curiosities whose only value

was as exhibition for profit. Such a mentality treats animals as merchandise and does not even consider whether it is 'bad' that they should be prevented from gathering their own food, establishing their own social orders and behaving in ways which were natural to them. A study of two hundred American zoos in 1974 catalogued an appalling list of animals with neuroses, overweight with synthetic 'junk' food (often prescribed by scientists) and underhoused in heated cells, with deformed feet caused by concrete floors. It is little wonder that there were frequent calls for the abolition of such places, not only because the treatment of inmates was overtly cruel but also because the zoo taught a false idea of man's place in the natural world, relative to other species. Such a sense of superiority has historically always been dangerous.

The morally proper and practically efficient ways of running zoos were not mutually exclusive, as the Director of the Basle Zoo, Dr Heini Hediger, tirelessly pointed out in books and papers. Hediger championed the principle of zoo biology, according to which the animal must live in conditions as near natural as possible; therefore he must eat not the most nutritious food, but the most natural to him. 'Nature knows nothing of early maturity, artificial fattening, sexual hypertrophy, the degeneration of the sense organs and the loss of the ability to move', he wrote. 'The zoo must be the opposite of a profitable farm; it must work in nature's direction and according to natural tendencies.' The essence of zoo biology was that 'the animal behaves in its artificial territory as a free-living animal behaves in its natural territory. In order that the zoo animal can behave like this, everything that is important to it as a species must be at its disposal within the enclosure.'

Just one example will indicate to what degree Aspinall has shared these ideals and how he has put them into practice. Elephants need to bathe daily in order to keep their skin (which is delicate, not as thick as popular belief has it) in good condition. Most zoos provide no such facility, either because the cost of building a pool would be prohibitive, or because it is regarded as a 'luxury' (an idiotically anthropomorphic concept – animals do not have 'luxuries'). At Howletts there is a large bathing-hole for the six African elephants, who towards the end of each afternoon literally submerge themselves in the water, lying on their sides; not only that, but they then have what is to humans a revolting wallow in mud *after* the bath, which moistens and feeds the skin.

Human abodes have for the most part been based on the cube, although it is impossible to imagine any less biological or natural construction. Completely flat surfaces at right angles to one another just do not occur in the wild, and to place animals in such artificial surroundings, presumably hoping to make them cosy, is an example of anthropomorphism gone mad. Hediger calls the zoo cube a 'monstrous humanization'. On the whole, there is strict avoidance of such absurdity at Port Lympne, and almost total absence of cubes at Howletts, although even there it is possible to find some smaller cats prowling up and down the straight line of their confinement.

The question of hygiene again marked a conflict between practice at Howletts and that which generally applied in zoos. As we have already seen, Aspinall disliked the paraphernalia of antiseptic precautions from the beginning; to him they represented interference with the dignity of animal life, and he preferred to allow animals to evolve their own mechanisms for immunity. Having paid the cost for this *laissez-faire* attitude with the untimely death in 1967 of Kulu and two other gorillas who fell victim to infection, he had somewhat to modify his principles and employ thenceforth a full-time veterinary surgeon.

There still exist zoo directors who swear by the value of concrete or glazed tile floors for apes because they cannot harbour bacteria and can be washed down several times a day to get rid of the animals' faeces. The idea is that in the wild animals can move away from the area where they have defecated, whereas in captivity they are obliged to stay close to their own waste matter and run the risk of constant reinfection from the intestinal parasites which they quite naturally carry, because the ground-cover on which they live is permanently contaminated. *Ergo*, a concrete floor may not be beautiful, but it acts in the animals' interest. Aspinall prefers the approach of providing an environment close to one they might recognise as natural to them, while still making sure that the straw is regularly replaced and kept reasonably free of excrement. The life of a keeper is not glamorous even at Howletts, the greater part of his time being employed in 'mucking out', fetching and carrying, ministering to the needs of his charges.

Some zoos pay exorbitant attention to the temperature of animal enclosures, keeping the apes warm at all times and regarding fresh air as hostile. This, again, is to confuse human comfort with optimum conditions for animals, and paradoxically it can encourage unhealthy air since bacteria proliferate in warmth. At Howletts the animals enjoy all the myriad seasons of an English year, and both gorillas and rhinoceroses have been seen to leave their sleeping quarters to come out into heavy snow through choice. It has done them no harm at all.

Gorillas in particular are susceptible to every disease which affects humans. For this reason, zoos occasionally separate animals from visitors with a glass screen in order to prevent human breath from reaching them. Such a practice would be anathema to John Aspinall (and, indeed, to all his keepers), but he is conscious of the danger and nobody with a cold is permitted to get close to the gorilla houses. The keepers know each animal so well that they can usually spot one which is ailing and secure immediate veterinary care. Still, the degree to which an animal may be suffering yet display no external evidence of anything untoward is quite alarming, as witness the sudden death of Gugis. Medical understanding of illness in wild animals (unlike that in domestic strains) is even now far from ideal, but at Howletts considerable advances have been made as the result of common-sense interpretations of experience. Tom Begg, the resident vet, is a far wiser man since he came to Howletts.

There is an irony inherent in the Howletts philosophy which can never be resolved. In the wild state animals are seldom as healthy as they are in captivity because they are exposed to greater natural dangers and cannot always be guaranteed abundant food; in zoos they are to a large extent cosseted. Moreover, a rigid natural selection takes place in the wild, where unhealthy specimens are banished from the group or herd, or linger behind and fall easily to predators, or even in certain cases are killed by other members of the group. The system in nature which keeps the species relatively pure is neither 'good' nor 'bad' in human terms, but efficient for the well-being of the species as a whole, and Aspinall has made no secret of his view that humans would benefit hugely from such remorseless weeding out of aberrant or inferior individuals. Yet natural selection cannot occur at Howletts or Port Lympne any more than it can in any other zoo, and Aspinall is therefore obliged to maintain a system of protection which he knows to be unnatural.*

It is also important to recognise that he does not confuse humaneness with sentimentality. Rabbits, chickens and crickets are reared at a nearby farm which he owns for the specific purpose of providing food for the animals, who get through about a hundred rabbits and two hundred chickens every week. This is a practical measure, of which visitors to either zoo are quite unaware. (In the eighteenth century, when the Tower of London held a 'menagerie', visitors were able to gain free entrance by bringing their own dogs and cats which they pushed through the bars for lions and tigers to tear apart; the senses of civilised man were considerably duller then than they are now.)

Many of the keepers at Howletts are adept at imitating greeting sounds which the animals will recognise and respond to. It is scarcely ever understood by the public that the popular mouthing of baby noises, the twittering and cooing, the clicking and tutting, are all distinctly unpleasant to most animals (and nauseating to a good many humans, too). Animals greet one another with a much more subtle sonic vocabulary, from the soft 'prousting' of the tiger to the deep contented

---

*Deformed or imperfect specimens are nevertheless destroyed soon after birth.

grunt of the gorilla. Captive gorillas have about eight different sounds which keepers quickly learn, although for the most part they are remarkably silent, appearing to signal to one another more by eye- and body-language. They grunt in short bursts when pleased or satiated (rather like belching), and to indicate where they are, which would be very useful in the dense undergrowth of the forest but is rarely called upon in Kent. They cough more loudly or bark when annoyed, and they scream when alarmed. The silverback leader is capable of a roar to make the trees tremble, shattering in its power; this he withholds for extremely special occasions, and no keeper attempts to imitate it. Nor, for that matter, is there any point in copying the loud yell of the siamang, which can be heard in neighbouring villages and was the original cause of neighbour Mount's displeasure. I can however testify personally to the satisfaction of an hour or two's gorilla company, and the reward of learning to communicate. Gorillas even giggle uncontrollably when tickled around the waist or stomach.

The visitor to Howletts and Port Lympne may on occasion be disappointed. What is listed as an animal enclosure appears to contain no living creature at all. This is simply because Aspinall understands the need that some animals have for severe privacy and will not compromise with their requirements. Enclosures which seem empty hide an animal in a far corner which is keeping itself apart from the common gaze. Those zoos which subject their inhabitants to permanent exhibition are perhaps fulfilling their obligations towards some municipal authority or other, or are earning their keep, or are contributing towards the education of humankind, but they are certainly not concerned in the first instance with the needs of the animals. (This is not to say, of course, that *all* the animals are shy *all* of the time.)

The days had long since passed when John Aspinall ran his zoo as a private indulgence. The number of people he employed grew from year to year (and was one of the factors which increased the drain on his resources after his 'retirement' in 1972). Also, the number of family members involved in one way or another in Aspers's enterprise mushroomed in like measure. Of Lady O.'s second family, Jennifer Osborne had married Anthony Little, who was responsible for designing and organising the various feasts at the Clermont Club and prepared a mighty Ball at Port Lympne for Amanda's coming-of-age. Little was in partnership with Sir Peter Osborne, his other brother-in-law, whose relations with his half-brother John Aspinall had never recovered from a row at Howletts when, typically, Aspinall had thoughtlessly insulted Sir Peter's wife; Aspinall abhors 'liberal' political views at the best of times, but when they are held by a woman, and a woman in the family to boot, then his responses are not rational. The two men did not meet each other again.

Aspinall's second sister, Carole, the only shy member of the family, married and settled quietly in Manchester where she raised two sons. The youngest brother, James Osborne, had been sixteen years old when the Clermont Club had opened. At that time he was a pupil at Seaford College in Chichester, where he betrayed his brother's influence upon his character by running the school book. The first time it was discovered he was a bookie he was severely beaten, a consequence which hurt him less than the win of the local tuckshop owner who had bet on a horse at 66–1 and cleaned him out. Ruin did not deter him, for James was again found with a pile of betting slips in his satchel and this time was summarily expelled. (The reader will recall that Aspinall himself had been 'invited not to return' to Rugby.)

James had attempted several business ventures, all of which failed sooner or later. One had been an office cleaning company, which involved him in scrubbing the steps and floors of public houses at six o'clock in the morning, and occasioned his being spotted so doing by Lord Lucan. Neither the job nor the circumstances were thought congenial. Eventually, Aspinall proposed to his brother that he should work as Zoo Manager at Howletts for a wage of £30 a week; James knew little about animals and manifested small desire to learn more, but as his duties consisted mainly in distributing the other wage packets and filling in PAYE forms, his ignorance of husbandry was not of crucial importance. Later, as we have seen, it was James who was entrusted with the task of taking pictures and *objets* to London every week in return for cash to feed the animals and pay the keepers. Gradually, James grew into the position of his brother's second-in-command in all his undertakings, the position held many years earlier by Ian Maxwell-Scott, as well as his confidant. Meanwhile, he had married Jane Boutwood, from Rustington in West Sussex, the daughter and granddaughter of dental surgeons.

Jane's younger brother, Robert Boutwood, was then a teenager at a respected public school in Cambridge. But it was not long before he, too, was subsumed into the complex feudal web which radiated out from John Aspinall, his sister's brother-in-law. In the school holidays, young Robert was employed on the gate, tearing public entrance tickets. Then he graduated to marketing, which meant distributing leaflets in Kentish towns and villages. Having passed his examinations with some distinction, he declined the offer of a full-time job at Howletts when he was nineteen, electing instead to study law. But two years later, Robert was again offered work at the zoo. This time he accepted. He was to be Marketing Manager and serve a year's apprenticeship under James Osborne. This arrangement lasted precisely twenty-four hours, for James was spirited away to London to help run the gaming club in Hans Place, leaving Robert Boutwood as Zoo Manager at the age of twenty-one with one day's experience.

Fortunately, Boutwood had the sagacity of the vet and zoo director Tom Begg at his side, but the story indicates the value Aspinall places upon nepotism. The word is not remotely pejorative in his vocabulary, but a natural expression of preference for one's own extended family, which he maintains is echoed amongst dozens of other species. He was disappointed his own two children, Amanda and Damian, who he hoped would carry on his work with the same devotion, chose at first to find their own respective ways to ambitions distinct from their father's. By 1987, however, Damian's passionate concern for the animals at Howletts became clear, and his determination that his father's work should not perish will eventually guide the colonies towards a long future.

James and Janie Osborne's twin sons might show some of the interest which is necessary to kindle enthusiasm (and zoo-keeping *cannot* be undertaken without enthusiasm), but Aspinall's nepotism will not extend to embrace them, as they are adopted, and he will not consider adoption a natural process; blood relations are the only ones he will accept in a family context.

One certain advantage of the involvement of Aspinall's relations in day-to-day administration was to free him for engagements in zoological circles elsewhere. The success of the Howletts experiment was now known so widely that he received dozens of invitations a year to write learned papers, address conferences, participate in the colloquy of scientific gatherings. Most of them he declined, not only because they were foreign to his independent nature, but because he felt he could achieve more in a day with the animals than in a month talking about them. Occasionally, however, he would make an exception, generally startling everyone by delivering an extempore speech stuffed with broad philosophy and rhetoric in marked contrast to other delegates, whose contributions might be smothered in detail and halted by jargon. An invitation that intrigued him was to speak at the International Centre for Medical Research in Franceville, Gabon.

The former French colony of Gabon held special attraction for anyone interested in the future of the gorilla, for purely accidental reasons. Whereas the mountain gorilla seemed doomed, reduced to little over two hundred individuals in the Virunga Volcanoes of Rwanda, the most heavily human-populated country in Africa, where greed for additional land remained unabated, the lowland gorilla in the forests of Gabon was undergoing a quite unexpected population expansion. Gabon, by contrast, had a population of under one million and a forest cover of some 70 per cent of the total land.

The oil company, Elf Acquitaine, had recently established a string of tiny cantonments along the river, surrounding small wharfs, at which a boat called regularly with provisions. As a result, the hunting tribes were sucked out of the thick forest, attracted by easy access to 'convenience' food, and left their habitual prey, the gorilla, in peace. There were estimates of twenty thousand gorillas in the dense forest.

Elf Acquitaine had also established the research station in Franceville, and it was from there that Professor Etienne Baulieu wrote to invite Aspinall to speak. Aspinall was suspicious of both the professorship and the scientific motives which might support the endeavours of the International Centre. His reply to Baulieu was ungracious but honest:

> As you are probably aware, I am 100% against medical research on primates for human benefit. It is not my nature to come as an invited guest and then possibly say something in my paper which would upset my hosts. As you know, I tend to speak my mind and am a very bad diplomat. Perhaps you could tell me exactly what goes on with these experiments. Secondly, I don't favourably regard the increase of the human population anywhere in the world other than as a step in the wrong direction, to put it mildly . . .

Professor Roger Short of the Medical Research Council wrote to reassure him that their purpose was to take advantage of possibly the last opportunity to study the behaviour of gorillas in the wild, before they disappeared entirely. Although the gorilla population was abundant in Gabon for the moment, the Gabonese had still to be persuaded that the animals should be left in their forests and not captured for the benefit of curious Westerners; each captured animal usually implied seven dead ones.

An indication of the stature which it was imagined Aspinall must enjoy in consequence of his work in England are the number of letters addressed to him as Dr (even once as Sir John). He rather gloried in his unqualified and unhonoured state; 'I would remind you, please', he wrote, 'that I am *not* a

Doctor but plain Mr John Aspinall.'

Plain or not, his reputation seemed more secure than ever before. No longer was he buffeted by carping remarks about his dilettantism or his questionable habit of encouraging keepers to mix freely with the animals. Memories of the unfortunate model whose arm had been mauled by a tiger nine years earlier had faded, and Aspinall's contention that eleven out of twelve tigers were entirely trustworthy was on the whole accepted. Of course, he and the keepers were adept at spotting the one out of twelve which was not, and they would treat such an animal with due caution.

The head keeper in the tiger compound was a remarkable man called Brian Stocks, brave and devoted to his job. At twenty-nine, he had served at Howletts virtually all his adult life, for the past seven years, and enjoyed Aspinall's total confidence. His second-in-command was a younger man, Robert Wilson, who had learnt all his skills from working with Stocks. In a letter to the renowned animal-man George Adamson (husband of the even more famous Joy), Aspinall had written inviting him to Howletts and had continued:

> I know of no one in the world I would rather show my tigers to, because you would understand the special relationship that we have. We can go in with nearly all the mothers, even the day they give birth, in fact they seem even more reliable when they have little cubs. Luckily, I am blessed with two fine keepers in Brian Stocks and Bob Wilson.

Both Brian and Bob noticed that one tigress, Zeya, was behaving unpredictably. Zeya had been at Howletts for twelve years, but had not been born there. She came from Winnipeg at the age of fourteen months, together with three others, one of which, her sister, had been the very animal which had mauled the model. On one occasion as Bob Wilson was passing food through the hatch, Zeya had snatched her paw through and grabbed him by the shoulder, ripping his shirt. It was decided to keep an even more wary eye upon her, and on no account did any keeper enter her enclosure alone. She had never been one of those animals with which one could forge bonds, even before she became troublesome. In August 1980 she had a six-week-old cub, and Brian Stocks told Aspinall she was getting 'bolder every day'. To Tom Begg he remarked that she was being 'tricky' and 'nasty', behaving unpleasantly to keepers she knew and recognised. He would not, he said, take any chances with her. Another keeper, Terry Whittaker, called her simply 'a bitch'.

On 21 August the keepers congregated as usual for their tea-break betwen 10.30 and 11 a.m. Brian Stocks was the first to leave. Shortly afterwards, the tea-lady, Pat, rushed in screaming that one of the tigers had got Brian. A junior keeper, Malcolm Bennett, immediately grabbed a chair and ran out as fast as he could, calling Brian's name. There was no answer. He met Bob Wilson on the way, and when they arrived at the tiger enclosure they saw Brian Stocks crouching forward on his knees about 6 feet inside. Zeya was standing over him. The door was open.

Bob Wilson hurled himself into the enclosure waving a broomstick and shouting at Zeya to back off, which she did. While the tigress retreated to the back, Bob stood between her and Brian's prostrate body so that Malcolm could drag him out. He was bleeding profusely from a deep wound to the neck. Peggy, the other tea-lady, arrived with hot water and began tending his wounds.

Within five minutes a police officer, alerted by radio, and an ambulance arrived. The ambulance man started mouth-to-mouth resuscitation and cardiac massage but very quickly decided Stocks should be taken to hospital without delay. He was vomiting. The police officer and Bob Wilson went in the ambulance to the Kent and Canterbury Hospital, where further resuscitation was attempted, but the bite to the neck was so deep that vomit was blocking the air-passage and Stocks was taking it into his lungs. He was unconscious all the time, probably from immediately after the initial bite. At 12.15 he was pronounced dead.

Bob Wilson was profoundly affected by the tragedy, and Aspinall, who was in London at the time, was driven at speed down to Canterbury in time for the cause of death to be pronounced: fracture dislocation of neck and multiple injuries due to mauling. Geoffrey Stocks, brother to the deceased and a local fireman, officially identified the body.

John Aspinall was visibly distraught for a long time afterwards. Not only was the personal disaster for the Stocks family, for himself, for Brian's colleagues at Howletts, difficult to bear when routine at the zoo had to continue, but an almost unblemished record for more than twenty-two years was finally and fatally compromised. The attacks on Robin Birley and the female model as well as Aspinall's own escape from one of his Himalayan bears had been dire omens which had caused him to hesitate, but his faith in the essential goodness of other species had not been shaken. Such faith would now more than ever be subject to critical scrutiny.

In accordance with a long-standing agreement with all the keepers that in the event of any accident the animal concerned should receive no blame, Aspinall did not kill Zeya. Yet he wondered how Brian Stocks came to be alone in the enclosure with Zeya and her cub, particularly since it had been he who gave the severest warnings of her character. It was inconceivable that he should have taken such a risk. There being no witnesses to the tragedy, no one would ever know how exactly it occurred, so no precise lessons could be learnt from it. They were to come a few weeks later.

Bob Wilson did not recover easily from the memory of his friend's death and decided that he must leave Howletts, at least for the time being, to work elsewhere. He told Aspinall of his decision, which was accepted without question. Aspinall then hired two new keepers in preparation for the reorganisation of staff on the cat section; these were Douglas Richardson and Billy Mathieson, both of whom had considerable experience with tigers at other zoos. They arrived in the second week of September and began working as assistants to Bob Wilson.

On 22 September, all three of them went to the tiger compound and set about the routine task of cleaning out Zeya's enclosure, which they did every two days and which would normally take about ten minutes. First they had to move Zeya out to an adjoining enclosure, which was not difficult and to which Zeya never objected. Her cub, now ten weeks old, was left behind in the first enclosure, as Bob Wilson and Billy Mathieson set about cleaning with bucket and spade. Doug Richardson remained at the entrance-gate to the compound, it being unnecessary for three people to accomplish such a mundane duty.

Suddenly, there was a sound of clanging. Zeya was attempting the impossible. She was clambering vertically up the internal chain-link fence, more than 10 feet high, which separated the two enclosures. As soon as Doug saw what was happening, he shouted, 'Bob, she's coming over!' Bob told Billy to 'Get out' and the two of them ran for their lives towards the gate, 50 feet away, Bob pushing Billy ahead of him. When Billy got to the gate he dived out head first, while Doug held it ready to slam shut as soon as Bob got through. Bob was barely 3 feet from the gate when Zeya leapt at him and pulled him down, then sank her canines into his neck. The others screamed for all they were worth and struck the tigress in frantic distress, but she would not loosen her grip on her victim, and dragged the body away by the neck to the pool, where she held it, head under water. The incident is best described in the vivid words of Billy Mathieson's statement to police:

I heard Bob call 'Get out' and I ran towards the door. I got through the door and turned and saw Bob on the ground with the tiger over him. The tiger shifted position and moved up to his neck, she bit him down into his neck from the back. Doug and I started shouting and screaming at the cat. Doug stepped in and hit her with a tool he was carrying [it was a pitch-fork]. The female lifted the body and carried it into the pool holding and gripping his neck all the while. I believe he was dead when he entered the pool. He appeared limp.

The grisly, efficient, murderous attack had taken only a few seconds from the moment Zeya began scaling the fence. It was scarcely believable that Fate could operate with such precise rapidity. Doug Richardson jumped on his bicycle and took thirty seconds to get to the mansion and raise the alarm. It was 11.45 in the morning. A tea-lady ran into the house. 'A tiger's got Bob,' she yelled, on the point of tears. John Aspinall biked down to the compound, where he saw Zeya still standing at the edge of the pool holding the obviously dead body of Bob Wilson under water. About three minutes had passed since the attack. He called to Jim Cronin to fetch a gun. Cronin ran both ways and returned with Aspinall's .303 with which he shot Zeya through the head at 11.58. Still, in death, the tigress held in her jaws the body of her victim. Aspinall and Cronin had to drag her out by the tail before they could release Bob from her grip.

It was too late for lessons to be grasped, and too tragic for recriminations. But certain conclusions could not be avoided. In the first place, Aspinall ought to have shot Zeya after she killed Brian Stocks one month earlier. The Siberian tigress was not one of those with whom keepers had a close affectionate relationship; indeed, she was the only one who was habitually aggressive, which was behaviour unheard of in the twenty-two years of tiger-breeding at Howletts. The pact which protected animals in the event of accident need not have applied in her case. Aspinall himself agreed with this assessment, and bitterly regretted that he had not shot her the first time. In the privacy of his study, he shook with distress over the fatal consequences of his own misjudgment. In the end, Bob Wilson's death was his responsibility, and he did not shirk the fearsome personal implications of culpability.

Second, Zeya was obviously not only a delinquent animal, but a treacherous one. Having found that humans were really quite helpless and that killing Brian Stocks was easy, she had become homicidal. She was not concerned about her cub in the smallest degree; she climbed the fence with intent to kill a human.

Third, the internal fence had been erected seventeen years

before, and it had never occurred to anyone that a tiger would or could scale it. There was no overhang as there was on external fences separating animals from public, but at 10 feet 2 inches it was higher than was thought necessary to deter a cat, and there was no record anywhere of a tiger attempting a feat such as Zeya had accomplished. In retrospect, the inexplicable fact of Stocks having been alone in the enclosure seemed to be solved. Zeya must have clambered over the fence on that occasion, too, although no one would ever know for certain. Henceforth long-accepted judgments on fencing would have to be reviewed, and not only at Howletts.

Fourth, Bob Wilson had made a cardinal error that was surprising in a keeper of his experience. He should not have run. Most of the keepers at Howletts would agree that the moment you turn and take flight, you become a prey object and can no longer be perceived by an unfriendly tiger as anything else. Once the predator/prey relationship is established, the speed of the tiger robs you of any chance whatever. Keepers are constantly aware of this danger and always face the animal squarely. Even in play it is as well not to run, except with a cub. Had Bob Wilson, Billy Mathieson and Doug Richardson faced Zeya when she came over the fence, the predator/prey relationship would have instantly evaporated, and she would have stopped. Tigers are intelligent, not stupid, and no tigress would take on three men. (Billy Singh, who knows tigers better than anyone in the world, independently confirmed this opinion when he wrote to Aspinall, 'the tigress would have backed down if all three had faced her'.)

This may be so in theory. No one can be surprised, however, that in the split-second that Zeya was seen to come over, mindful of her reputation and his friend's death, Bob Wilson made a dash for his life. To his credit, John Aspinall made no mention at the inquest of Bob's miscalculation in running (and to this day does not allude to it – other keepers hold the opinion, not him). He accepted full responsibility. 'I am prepared to be blamed,' he said; and later, 'If there's anyone to blame, it's got to be me for not realising about the fence.'

The outcry in newspapers of every hue soon made it clear that editors found Aspinall guilty on rather more counts than that. The *Spectator* devoted a leading editorial to the disasters at Howletts, attacking him for his absurd idea that a tiger could 'decide' whether or not to attack a human, and for his alleged preference for animals at the expense of humankind. 'The cult of the wild is a dangerous folly,' it stated. Aspinall had this to say in reply:

> Hubris seems to blind the writer to the common know-ledge that high mammals are quite as capable of taking decisions and that their behaviour is not merely confined to Pavlovian responses . . .
>
> I love my species and if I would wish to see a decline in our numbers, that is because I would like the human race to survive, along with the other great mammals, for as long as possible . . .

John Junor in the *Sunday Express* and Jean Rook in the *Daily Express* both launched petulant attacks, possibly scribbled in a few minutes with little reflection, and *The Times* printed a letter from Lady Medawar which berated Aspinall for the opposite transgression – he ought not to have shot the tigress at all!

For the first time, John Aspinall was known to the country at large not for his gambling, still less for his achievements in breeding, but for his misfortunes. A deluge of letters fell upon him, two-thirds of which were supportive and around a quarter critical of his decision to shoot Zeya. Fortunately, they were sifted by his trusted secretary, Susan Hunt, and his brother James Osborne, for about 10 per cent was 'hate mail' which he was not allowed to see. This batch of extra-ordinarily vituperative correspondence advised him to shoot himself, wished a cancer of the throat upon him, and called him 'scum', 'brainless', 'not fit to be in charge of a shit-house let alone a zoo'. Typical of many was a letter from Scotland which said; 'I presume you shot the tigress to protect your public image and the income from your zoo. So you now have three lives and an orphan cub on your conscience. I hope they weigh heavily. You don't bloody well deserve to sleep in peace again.' Aspinall was so upset by events that letters such as this would almost certainly have punctured his natural resilience in spite of their being written by evidently unstable people. The decision to keep them from him was a wise one.

He was encouraged by letters from Dian Fossey and Billy Singh, by unexpected support from the Parish Council of Bekesbourne, and by the views of strangers exhorting him not to be deflected from his unique and priceless work. More than any other testament Aspinall treasured the understanding of Bob Wilson's parents who, in the midst of their own sorrow, found cause to express their sympathy with his. To Mr and Mrs Wilson he wrote simply, 'I am moved and touched by the way you have stood by me in my hour of need.'

Any visitor to Howletts today is confronted soon after passing through the entrance turnstile by an eighteenth century well-head from which is suspended a bronze plaque commemorating Brian Stocks and Robert Wilson. Surrounding the inscription are the names of fourteen tigers of whom the two keepers were especially fond and to whose comfort and welfare they devoted their lives. The tiger compound beyond is likewise named in their honour. In the newsletter sent to Friends of Howletts and Port Lympne Aspinall wrote, 'What would have hurt Brian and Bob most would be if the tiger in general got a bad name through the errant nature of one animal.'

A man of deed as well as word, John Aspinall continued to make it his purpose that the tiger's pacific character be demonstrated in defiance of its ferocious reputation, and he shortly resumed his games with fully-grown trusted individuals who would leap upon his back and occasionally knock him to the ground. Thereupon the tigers would nuzzle his neck, purring, while he 'played dead'.

12

The Canterbury Trial

One of the first fruits of John Aspinall's visit to Gabon was a happy, one might even say an historic, exchange of gorillas. Having satisfied himself that the scientific purposes of the Primatology Centre were, in his eyes, innocuous, Aspinall was eager to co-operate in a venture which would prove beneficial to his colony, to the Centre, and to the gorillas themselves. There had never yet been a birth among the animals kept under observation in Gabon, hence they looked with some envy upon the successes at Howletts. Aspinall agreed to send out to Gabon an eleven-year-old breeding male named Toumbi.

When news of this intention was released to the press, *The Times* took the opportunity to question the much vaunted integrity of the Howletts ethic. The unfortunate Toumbi, it suggested, would be subjected to undignified research into human fertility, since it was well known that the Gabonese treated gorillas as vermin; it was a sorry fate for one of the Kentish clan. Aspinall rose to the awful insinuation with that mixture of indignation and charm which was his *forte*. In a letter to the editor, he said he was 'not the type of man to send a close personal friend to such a grisly rendezvous'. This cannot have been quite the rejoinder the journalist expected. Toumbi was sent by lorry to Paris, thence by air to Franceville, all at Aspinall's expense. He was accompanied by the gorilla keeper Richard Woods, who Aspinall additionally arranged should stay in Gabon for eighteen months to show the French something of the Howletts methods.

In exchange, Howletts received an infant female whose start in life had been harsh and whose future seemed brief and bleak. The baby was found in a small village near Akondja, three hours north of Franceville, by two French physicians who immediately alerted Bob Cooper, the veterinary surgeon in charge of the Primatology Centre. Cooper drove to the village and found 'a very weak, emaciated, dehydrated, louse-covered infant female gorilla no more than six months old'. She was in the care of an old woman who said she had been given to her a month previously by relations from the village of Tebi, since when she had been fed only on bananas! The old woman was reluctant to part with her, for the infant would eventually grow fat enough, she thought, to provide several wholesome meals. (It was still then legal in Gabon to kill gorillas for meat or as punishment for crop destruction.) However, she realised she was not having much success and the gorilla was near death, so she accepted a small amount of money for her. Cooper did not enquire what had been the fate of the mother; such enquiries invariably met with the reply that the mother had dropped and abandoned the infant, but Cooper well knew that no gorilla would behave in such a way. The mother had almost certainly been killed and eaten.

Having rescued the ailing creature, Cooper recognised that she not only needed proper diet, but to escape the consequences of her miserable life so far she needed to be properly socialised with other gorillas, 'and the opportunity to become so, afforded by the Howletts collection, is unparalleled anywhere else in captivity.' He sent a telegram to Aspinall, who immediately agreed to accept her. In memory of the presumed place of her birth, she was called 'Tebe'.

Before she could be welcomed in Kent, the Ministry had to be satisfied that the animal's mother had not been slaughtered as an excuse to import it. Dr Brambell, Chairman of the Advisory Committee on animals, was almost apologetic in having to raise the condition. 'Your gorilla breeding record is excellent', he wrote, 'and your colony is far superior to any other I know.' On the advice of Richard Woods, who reported on the case from Gabon, Dr Brambell was happy to declare his satisfaction. It only remained for Tebe to complete her obligatory period of quarantine.

A bedroom on the top floor of the mansion was converted into a gorilla den, with ropes and frames to climb, and Lady Sarah prepared to rear Tebe by hand. As it happened, she was lucky enough to have a companion from the beginning. Another female, Mushie, had recently given birth to Shumba, whom she treated somewhat erratically. Having cared for her baby for thirty days, she then lost interest in it, and on the thirty-third day she actually pulled Shumba from her nipple and prevented her suckling, despite eloquent cries of protest from the infant. In the late afternoon she buried the baby in the straw, placed a tyre and a piece of wood on top, and happily jumped up and down on the construction to the consternation of her keepers. The next day, when Mushie continued to bury Shumba under straw, it was decided the baby should be removed. So Shumba and Tebe were brought up together in a bedroom at Howletts by Lady Sarah.

Today both Shumba and Tebe are happily integrated into the gorilla colony. Tebe, in fact, is one of the finest animals in the collection, healthy and strong and blessed with a delightful personality which makes her agreeable company for both humans and gorillas, a far cry from her terrifying beginnings. Meanwhile, in Gabon, Toumbi bred successfully, and his progeny is still the only gorilla born in captivity in Africa. There was more cause for rejoicing when Lomie, the female on loan from London Zoo gave birth to an infant by Djoum, not only because this was Djoum's first paternity, but because the event had the most beneficent effect upon Lomie herself. She often placed the baby, called Jomie, on her back and allowed it to slide down into her hand. Her response to motherhood is best recorded in the words of her keeper, Peter Halliday. 'From the day of Jomie's birth', he wrote, 'Lomie's character changed dramatically, she ceased to be aggressive and argumentative and the whole colony seemed to notice.' Other gorillas who had until then threatened the luckless Lomie at every opportunity showed great interest in the baby and grunted their approval at its mother, a veritable volte-face in social conduct.

Peter Halliday was gradually earning universal respect as one of the finest gorilla keepers working today. His entire learning experience has been in the employ of John Aspinall. The son of a plumber in Whitstable, he came to Howletts in half-hearted fashion (having nothing else to do), but over the years his appreciation of the subtleties of character and varieties of personality among gorillas, as well as his dedication to their well-being, brought recognition from far beyond Kent. Halliday, who is married, does not envisage doing anything else; his commitment is for life.

It was ironic that Howletts should now enjoy such fame, and its owner such prestige, as to bring invitations to John Aspinall to deliver the kind of solemn academic 'papers' that he had disregarded all his life. One learned assembly that he could not resist was the Great Ape Conference at Hanover Zoological Gardens towards the end of 1982. In truth, he was privately flattered that he should be asked to address such a body, as his was the only unqualified voice among a chorus of 'experts', who were prepared to acknowledge they had something to learn from him. Aspinall's paper was given a suitably ponderous title by the organisers of the symposium: 'Some Aspects of Behaviour in the Howletts Gorilla Colony with Special Reference to the Reaction of Males to their Infant Progeny'.

Based on his own lengthy experience as well as copious notes taken by Peter Halliday, Aspinall concentrated on useful observations which were not easily obtained elsewhere, as that there existed a definite hierarchy among mothers which appeared to rub off on their children, 'status' thereby passing down matrilineally; that mothers and daughters spend much time practising the art of bed-making. Or that siblings betray no jealousy when a new baby arrives: 'having spent every night of their lives in their mother's arms they moved away without resentment from the first night of the births, and rested down adjacent to their mothers.' On the status of males born into the colony who must later establish their authority, Aspinall pointed out that this was a far from easy task. 'The mothers accept no god-given right of male over female and each step upwards has to be hardly won.'

The paper is packed with data of the comprehensible kind, and mercifully free of both jargon and statistical analysis. Very quickly, Aspinall makes clear that he has in mind much less an arid report than an up-to-date chat about his friends. He tells how the proud young male, Djoum, once fell 22 feet to land head first on a wooden platform, with a mighty thud, then leapt to his feet as if nothing had happened. There is indeed a whole central section to the paper which celebrates the progress of Djoum with the pride of a father whose son has just captained the school and become heavyweight champion of Middlesex; the voice could not belong to any other zoo-keeper. Having remarked that Djoum was astonishingly gentle in playing with his son Jomie, Aspinall continues:

> I am sure that Djoum loves his wife and children and I have no doubt in my mind that he would sacrifice his life for them if the occasion arose. Apart from his majestic personality and appearance he is the possessor of a rare courage. I have known him for 13 of his 14 years of life and have watched him grow from 12 to 408 lb. in weight . . . his females trust him and seem more relaxed in his company than those of Kisoro. His temperament is so stable that his two keepers and I play with him each week in the presence of his family . . . The great question was when Djoum reached full silver-backed adulthood and became a father, would he still remain gentle with us? The question has been answered in full. He is gentler and more playful now than he ever was.

So much, one may hear him thinking, for received opinion! Aspinall concludes with advice (for which, after all, he was summoned to Hanover) on prerequisites for successful breeding. These include housing and outdoor play-foraging area to accommodate a whole family of between ten and twenty apes; twenty bales of fresh straw a week; a roof equipped for brachiation; and at least a hundred types of food a year.

The sustained joy which simmers beneath such advice was evident in the third (and best) of Roy Deverell's films about Aspinall, *A Passion to Protect*, which was shown in the same year. Much praised by critics normally hostile to Aspinall's philosophy, this television documentary won the top prize at the Chicago International Film Festival and has since been seen by more millions than Aspinall could possibly hope to reach through publication or personal proselytising. It is significant that, realising this, he chose to do the commentary himself. One of the reasons the film is so successful is that Aspinall, like one of his gorillas, withholds his strength; his words are less strident than usual, calmer, more reflective, and all the more devastating for a restraint which cannot have come naturally to him. Another reason is, of course, the scarcely believable scenes of Aspinall having his eyelashes picked with exquisite delicacy by the vast and mighty gorilla, Djoum; Aspinall having dumped in his lap newly-born tiger cubs by the tired mother, who licks his cheek in gratitude; Aspinall surrounded by an ecstatic wolf-pack. There could be no more eloquent scenes than these to support the contention that at Howletts existed a kind of Kiplingesque harmony between keeper and kept. The film is intensely moving.

Aspinall's primary purpose is to alert the viewer to certain uncomfortable but important truths; this time, however, he jogs his audience into attention, he does not shock them. By this time well into his fifties, John Aspinall is a much mellower figure.

The first of these truths is the familiar one that mankind is the result of 'evolutionary miscarriage', that we have neither the competence nor the responsibility to use the planet for our own or any other creature's benefit. In contrast, the gorilla never went on a rampage against nature, destroying everything in sight, and the first explorers were astonished at the richness and variety of life in a gorilla-dominated forest. Similarly, untouched tiger country is full, verdant, vibrant, the tiger a responsible overlord who benefits the animals he preys upon.

The moral established, Aspinall then goes on to sing the virtues of emotional bonding with higher mammals. 'To reveal the true nature of these animals is my most exhilarating task.' The tiger, for example, has an unmatched capacity for loyalty and affection 'and an almost bottomless fund of good nature'. It is sad that no animal today has any 'rights', save those we are prepared to extend to them; they have no future, unless far-seeing zoos can breed them in sufficient numbers to protect the gene pool.

The timing of *A Passion to Protect* could hardly have been better, in so far as the film was able to capture the first-ever birth of an African elephant in the United Kingdom. Elephants are notoriously difficult, responding only to a keeper they have known all their lives, and even then fitfully. Bull elephants in particular are nearly impossible, so that zoos scarcely make the effort to deal with them. Of only six bull elephants in captivity in Britain, four were at Howletts and Port Lympne. Unending patience was needed if breeding were to be attempted, for the elephant did not reach breeding age until fourteen years. Therefore, to aim for an elephant birth was no frivolous endeavour, undertaken for amusement or fame, but a long-term, expensive and uncertain gamble. When Sabi was born, and her first steps recorded on this remarkable film, the event was the first dividend of a ten-year programme. It was also, of course, cause of considerable rejoicing.

Ernst Lang came from Basle to appear before camera and to advise on the transportation of the Indian elephants from Howletts to their expansive new home at Port Lympne. Aspinall's zoos, he said, were built entirely for the animals and their welfare, which made them virtually unique. As for the African elephant, the birth of Sabi was of crucial importance, showing that breeding was after all possible in captive conditions; without this knowledge, said Dr Lang, there could be no hope of saving the African elephant from premature extinction.

Roy Deverell's film also gave Aspinall his first chance to address the world directly since the deaths of Brian Stocks and Bob Wilson, and there was some curiosity as to how he would deal with these setbacks. He did so with the succinct avowal that they had not diminished his faith in the character of the tiger. There was no defiance, no braggadocio, no flamboyance. Quite clearly, he would not allow tragedy to deflect him from what had amounted to a personal crusade against the vilification of wildlife.

And yet, in the closing frames of *A Passion to Protect* are the first signs of real pessimism, the first glimpse of a possible surrender to the inevitable. It is a new Aspinall who can say that 'the general trend is against us' and that the pressure upon wild animals was too great to resist. At fifty-six the will to fight was not so strong in his breast at it had been at twenty-six and a note of despondency was for the first time allowed to dominate the closing words. Also, a note of humility. Talking of the future of wildlife, John Aspinall could not mention his contribution without interposing the qualification 'if any'.

Shortly afterwards, he received the news that he was to be prosecuted by the Ministry of Agriculture, Fisheries and Food, Health and Safety Department, for infringements against the Health and Safety at Work Act, 1974. The gravamen of the charges levied was that professional negligence had contributed towards the deaths of Brian Stocks and Bob Wilson. The case would be heard in Canterbury in 1983.

In the meantime, Aspinall was engaged on the one final gamble which might ensure the continuation of his vision after his death. He had behaved for thirty-five years as if he were a rich man. He had spent lavishly, entertained outrageously, given generously, but it had all been done with the gambler's dexterity. Borrowing, juggling with creditors, leap-frogging with debts had enabled him through good years and bad not only to keep the zoos going but constantly to expand their potential. With escalating costs they had reached the point where their chances of survival would be slim if they were to depend solely upon his assets. The idea that the zoos might be forced to close and the animals be dispersed when he was no longer the fount of all resources was acutely painful and would make a mockery of his dream, reducing it to the ephemeral achievement of one lifetime. Besides which, such an outcome would let down the animals whose continued welfare had become the ruling passion of his life. He could not abandon his friends in this way.

It was essential that the zoos be endowed for an indefinite future, and for this Aspinall would need to be seriously rich for the first time. His gambling instincts must finally be contained in favour of old-fashioned bourgeois planning.

At the beginning, of course, the zoos were merely a group of animals in the garden of a private house. As the collection grew it remained for an astonishing time (nearly twenty years) the private property of one man, paid for out of that man's taxable income. With the purchase of Port Lympne in 1973, the lean years that followed, and the opening of Aspinall's Club in Hans Place in 1978, this cosy state of affairs could not continue. Howletts and Port Lympne Estates Ltd had been set up, and was now wholly owned by Aspinall's Club, so that the increasing costs of feeding, housing and servicing the animals were borne by the Club and set against profits from gambling. The Club also owned the house in London, 1 Lyall Street. The virtue of this arrangement was that the operating costs of the zoos no longer came from private income, but from punters' folly; on the other hand, John Aspinall himself no longer owned anything.

There then followed a complex series of events and negotiations which completely altered the perspective. In the first place, the profits of Aspinall's Club were looking rosier each year. Since the granting of the original licence in 1978, profits had risen from £732,000 to £1.5 million in the second year, nearly £3 million in the third year, and well over £8 million in the fourth. The anticipated operating profit in the year to come was in the region of £12 million.

Incidentally, no one quite knows how these profits are made against all mathematical logic, either in Aspinall's Club or in any other casino. The 'drop', which is the value of gambling chips purchased and the best indicator of volume of business, bears only a superficial relationship to the profit. It has been precisely calculated that the casino *must* make a win on roulette, for example, of 2.67 per cent of the drop; in fact, every casino expects to make between 19 per cent and 21 per cent, and invariably does. Again, according to averages, ratios, the mathematics of chance and so on, profit from blackjack is less than 1 per cent of the drop; historically, however, it exceeds 20 per cent. Even the Gaming Board is mystified by this incongruity, but has become resigned to it.

Another measurement of the success of Little Aspinall's then, should be the drop. This had risen from £26 million in the first year to nearly £80 million. As there were nineteen casinos in Greater London with a total drop of £893 million, this meant that Aspinall's Club took nearly 10 per cent of the drop for the whole city, although, being one among nineteen and on very small premises, it should expect to have a share far less than 5 per cent. Put another way, it took three times the drop of any other single gaming house. The upshot of all this was that Aspinall's Club was doing very well indeed. The reader will recall that Sir James Goldsmith had put up £625,000 in 1978 in return for convertible loan stock; John Aspinall himself had put up virtually nothing, yet he was now sole owner of ordinary shares with a business which could be converted into cash. There were two ways of doing this. The first to be considered was to sell the club altogether for a handsome sum, thereby releasing Aspinall to his second retirement. The second plan was to seek larger premises and then offer a percentage of shares to the public through flotation on the Stock Market.

Once more through a sequence of fortunate coincidences it was the second plan which was adopted. The Curzon House Club in Curzon Street, owned and operated by Corals, had fallen victim to the Gaming Board's more vigilant application of rules and had lost its licence before the local magistrates (application for renewal of gaming licences must be made annually). Corals appealed against the decision and lost. They had no alternative but to sell their casinos, which were little more than empty houses without the licence to use the furnishings for their obvious purpose. The Curzon House Club seemed therefore the most colossal white elephant, a guaranteed drain with no compensating income – to everyone, that is, except John Aspinall.

Aspinall was attracted by the house in Curzon Street not only because of its size and architectural distinction, not only because it was in the heart of fashionable Mayfair, but also, coincidentally, because it had once been the ancestral home of the Earls Howe. His wife Sally was a daughter of the 5th Earl Howe. To buy Curzon Street would be like going home.

Aspinall bought the freehold property for the knock-down price of £2.85 million and determined to keep it in repair, redecorate it entirely, and sit tight until the licence to use the premises for the purposes of gaming was re-granted.* He was not to know that the process would take three years and involve many costly hearings in court but, had he known, he would have been unlikely to surrender his ambitions even so. The plan injected him with new vigour and renewed eagerness for the fight.

With excellent new premises, a splendid record of profit in Hans Place, and the justified expectation of a gaming licence, Aspinall's business ventures appeared a juicy plum to offer the public. In anticipation of the flotation (and as a condition of it), John Aspinall himself bought back the zoos from the club, thus making them once more a private enterprise. This was gambling with real nerve, for he could not possibly afford to buy the zoos (he had borrowed the money in the meantime), or maintain them, without the flotation of the new company, Aspinall Holdings plc, and the flotation would not be successful enough to give him the profit he needed to implement these plans unless the gaming licence were granted. It was a perfect circle, the carts and the horses following and preceding one another *ad infinitum*. In a

---

*To be precise of course, it was Aspinall's Club which bought the Curzon House premises, but the decision and, as usual, the foresight, were John Aspinall's.

very real sense, the future of Howletts and Port Lympne, of Djoum and his colony of gorillas, of the elephant calves, the wild horses, and the five hundred other animals who looked to Aspinall for their survival, depended upon the discreet and decorous magistrates of Mayfair.

Typically, Aspinall decided to make no secret of this but rather to trumpet it; at least the magistrates would be unlikely ever to hear a similar justification for gambling. The sequence of hearings is complicated, and the methods adopted by Aspinall are best illustrated by a summary. The first application failed, because he was unable to satisfy one of the two main conditions, namely that there was an unstimulated demand for a gaming house in Mayfair. Not surprisingly, the Gaming Board said there were quite enough already, which on the face of it appeared glaringly obvious. The second requirement, that Aspinall and his fellow directors were fit and proper persons, was, however, readily accepted by the Gaming Board.

Objections were raised by the Mayfair Residents' Association, but since they habitually objected to everything, the court did not pay more than token attention to their remarks. Aspinall, on the other hand, did: the Chairman of the Mayfair Residents' Association suddenly found himself invited to dinner, to sit in on important discussions, to proffer his advice.

Aspinall also heard that Corals had used a small room upstairs in Curzon House for afternoon bridge and that this facility had been much missed by little old ladies with nothing to do. He submitted plans at the next hearing (his appeal against the refusal) to show how this valuable service to the community would be reintroduced, and called some elegantly-dressed and visibly elderly women to state in evidence how much they were looking forward to it. Aspinall also called some 'flash' witnesses, impressively grand gamblers who charmed the magistrates. Not content to announce his plans for renovation at Curzon House, he brought along large samples of curtains, luxurious carpets, upholstery fabric, wallpaper, and a beautiful watercolour impression of how the finished house would look, so turning the courtroom into

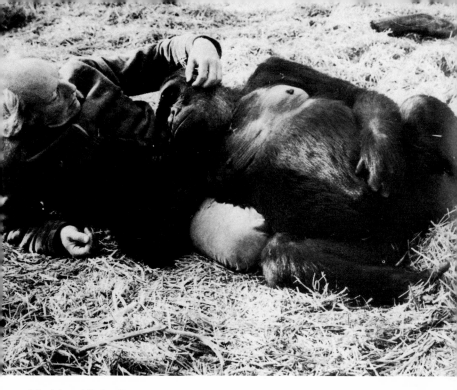

26 *(above)* Relaxing

27 *(below)* Greeting

28 *(above)* Aspinall with Juju and Kijo

29 *(below)* The author with Djala

30 *(above)* A mock attack by a group of one-year-old Indian tigers

31 *(below)* Aspinall with the silverback male, Djoum

32 A bond of trust

a rather exciting bazaar. The magistrates almost felt they were being consulted. There could be no doubt, at the very least, that Curzon House would boast a degree of elegance which other chrome-plated clubs would never be able to match, and the Mayfair magistrates would have contributed to this historic revival. The architect to be consulted was again Philip Jebb, the decorator this time David Mlinaric. By far the most effective witness was John Aspinall himself, who spoke with conviction and ardour of his love of animals, making it abundantly clear, for the second time, that the only reason he wanted to expand his gambling activities was to protect and feed them. The licence was duly granted.

That was not the end of the matter, however, because the Gaming Board appealed against the decision, the first (and last) time they have ever exercised this right. Quite why they were opposed to Aspinall to such a dramatic extent is not clear, unless it be that he was the only survivor from the early days immediately after the Gaming Act of 1968, that so much legislation had been introduced in direct response to his activities, and that he had never once been accused of any infringements.

The Gaming Board took the case to the Crown Court before Mr Justice Friend. Though Aspinall argued vigorously, he lost the appeal, and the future was placed in very precarious abeyance. More than £4 million was in the process of being lavished on Curzon Street, with, as yet, no certain prospect that it would serve any purpose whatever.

When Aspinall lost a further hearing at the Divisional Court, he decided on advice from lawyers to make an entirely new application, namely that his existing licence to operate the club in Hans Place, which had been granted for four years without any objection being raised, be transferred to Curzon Street, and that Hans Place be closed. By this time, the magistrates were almost palpably biased in his favour and gave the impression they felt he had been hard done by. Aspinall's application was the last out of eight to be heard that day, and might be thought to have had odds stacked against it for that reason alone, as there was a reasonable limit to the number of licences which could be granted. Counsel suggested that all eight should be heard simultaneously. The Chairman of the Justices, refusing the request, said, 'I give you my word that your application will not be influenced by any others granted in advance of it.' It may also have been noticed that while the Gaming Board still objected to Aspinall, they made no objection to the other seven.

The magistrates duly granted the licence for Aspinall's Curzon Club and actually improved it, for they gave permission for eleven gaming tables at the new club, practically double the six tables which existed at the old. 'You have every reason to feel aggrieved,' Aspinall was told. The Gaming Board made no appeal.

All was now set for the flotation of Aspinall Holdings plc. Aspinall himself would retain just over 40 per cent of the shares, Sir James Goldsmith an equal amount and the remainder of almost 20 per cent was offered on the Unlisted Shares Market at 115p per share, with a market capitalisation of between £5 and £6 million (the value of the whole company was £60 million). Whether it was Goldsmith's fame, or Aspinall's eccentricity, or the latent sniff of gambling among city gentlemen, Aspinall Holdings was besieged by an avalanche of investors who applied for fifty-seven times the volume of shares available. In the whole history of the Stock Exchange only one other new issue had been oversubscribed to this extent.

Aspinall was thus enabled to complete his purchase of the zoos (i.e. of Howletts and Port Lympne Estates Ltd), the entire shareholding of which came back to him. He also bought back the house in Lyall Street, a flat in Bina Gardens where his daughter Amanda was living, and the flat in Sloane Street occupied by his mother Lady O., all out of the 20 per cent shareholding sold to the public. Because the price had been topped by a premium, Aspinall's personal gain from the sale was nearly £20 million, representing the first real wealth he had ever known. Of this £1 million was used to set up a trust for his three children, Amanda, Damian and Bassa, and for his half-brother James Osborne. The rest would be for the exclusive use of the animals.

The last act was to turn the zoos into a charity. The Inland Revenue took the sensible view that neither Howletts nor Port Lympne would ever make a profit, and now that they were privately owned once again, their losses were not available for tax relief purposes. There was only one way to fund the zoo losses of well over £1 million a year without the sums coming from Aspinall's taxed income. Hence the establishment of the charitable foundation which swallowed the whole of the remainder of John Aspinall's personal gain from the flotation of his company, some £18.5 million. The objectives of the charity were to preserve rare species and to educate the public. There was never a more overt display of proof that John Aspinall was in earnest, that he meant what he said. The charity was thenceforward able to fund the zoo losses as an appropriate expenditure of charitable funds, subject to the approval of trustees. These were, by the way (and still are), John Victor Aspinall, Sir James Goldsmith, the Marquess of Londonderry, the international businessman Selim Zilkha, Simon Fraser and James Osborne.

Aspinall's name came up in the House of Commons again later that year. In a debate on the Zoo Licensing Bill, introduced by John Blackburn MP, and given an unopposed second reading with full government backing, David Crouch, the Member for Canterbury, opened his remarks with an enigmatic reference to a rare species which dwelt in his constituency; it was, he said, bred in Mayfair but had developed and matured in Kent, and it was a species of *Homo sapiens* called the Aspinall species. After giving fulsome praise for Aspinall, in every way a 'remarkable' man, Crouch none the less drew the government's attention to the deaths of Brian Stocks and Bob Wilson at Howletts as well as a number of escapes from the estate over the years. In reply, the under-secretary at the Ministry of the Environment, Hector Munro, said that the 'sad events' at Howletts had been exceptional and did not reflect upon the zoo world in general. Moreover, the

Ministry intended to prosecute the zoo at Howletts under health and safety laws. Thus was the stage set for the most sustained bombardment of publicity John Aspinall had ever received.

The case came up before Judge Giles Rook QC at Canterbury Crown Court in July 1983. The indictment brought by Peter Bishop, HM Agricultural Inspector with the Health and Safety Executive, read that,

> you, being an employer within the meaning of the Health and Safety at Work Act 1974, failed to discharge a duty imposed by Section 2(1) of the said Act, in that, on 21 August 1980 you caused and permitted Brian Stocks to enter alone the enclosure of Zeya, a Siberian tigress, although she was in that enclosure, or separated from it by a fence of inadequate design and height, and failed to take sufficient or any steps to ensure that he did not do so, contrary to Section 33 of the said Act.

Aspinall was keenly aware of the dire implications of a guilty verdict, and of the suppressed delight which it would afford some sections of the zoological establishment. Not only was there no limit on the penalty which the Crown Court could impose, but a guilty verdict might invite applications for damages from at least one of the families of the dead keepers. There might be no recovery from financial consequences of such magnitude, forcing the zoos to close. Furthermore, Aspinall's philosophy and approach would be scrutinised under attack, and he would be expected to justify both. While he was, as ever, quite ready to do so, his congenital assumption of conspiracy led him to suspect that the ultimate purpose was to put an end to his dream. Although the indictment was brought against Howletts and Port Lympne Estates Ltd, Aspinall knew that it was he who was on trial.

The two points at issue were whether or not he should have killed Zeya after her first attack on Stocks, and whether or not the internal dividing fences were high enough. On either count he could be held negligent of human life.

The corollary of the first accusation is that the tigress should be held to blame for what she did and that Aspinall should have punished her with death. This strangely anthropomorphic view of the moral code which wild animals must be expected to obey is deeply ingrained and, it must be said, absurdly arrogant. The idea that animals must be held to account for their actions dates from the Middle Ages, perhaps earlier. In 1546 the French Parliament ordered the execution of a cow, which was duly hanged and then burnt at the stake in the manner of a devil's disciple. Even within the present century, in 1906, a Swiss man and his son, accompanied by their dog, robbed and killed a householder; the two men were sentenced to life imprisonment, but the dog was condemned to death because the court decreed that the crime would not have been committed without the animal's complicity.

Hundreds of similar cases may be found in the annals, with beasts subjected to the same capital punishment as humans. They were hanged or beheaded and occasionally, in mute recognition of the subterranean powers at work, were dressed in human clothes for their execution. Nor was homicide the only crime for which animals stood trial. In Germany an innkeeper's dog bit the leg of a town councillor. The innkeeper was first imprisoned, then released by the judge who decided that the real culprit should pay his dues to society; the dog was sent to prison for a year, sharing his cell with two human inmates. In Russia a goat who butted an official as he was fastening his shoe-lace was banished to Siberia.

The idea that Zeya should have been executed for her first crime was not far removed from these idiocies, but it ran counter to enlightened practice in twentieth-century zoos where fatalities among keepers were a regular hazard (even domestic animals, after ten thousand years of guided selected breeding for docility, kill seven or eight farm-hands a year in Britain alone). Aspinall assembled an array of evidence to support his contention that the life of a tigress is not normally forfeited for homicide.

In 1981, a member of the public jumped into the lions' den at Los Angeles Zoo, was killed and partially eaten. Nothing was done to the lions. In Washington, DC, another lion ripped the head off a girl being held up to the cage by her grandfather. The grandfather immediately dropped dead of a heart attack, but nothing happened to the lion. An intruder made his way into the lion enclosure at Portland, Oregon, and was killed. The authorities did not punish the lion, but some of the intruder's friends came back the following night and shot it. A girl's parents allowed her to crawl under two fences into the elephant enclosure in Madison, Wisconsin, then watched her being crushed to death. The elephant is still there. Cassowaries, giraffes and snakes have all been known to kill zoo-keepers without any of them being slaughtered as a result. It is noticeable, too, that all these examples occurred in the United States of America, where the sanctity of human life is held in greatest awe and where one might more readily anticipate a spirit of retribution. Counsel would therefore submit that Aspinall behaved with perfect propriety in not shooting Zeya after the death of Brian Stocks and could not be held negligent on that account.

Warren Thomas, director of the Los Angeles Zoo, wrote to say that the blame must be turned to the keeper rather than the kept, and that the idea of destroying the animal was wholly and totally unjustified. Warren Iliffe of the Dallas Zoo said that a chimpanzee had bitten off two-thirds of his middle finger; 'he was far more surprised than I was, and much sorrier'.

The other question related to the height of the internal fence. In Alberta, Canada, the fence which had stood for twenty years was 10 feet 2 inches high. There had been no incidence of animals leaping over it. In Nairobi, the fences were 6 feet 9 inches high, with no overhang, and had proved satisfactory. In short, there was no record of a tiger ever leaping a fence anywhere near as high as the one at Howletts, nearly 11 feet, and no experienced zoo-keeper would ever have thought it possible. Zeya's feat was unique; it could not have been foreseen. Nicolas Marx, one of the Howletts tiger-keepers, said he thought it far more likely a tiger might try to rush through the fence than clamber over it. The one dissenting voice came from Professor Doctor Dittrich of Hanover Zoo. While agreeing with the ethical point that no animal, not even an anthropoid ape, has the consciousness to do right or wrong, he thought the interior fences should reach at least 5 metres, and with overhang.

Graham Dangerfield of the Wildlife Breeding Centre ventured a wholly novel interpretation of events, in a written deposition. Forget about fences and overhangs, he said; Brian Stocks was depressed and the tigress noticed. Angry at Brian's death, Bob Wilson beat her in anger. The tigress remembered; Wilson was a marked man. Dangerfield was not called to give evidence.

Those who were called kept the trial going for a week. Prosecution, led by Mr John Reide, made much of the fact that there were no written safety codes to be followed by all employees at Howletts, and that it was a 'golden rule' one never separated a big cat from her cub. Under cross-examination, Aspinall disputed this with some scorn (causing his own counsel a moment of anxiety), and said that the adherents of such golden rules probably fed the tigers with milk-bottles and otherwise treated them like dog-pets. He volunteered the information that he still visited his tigers, 'to reacquaint myself with them, to see them, feel them and play with them'.

Defending, John Matthew QC maintained that the prosecution case was based entirely on hindsight. 'We know in the particular circumstances that prevailed on that unfortunate day that the fence was inadequate because Zeya got over it and killed.' The important point was that the fence had been constructed on the best, most professional advice and was considered more than sufficient deterrent. In his own defence, Aspinall advanced the new information that Brian Stocks had been trying to say something just before he died; he thought the keeper was probably about to warn him that Zeya was capable of jumping unheard-of heights, and that such knowledge would have saved Bob Wilson.

In his summing-up, Judge Giles Rook QC told the jury it would be perilous to convict when there were no witnesses to the death of Brian Stocks. Nobody knew for certain if he went into the enclosure alone with the tigress, or if she had jumped. Further, the jury must dismiss from their minds any sentimentality about animals or opinions as to their nature; in this regard the defendants were 'blinkered by the wisdom of their own conceits'. The sole issue in the case was the safety of an employee. The jury was out for nearly four hours before returning a verdict of 'Not Guilty'.

The relief of the entire Howletts staff was palpable. Aspinall himself was freed from *sub judice* restraints against comment, which he undeniably found irksome, and spoke at length to reporters about his own feelings. Two points he specifically wanted to make. He had been shocked and distressed by the keepers' deaths. 'The cats loved Brian and they miss him,' he said. 'I also miss him a great deal. He was a great keeper and a fantastic friend. His death left me thunderstruck.' To another reporter he said, 'I feel responsible for the deaths but I don't feel guilty about them. They were good, loyal people doing their duty.'

The view of Peter Karsten, Director of Calgary Zoo, made a fitting epilogue to the trial. 'To live and work with these animals is our choice,' he wrote. 'It harbours known risks . . . the aftermath of a fatal car accident is not to destroy the car.' Someone else pointed out the relevance of George Bernard Shaw's dictum, 'When a man wants to murder a tiger he calls it sport but when a tiger wants to murder him he calls it ferocity.'

Some time later, Aspinall's insurance brokers paid £38,000 to the estate of Brian Stocks, for the benefit and education of his son. He had in addition supported Stocks's common-law wife and mother financially without the circus of press attention.

Aspinall was also worried by the proposed Zoo Licensing Act, which he ridiculed with some vehemence. It would do immense harm to zoos, he said. 'It will enable civil servants to exert absolute power over the owners. The whole Act has been dressed up in a veneer. People believe that it is for the benefit of animals, but only about 5 per cent is for the benefit of animals. The rest is for the benefit of the State . . . the case I've had hanging over me was instigated by civil servants who know little about zoos.'

This last remark is certainly justified. There arose an antipathy between the civil servants and John Aspinall as a result of this trial which would not abate; on their side it developed into unreasoning hostility, directed as much against his manner and confidence as his apparent ability to 'get away with it'. On his side, it fed on congenital contempt for people who make a living out of arranging and obeying rules. The only way to learn about animals and how to treat them is by experience. Most of the regulation–drafters had not been near a wild animal in their lives. Such people were to Aspinall narrow, prejudiced and stubborn. To them, Aspinall was arrogant, irresponsible and wilful. There was little possibility of compromise and the fires were merely stoked for a future confrontation.

On the other hand, Aspinall did not understand the proposals of the Zoo Licensing Bill until he asked lawyers to translate its arcane verbiage into colloquial language. He was too idle to make the attempt himself. 'I have given this Bill over to experts,' he told Jeremy Mallison of the Jersey Wildlife Park, 'to try and interpret the phraseology that our legislators love to use so that I can have some idea what it is all about.' Once it had been explained to him that he would thenceforth be obliged to submit to regular examinations, that every screw in every fence and every ounce of every feed would have to be in accordance with rules formulated in Whitehall, he declared that he would rather close the zoos to the public than permit outside interference. As usual, Aspinall knew what he was talking about, emotionally, and he was right, but he was incapable of that Machiavellian strategy of compromise which would enable him to have his way while appearing to concede it to others.

In the meantime, there was plenty to occupy his attention at the zoos. To his great chagrin, he lost his senior gorilla keeper, Richard Johnstone-Scott, enticed away by an offer from the famous zoo in Jersey. Not long afterwards,

Johnstone-Scott wrote to say, 'It's pathetic that to fully appreciate working for you I have first to leave.' The top position was taken by Peter Halliday, with whom he maintained some correspondence to keep abreast of developments at Howletts, referring often to the gorilla colony as his 'family'.

At the same time, the behaviour of Kisoro was causing some concern. Nine years had passed since his historic loan from Lincoln Park, Chicago, and two of his male offspring had been sent to Chicago (with Peter Halliday) in accordance with their agreement. Aspinall had since visited Chicago and had been touchingly welcomed by the two young males when he went into their enclosure. Now, two of the other males, Djoum and Mumbah, had reached silverback maturity, a fact which made Kisoro restless, resentful, and harmful to the females ('the women', as Aspinall put it in a letter). Reluctantly, it was decided the time had come for him to move elsewhere. To Lincoln Park he wrote,

> The great experiment we tried with Kisoro has now come to an end. You sent him over to us when he was badly needed and he has done his work and become world champion breeding male gorilla. We have had twelve births here from him, nine of which survived (two with you).

Kisoro went to Denver Zoo in Colorado on 5 October 1983. Peter Halliday travelled with him and stayed for three days. In Denver, where I saw him in 1986, he was placed with two females in a relatively small enclosure. He copulated with one of the females, but she did not conceive. He was moody and difficult, never accepting the keepers as friends but keeping them at a distance. They, of course, did not commune with him in the enclosure as had the keepers at Howletts, largely because city regulations forbade it. Kisoro died at Denver in October 1986.

In another development, Aspinall received an encouraging letter from the zoo in Columbus, Ohio. Melvin Dodge of the Columbus Recreation and Parks Department wrote, 'I am convinced that you are the world leader in breeding gorillas in captivity . . . If you would help us we would like to duplicate your facility here in Columbus, Ohio.' Aspinall sent Mumbah to Ohio, again with Peter Halliday, and advised on the practice of gorilla husbandry, with the happy consequence that today the gorilla enclosure there is named after him.

One particular incident may serve as a fitting epitaph to the unwelcome publicity of the Canterbury trial which had dominated this year. An Indian tigress, Zorra, was taken ill. She had difficulty in breathing and showed signs of general debility occasioned by her advanced age. Zorra had been one of triplets raised by Aspinall's second wife, Min, and the nanny to his children, Beryl, since when the tigress had lived happily in the Howletts enclosure and given birth a number of times. When he first noticed she was ill, Aspinall spent two nights sleeping beside her in her den, wrapped in a blanket with a flask of hot chocolate to sustain him. Zorra obviously welcomed the comfort, but did not improve.

Aspinall decided to consult his vet and zoo director Tom Begg with the words, 'Please take a look at dear old Zorra.' On observation, Begg thought a likely diagnosis was some form of pneumonia, but he suspected something else might be going on, which he could only discover with the aid of anaesthetic. This was of course dangerous, as it might well embarrass the breathing further, but he was of the opinion that the risk must be taken if any progress was to occur. He would need to examine her carefully. Aspinall agreed, but said, 'Only one incision. I've known her for twenty years and I don't want her cut up.'

Zorra was anaesthetised and examined, Begg making the gravest diagnosis. He found a lung tumour which he thought was probably malignant. He telephoned Aspinall and told him that she was in deep trouble. In his frank opinion, it would be kinder to put her down. 'If you must,' said Aspinall, 'but don't do it for ten minutes. I want to see her.' He then spent time alone with the ailing tigress, out of respect for her as much as to give expression to his own sadness. Over the years he had been with her countless hundreds of times, had watched her grow and had handled her cubs with her consent. Their mutual trust had been profound and touching to behold. He left the den manifestly distressed.

13
Julie and Djala

As John Aspinall approached the age of sixty he could reflect upon the direction his life had taken with no small satisfaction. The Curzon Club opened in 1984 with three consecutive evenings of lavish entertainment, the culmination of a gambling career which had begun nearly forty years earlier in the modest digs of Walton Street, Oxford, and which had forced a profound change in the law. After triumphs and calamities in such giddy succession as to drive any ordinary man to neurosis, Aspinall had finally made fortune enough to guarantee the future of his animal sanctuaries for a very long time (dependent though it was on the price of Aspinall stock). At Howletts, work was advanced on a new gorillarium, the third, which would be the Chatsworth of accommodation for captive gorillas, and Aspinall would soon have three entire breeding groups. Before long, he would be invited to address yet another assembly of experts, this time in San Diego, California, as his achievements were now widely recognised despite their unorthodox roots. The most ambitious scheme yet imagined, foolhardy even for Aspinall, would be launched in 1985 – the capture, rescue and long-term breeding of the extremely scarce Sumatran rhinoceros. If the first rhino could be welcomed at Port Lympne in time for Aspinall's sixtieth birthday, he would throw a gigantic party in joint celebration.

Still, events did not proceed as smoothly as this happy

summary might suggest and further setbacks were to
intervene to sour the celebrations. The African elephants
at Howletts were a source of especial pride; not content
with producing the first calf ever to be born in Britain, Masa
produced the second as well, the father of both being Bwana.
The second baby, Swana, was (and still is) a particular delight
– a frolicsome friendly infant who displays inordinate pleasure in the company of humans. It was all the more upsetting,
then, when Bwana began to show signs of deterioration. For
nearly six months the bull elephant did not lie down; once he
fell over and had to be picked up by a crane. He was moving
badly and was quite clearly in trouble. Eventually, Aspinall
consulted Tom Begg as to his condition, who gave the opinion that they could not long leave him in this state as he was
obviously in pain. It was decided that Bwana would have to
be put down. Aspinall decreed that this be achieved with
expedition and discretion, since many visitors to Howletts
had grown to know and love Bwana. He also said that he
would first like to spend a weekend with the elephant whom
he had known for fourteen years. A gigantic hole was dug in
the car park at Port Lympne, where Bwana, the only breeding African bull elephant in Britain, now lies.

The Indian elephants were kept at Port Lympne where
they had vast space and eventful days. It had always been
assumed that Indian bull elephants were less awkward guests
in captivity, since unlike the African variety they had been
domesticated for generations. It none the less remained true
that the bull was, even at his best, an unpredictable creature.
During the dangerous period of *musth*, when elephants weep
from the temples, experienced keepers maintain a sensible
distance from the afflicted bull (if indeed *musth* be an affliction
– nobody knows). Whereas most animals who act alarmingly
are seeking safety by flight, establishing the greatest possible
distance between themselves and the human intruder, a bull
elephant will show symptoms of a fit for no apparent reason
at all, and for the briefest possible time.

The Indian bull elephant, Bindu, was well known and
well respected by Martin Smith and Mark Aitken, the joint

head keepers. He had not given cause for concern until early in 1984 when he was observed to behave roughly with the females, though not for long. By mischance, the whole group had to be shut in for five days at the beginning of April while building work was in progress on the yard outside. The first day of their release once more into the open air, both keepers helped to contain the general excitement. On the second day, Mark Aitken was on duty while Martin Smith had a day off. Working with Mark was a junior assistant.

Mark Aitken was a typical Howletts recruit, a regular visitor to the zoo since the age of ten and ambitious only to work with animals. When he joined the staff as a keeper he found his role in life. Mark lived in a cottage on the estate with his girlfriend, Julie Battersea, with whom he would spend many evening hours sitting on the grass bank overlooking the elephant paddock, watching his charges even when he was not working. He and Julie planned to marry soon, and she was happy to see him so evidently fulfilled in the work which he loved. The daughter of a police inspector, she intended to become a hairdresser and beautician. The zoo did not attract her in itself, and Aspinall scarcely noticed her.

Mark habitually left the house at 8 a.m., returning at 10.15 for the breakfast which Julie prepared. He then went back to the elephants at 11 a.m. On 7 April, Mark did not come home for breakfast. Julie assumed he had encountered a problem which kept him away and that she would see him at lunchtime. In fact, she never saw him again. One of the catkeepers, Terry Whittaker, an impressive man deeply committed to conservation, who was also the couple's closest friend, came instead to tell her Mark was dead. She begged to be taken to him, but Terry in his distress thought it better that she should not, lest the shock be made more acute by Mark's condition.

No one had witnessed Mark's death. He was outside the yard, which was surrounded by a strong fence of horizontal iron girders of the kind used in railway construction. He was about to go in, as he did routinely three times a day, to remove dung; Martin Smith said he had done this thousands

of times without the slightest hint of threat or irritation from
Bindu. Mark was heard to shout 'Bindu' loudly and sharply,
and when the assistant keeper went to investigate, two seconds later, he was lying dead by the fence. By his injuries it
seemed likely that Bindu had crushed him against the iron
girder in one sudden grip, and that Mark had died instantly.
Bindu was fifty times heavier than his keeper, a fact which
must always be kept in mind by anyone who has dealings
with these mighty animals. When an elephant decides to do
something, no human can stop him.

'Decide' is almost certainly the wrong verb to use in such
a circumstance. As John Aspinall wrote in a message to the
supporters of his zoo, 'an elephant of his age and experience
would know nothing of the concept of "killing" so he was
probably barely aware of what he was doing. A similar tan-
trum with another elephant even half his size would have left
no ill effects and inflicted no physical damage.' For the rest of
the day, and ever afterwards, Bindu behaved quite normally.
He is still a star attraction at Port Lympne.

Martin Smith's attitude towards the elephant underwent
a radical change and he never again could bring himself to
trust him. The notion that elephant behaviour is blameless
even when it results in tragedy was no comfort to a man
whose colleague had been snuffed out in a second. As for
Julie, whose future and mental equilibrium were crushed
along with Mark's bones, she descended into bleak numb
despair. At first she was embittered and angry because no one
appeared to be ready even to chastise Bindu. Her resentment
grew worse when she discovered Mark's diary, in which he
had noted two weeks earlier that Bindu was getting rough
and that he would need to keep a wary eye on him. That life
should continue at both zoos as if nothing had happened felt
like the deepest insult to her. Her life had changed irrevocably
between breakfast and lunch one Saturday in April, and she
wanted someone, anyone, to notice.

The reader will shortly hear Julie Battersea's subsequent
story. But her gradual emergence from grief and the totally
unexpected therapy she discovered to assuage it have to be

seen in their context, as an integral part of the Howletts influence and a vivid expression of its power.

Aspinall was so keenly alive to this influence and power that, by an odd paradox, he found the task of putting them into words progressively more difficult. They need to be experienced rather than described, as I have myself discovered. Yet description must be attempted if the experiment is to be understood. At the Primate Conference in San Diego in 1985, Aspinall delivered a paper which sought to answer his own question, 'Why has a poorly funded zoo in Kent owned by a part-time dilettante and supported by a cast of unqualified personnel made such satisfactory progress in gorilla husbandry?'

We already know that neither Aspinall nor his keepers can boast a degree in zoology, that on the contrary they would consider such a decoration as an impediment to their work. But poorly funded? Though the survival of the zoos has always depended upon the ability of John Aspinall to raise large sums of money with the deceptive regularity of an Aladdin, it is none the less true that neither Howletts nor Port Lympne has been blessed with financial encouragement from either central government or local municipalities. In contrast, the famous zoos of the world are nearly all supported by the taxpayer, and are thereby obliged to exist for the benefit of the taxpayer. Aspinall pointed out at San Diego that his zoos could not be counted equal to any of the top fifty in the United States if the measure of comparison were the level of financial resources. Howletts has grown to its present eminence on funding which most zoos would regard as risible.

It has also been free of the need to demonstrate a return on investment. Howletts is an enterprise which could only have been undertaken by a gambler indifferent to losses.

On the vexed and more important matter of contact between man and beast, Aspinall said that the keepers benefited from such contact because when they were with the animals they were acutely alive to all that was happening around them. Terry Whittaker is emphatic in his belief that going in with tigers is not done for fun, it is done to learn, and the keeper who is deprived of this contact must needs know less than the one who enjoys it as a regular event. Whittaker appreciates the privilege of working closely with other species but emphasises the privilege has to be worked for. It is not simply bestowed.

There were practical consequences of such close relationships which time and again had proven crucial to the animals. A three-year-old gorilla had once caught his neck between the bars, and his mother, Lomie, was trying to release him by pulling him the wrong way. Ian Williams rushed in and corrected Lomie's efforts. Peter Halliday was on another occasion able to cut the umbilical cord wrapped around a baby's neck before its mother, Juju, unwittingly strangled it at birth. In both cases, lives were saved because gorillas were accustomed to the approach of humans and made no objection to help offered; they might have panicked in a more orthodox zoo.

A further positive example of contact was afforded by the necessity of introducing a newly-arrived infant into the group. Aspinall told how keepers at Howletts do this gradually, presenting the strange gorilla first to one female, then to another, then to a young male, and finally into an already integrated family, in the manner of a trusted friend whose motives are not suspect. When animals and keepers are kept apart, the infant must either be abandoned to a solitary life in its own cage, which is not the point of a breeding colony, or be chucked in with fingers crossed, which is likely to court disaster.

Observation was also made easier by the establishment of trust, and Peter Halliday had been able to draw certain conclusions relating to gorilla behaviour which were valuable far beyond the confines of Howletts. He had noticed, for example, that a silverback took longer to assert his patriarchal status than he would in the wild state, since his first function, to protect the family from external threat and make all decisions concerning the family's well-being, was unfortunately redundant in the zoo. Even at Howletts, they are not able to pretend that the silverback must concentrate his energies on keeping the group out of harm's way. There was also the opportunity to observe the gorilla's essentially forgiving nature. A quarrel is always followed very shortly afterwards by conciliatory gestures, 'making up', which involves a great deal of back-patting, gurgling and embracing. The gorilla does not normally bear grudges. I have myself seen this need for *rapprochement* when a gorilla has given an ill-judged bite and I have retaliated with a cuff or sharp word. The virtually instant renewal of ties, expressed in much hugging, is no expression of remorse or submission, but a desire to 'return to normal' as it were, which carries with it an indescribable feeling of goodness.

That a gorilla should submit to his human companions is, of course, quite out of the question. As Aspinall put it, 'The gorillas have long ago rumbled that we are not as strong as we are tall,' and accordingly they withhold their strength when dealing with us. Since some of them are subtle enough even to know when humans are making remarks about them which may be unflattering, their good nature is a boon to be cherished.

All of which sounds sinister and suspicious to the denigrators of 'anthropomorphism' (or to use the equally ugly terms prevalent in the nineteenth century, 'zoophily' and 'philobrutism'). In San Diego as elsewhere, Aspinall slipped so easily into colloquial parlance when referring to his animals that he was thought by some to be not quite 'serious'. The desperate desire to be serious has led even some ethologists into craven avoidance of the obvious by using words like 'pain', 'fear', 'hunger' in quotation marks when speaking of animals; the quotation marks are a safety barrier to prevent the professors from being subjected to derision, for everyone knows this vocabulary should be reserved for human beings. In a journal called *The Advancement of Science* in 1952, R.J. Pumphrey pointed out that 'when the accurate and proper use of language has entrapped the zoologist into a statement that seems to him heretical, it is quite usual to hear him apologise for speaking teleologically, and he generally looks as sheepish and embarrassed about it as if his bedroom had been found full of empty whiskey bottles.' Hence he will prefer language which has been anaesthetised, saying that animals are photo-receptive to avoid saying they can see. To such idiotic circumlocutions has the fear of anthropomorphism reduced us.

John Aspinall has never known this fear, still less felt impelled to apologise for its absence. Without examining the concept of anthropomorphism in any organised philosophic way he has shown himself to be one of the greatest sinners in this regard, one of the firmest adherents to the principle that one understands animals by understanding oneself.

He says, for example, that animals do not yearn for the wide open spaces as we imagine them to. On the contrary, a zoo animal that is contented will consider himself a property owner more than a prisoner, if we must draw human parallels; his territory is a comfort, not a denial of something else. He further maintains that prolonged observation of animals enables one to posit by analogy their subjective experiences. This is not to treat animals as though they were humans, but to recognise that humans have inherited animal behaviour to a degree still not entirely appreciated.

It could hardly be otherwise. The capacity for sensation and emotion is primitive, predating the evolution of *Homo sapiens*. The similarity between man and animals is not only functional, but historical, and it would be an actual fallacy not to express one's observations anthropomorphically. The recognition of this inheritance is pre-eminently intuitive, and every zoo-keeper who lacks it is no more than a museum curator. John Aspinall's intuitive response to animals has been honed over the years to the point where some other zoo-keepers frankly believe that he should be studied with as much attention as the animals, so many are the windows he has opened.

The ultimate philosophy of Howletts, for which that Kentish mansion and its surroundings will be remembered, is that there is no barrier between primates save those which have been falsely erected by human pride. We must now return to the story of Julie Battersea, on the strict condition that none of what follows should be interpreted as simple sentimentality.

Julie was stunned by Mark Aitken's death as if she had been struck on the brow by a mallet. Her father drove to the cottage at Port Lympne and took her home, where she lay in bed for three whole weeks and would not eat. Nobody was willing to tell her the results of Mark's post-mortem examination, presumably to protect her from further hurt, so she went downstairs and read them in a newspaper report, which upset her even more. Death had been due to a broken neck and multiple rib injuries.

For the next six months Julie was hardly living at all. She suffered drastic loss of weight and was frequently sick for days on end. Occasionally she went to stay with friends among the other keepers, but they mistakenly thought it best not to allude to Mark's death, whereas she wanted to hear about it, wanted to know as much as she could learn. Their diffidence on the subject was an additional burden, though she well understood that it was difficult for them to talk about it for their own sakes as well as hers. She could not bring herself to enter the zoo during those six months, but would visit the cottage she had shared with Mark and sit there alone, remembering. Otherwise she did nothing, went nowhere, grew thinner.

Salvation arrived in the shape of a gorilla. A telephone call from Paris alerted Aspinall to the plight of an infant male, two and a half years old, called Albin. He had been found by the prospector of a mineral company in Djala, a village in the Congo, orphaned and miserable. The villagers were, as usual, waiting for him to grow fat enough for a meal, and in the meantime were teasing and torturing him; when the prospector came upon him, the villagers had tied him to a post and were using him as a dartboard. He was rescued in exchange for a small sum of money and taken to Brazzaville, where he was cared for by a Madame Leroy. As he grew larger, the gorilla became difficult to handle and Madame Leroy was at a loss what to do with him. Then, while on holiday in Paris, she watched by chance a film on television which was devoted to Howletts (it was the third of Roy Deverell's films, *A Passion to Protect*) and recognised at once that a permanent home might at last be possible for her small but intractable gorilla. Madame Leroy contacted the directory enquiries service and was shortly on the telephone to John Aspinall with her story.

Plans were immediately set in motion for the gorilla to be imported into England. His name was changed to Djala, after the village of his presumed birth, and the bedroom at the top of the mansion prepared to accommodate him for his six-month quarantine. He was hopping lame when he arrived, and Tom Begg diagnosed an arthritic condition, probably caught by infection rather than the traumatic or ageing variety. A large amount of fluid was removed from his knee joints. Djala would be restored to health at Howletts, it was hoped, in a relatively short time, but the damage to his mental well-being could only be reversed by sustained personal attention. Djala's confidence needed to be restored, and someone would have to spend all his waking hours with the gorilla in the months ahead, would literally have to live with him.

It was Mark Atwater, a junior keeper in the gorilla house, who first thought to suggest that the still-grieving Julie Battersea might be willing to undertake the task. He mentioned it to Peter Halliday, who told John Aspinall, and Julie was duly invited to look after Djala. Aspinall was in favour principally because Julie's maternal nature, currently frustrated and deadened, would be of enormous value to Djala; only secondarily did he consider the experience might also benefit her. She accepted without enthusiasm. Though she could still not bear the thought of people around her, she wondered whether the companionship of a gorilla might do her some good. She was entirely without experience.

Julie's new life consisted in being with Djala in a straw-filled room festooned with ropes and climbing equipment for eight hours every day. There was no room or time for any personal pursuits independent of the gorilla; total unselfish dedication to his future was required. At first, Julie found that her presence within the confines of the zoo, albeit in the house, was too difficult to bear. Every time she approached the place she thought of Mark. She was frequently ill and had to take days off; even when she was in good health, she feigned illness rather than face the gates of Howletts. Gradually, however, Djala became dependent on her, and she could not stay away in the knowledge that she was letting him down. She forced herself to turn up for duty.

As the months went by, Julie no longer had to fight with herself and no longer took days off. She did not consider that she was working for the zoo, and such an outcome was still intolerable to her, unthinkable. Yet she positively looked forward to her long hours alone with Djala. Frequently she would succumb to her grief and have a quiet weep with the gorilla. He in turn would hold her, hug her, comfort her. Where all else had failed, she came to acknowledge that Djala aided her recovery more than any words of condolence or sympathy, more than all the brave attempts of friends to edge her towards a normal life. 'I had so much to give', Julie said, 'and I gave it all totally without reserve to Djala and to no one else. People may say what they like, he became the main point of my life. Nothing else mattered.'

The gorilla naturally flourished under the sun of this undivided attention and was soon a vigorous and energetic youngster, despite the sporadic resurgence of his arthritis. Once his quarantine reached its term it became imperative that he should be introduced to others of his species in order to reduce the effect of imprinting which had inevitably ensued as a result of his being constantly in the company of a human female. Julie meant as much to Djala as he did to her. His steps towards independence had to be managed with delicacy and tact.

It was Julie who first opened the door to his room and instead of closing it behind her invited him to venture out into the corridor. Djala could not believe his luck. He ran into the bathroom, then into the kitchen, his chest puffed up, and repeatedly smacked with the open palm of his hands to produce the proud 'pok pok' sound so typical of gorillas who wish to give expression to their feelings. The chest-beating continued almost without interruption until Julie showed him the way downstairs. This was too much. He would not be so bold as to walk down, so Julie had to carry him and place him by the front door. When the door was opened, Djala held her hand insistently. He would not move without her. They went out together to explore the park. Djala bent down and touched the grass, wonderingly. He did not wander far from Julie's side and clung to her at the slightest strange sound, but he was obviously very excited by the adventure.

Shortly afterwards Djala had to meet the gorillas. The first time he saw them he did not like them at all. In fact, he was terrified. Julie took him in to show him to Tebe and Shumba, who were mildly curious but otherwise tolerant and calm. Djala puffed himself up and gave the gorilla bark, or cough, to show displeasure when the others went anywhere near Julie; he wanted them to leave her alone. When she left the enclosure for a while, he cried piteously for her to return. As the days went by, Djala grew used to his new companions, and would only weep for Julie in the evenings. The sense of loss worked in both directions. If Julie saw him playing with the other gorillas and apparently indifferent to her, she felt jealous.

Now, the period of rehabilitation is complete and Djala forms part of an embryonic group which will eventually reach the proportions of Djoum's family. He has no difficulty in viewing himself as a gorilla amongst gorillas and has accustomed himself to life without a surrogate mother. He is full of mischief and character, a lively and amusing companion. His attitude towards humans remains friendly, even affectionate. I first met him when he was incarcerated in his top-floor redoubt with Julie Battersea, and now regularly spend an hour or so with him whenever I visit, either sitting and contemplating, or indulging in some rough play. He is now large enough for me to respect his wishes and play when he wants to.

As for Julie, she subsequently accepted a post as assistant keeper of gorillas.

Two aspects of this story make it remarkable. On a personal level it is, to say the least, unexpected that an extremely pretty girl whose fiancé is killed in a zoo should find renewal of life within that zoo, and it must say something for the peculiar quality of Howletts that she was not tempted to nurse a lifelong hatred for the place. Secondly, and this is why the story is worth telling in some detail, that renewal was effected by the care of an animal. A gorilla is not and can never be a human's pet, in the manner of a dog. There is no symbiotic relationship between the species born of hundreds of generations of mutual dependence which, as it has the domestic animal, makes him subservient and obedient. Julie's experience with Djala was nothing less than a demonstration of that interspecific contact, at the deepest level, which the Howletts colony was founded to encourage. Supposed barriers melted away to reveal a communion of interest, the kindling of affection and the nurturing of optimism which were essential to both gorilla and human and of which they shared the beneficent effects. Each moved on to a life less concerned with the other, but that the bond was possible in the first place vindicates one of the most contentious tenets of John Aspinall's dream.

The other side of that dream, to protect species of mammal from the vicious and vulgar spread of humankind (what Aspinall called, slightly more decorously, 'the approaching avalanche of human biomass that is now sweeping away what is left of the natural world'), also received encouragement later that year. The breeding record at Howletts and Port Lympne was by now so spectacular that he could claim 95 per cent of his animals were reproducing regularly, no doubt because, genetically, they knew it was worthwhile. The latest success was with the black rhinoceroses, breeding faster than they were dying. Of twelve in the United Kingdom, six were at Port Lympne, three of them born there; no other British zoo could match success of this order. Emboldened, Aspinall was now able to launch his most ambitious project yet: the rescue of the poor, beleaguered, virtually unknown Sumatran rhinoceros (*Dicerorhinus sumatrensis*). The idea was typically reckless and romantic.

Of the five species of rhinoceros left in the world, one of the rarest is the Sumatran. It was first seen two hundred years ago and until recent times roamed the dense forests in Sumatra, Borneo, Thailand, Burma and Malaya. In the past thirty years the rhinoceros has entirely disappeared from Burma and Thailand, and its days in Sumatra are hideously numbered. Wars in Laos, Cambodia and Vietnam wiped out what was left of the species in those countries. There was only one in captivity when Aspinall first declared his intention, and that was a lone cow caught by accident, now residing in Malacca Zoo, Malaysia. In the nineteenth century there had been several specimens in zoos, and even some births had been recorded – two in Calcutta in 1889 and 1895, and one on board a steamer in London in 1972. As far as living memory was concerned, however, the animal was practically unknown, sliding rapidly into the category of the extinct. There was not even a photograph of one in the wild state.

It was known that the Sumatran rhinoceros was hairy, two-horned, small and russet-coloured, its thick and somewhat delicate skin overlapping in folds. It was rarely seen for a variety of reasons. First, it inhabited dense rain-forest almost impenetrable by man where visibility was barely 20 yards. Second, it was nocturnal and solitary, the bull and cow only meeting to copulate once every three or four years. A field study begun in 1973 involved observers hiding in trees day and night for three years without spotting one animal. Estimates of numbers surviving varied from over 500 to under 150, scattered in pockets of between 20 and 40 animals in different corners of Sumatra. All were agreed that it was one of the rarest animals in the world, so scarce that every individual mattered.

The rhinoceros was doomed on two counts. Enormous irreversible changes in the ecosystem of Sumatra were destroying its habitat at an alarming rate. Timber extraction was changing the face of an island once entirely covered by forest of one type or another, and the forests were also being cleared to facilitate access to areas thought suitable for palm-oil plantations. There was a grave risk there would be no forested districts left at all within a few years. As rains washed away the thin layer of humus, they left behind land unfit for cultivation, useless to wildlife and humans alike. Already a quarter of the island is barren.

Furthermore, the rhinoceros had always been prey to commercial advantage, every part of its body – horns, teeth, nails, even faeces – possessed of supposed magical or medicinal properties. Its shoulder-blade served as a cigarette-holder. Animals were customarily caught in spear-traps where they would die of internal injuries, often disappearing into the forest with the spears lodged in their backs. Other traps disembowelled them. Only half of those killed were actually caught, which meant that two animals died for each pair of horns to reach the market. Thai hunters exterminated the rhinoceros in their own country and in Burma in this manner.

As the female gave birth to only one calf at a time, which would then remain with its mother for eighteen months during which time no other calves were born, the rate of increase among the population could not possibly keep pace with its annihilation at the hands of its only predator, the human.

It was Francesco Nardelli, the curator at Howletts, who first alerted Aspinall to the imminent fate of this hairy rhinoceros. His plan to save it by founding a breeding colony at Port Lympne met with Aspinall's enthusiastic approval, and approaches to the International Union for the Conservation of Nature, to the Species Survival Commission, and to the Indonesian government, were immediately set in motion. The sheer glamour of the idea enticed Aspinall, and he relished the knowledge that he was probably the only man who could, if necessary, countenance the enormous cost involved without having to resort to committees and fund-raising. At a conference to consider the proposal, held in Singapore in 1984, the Howletts project was matched by a similar one from the United States, sponsored by a consortium of five large and powerful zoos. Both were approved in principle, but the American consortium was obliged to withdraw when it encountered difficulties with the Malaysian authorities. Aspinall was left as the lone champion of *Dicerorhinus sumatrensis*. The agreement between Aspinall and the Indonesian government was signed in the presence of the British ambassador and lauded as a most imaginative venture in keeping with the co-operation established by Prime Minister Margaret Thatcher. Aspinall was also free, unlike his American counterparts, to make handsome gifts of cash to the Indonesian Wildlife Department, which were written into the agreement.

The project would cost about £1.5 million with at most a 50 per cent chance of success. Only a seasoned gambler could possibly face such odds. The agreement stipulated that the first and fourth pair to be captured would go to Howletts, the second and third to a zoo in Jakarta; subsequent captures would be necessary to protect the gene pool of the eventual colony. The expense included building living quarters in the forest for Nardelli and other European assistants, employing local men, constructing humane equipment for the capture, and transporting animals across land and by air to England. Nardelli went to Sumatra in 1985, while the catchers prepared for a lonely sojourn in dank submontane forest for up to two years. The area chosen for the search was a doomed stretch on the north-east of the island called Torgamba.

Success came within the first year. Jimmy Shave, the senior rhino keeper, flew out to Sumatra when a bull rhinoceros, naturally named Torgamba, was caught in the spring of 1986, and he accompanied the animal on its flight to England after a few weeks of adjustment. Torgamba took up residence at Port Lympne in special quarters constructed with the essential wallow the animal needed to keep its skin healthy, free from parasites, cracks and inflammation. Having settled in remarkably quickly, he was much admired for his unusual hue and pleasant disposition. Aspinall's excitement could only be harnessed by a gigantic celebration, and thus took place the headiest party he had ever given, a lavish dinner to welcome Torgamba to his new home.

The dinner, at Port Lympne, was neatly contrived to mark Aspinall's sixtieth birthday as well, and Lady Sarah took charge of the detailed preparations with a personal zest. It was, however, evident from the elaborate invitation card (which alone cost £25 a copy to produce) and, later, from the complex reconstruction of a Sumatran rain-forest in Kent, that the real star of the occasion was the incongruous hairy rhinoceros munching happily half a mile from the festivities.

Five years previously Aspinall had given a Ball at Port Lympne for his daughter Amanda's coming-of-age, for which 5 acres of garden had been replanted by twenty gardeners; two marquees of specially designed printed fabric had been erected; and 10 kilos of caviare had been concealed inside a huge ice-bear. A touch of the eccentric had been added by the lines of Boy Scouts who lit the long drive up to the house with torches. Aspinall needed something spectacular to surpass this earlier event.

In the first place, he invited 450 people to dine, and booked all the hotels within a 30 mile radius to accommodate guests at his expense, it being assumed none would be fit to drive back to London, or would want to. Moreover, the hotel rooms were booked for two nights, enabling guests to extend their stay to a weekend if they felt inclined. A fleet of chauffeured Rolls-Royces was brought in to ferry guests from their various points of origin to Port Lympne. Between eight and nine o'clock on the evening of 6 July 1986, the roads of southern Kent were spattered with gleaming black cars converging on Sassoon's house from all directions.

As guests arrived, they alighted from their cars to the music of the Grenadier Guards, in bearskins, and began their long walk on special matting through the grounds. To their right, Siberian tigers peered nonchalantly; to their left, Canadian timber wolves fixed them with silver-grey eyes. The entire walk was festooned with lanterns and Sumatran artefacts, and lined on both sides with exotic jungle plants which had been flown in for the occasion. The walk ended with arrival at the top of the famous flight of York stone steps, 125 of them in steep descent through cascading gardens to the house.

Progress down the steps, slow for ladies in long dresses, was further hindered by the presence of a dozen dwarfs in gold lamé trousers and elaborate head-dress as high as themselves, whose instructions appeared to include hurling soft objects at *les invités*, plus twenty male and female dancers weaving between them with undulating gestures of welcome. At the foot stood John and Lady Sarah Aspinall to greet each guest and congratulate him on having survived the obstacles to his descent. One then passed to a champagne reception on the terrace (fortunately it was a warm evening).

Dinner was served in the garden, in a vast marquee around a stage where jugglers, sword-swallowers and acrobats cavorted beneath a ceiling of jungle vegetation. Fifty-six round tables accommodated the diners, who sat down to a meal of seemingly endless variety and fathomless sophistication, accompanied by the finest claret. After dinner, everyone repaired to a different terrace on the other side of the house where the full complement of the London Symphony Orchestra prepared to entertain with a confection of Smetana and Strauss. Robert Tear came on to sing some of Richard Tauber's most celebrated numbers. As there were not seats for 450 people in front of the terrace before this occasion, special cushions had been made for guests to recline upon as they listened. Aspinall intended to follow Robert Tear at the end of the concert and exercise his own vocal talents (it was hinted, to sing Hitler's favourite songs), but a slight shower of rain sent the musicians into panic, and they quite properly scuttled indoors with their valuable instruments.

By this time, the stage in the marquee had been cleared for dancing, to a twelve-piece dance orchestra imported from Palm Beach, Florida. Tables were also being laid for breakfast, to be served when the display of fireworks began.

To many, such extravagance might seem wasteful, a meretricious parade of unearned income. Needless to say, people attracted by such a view were not invited. Anyway, they would have missed the point. The party was in no sense a public relations exercise (and many of these cost as much without giving an equivalent degree of pleasure); it was not designed to win friends, influence people, raise funds. The press was not present. Every one of the 450 guests had something to do with Aspinall's unusual career. There was a table of old cronies from Oxford days; another table of architects; another of zoo people; more than one for gamblers; a collection of financial advisers; and many composed of friends gathered over the years. The total represented the dramatis personae of Aspinall's life from the age of twenty to sixty. They had been the décor of his existence, the spectators of his vertiginous rises and falls assembled in one place to pay homage to his influence upon their own lives. Ultimately, the evening was the most outrageous example of self-indulgence, of Aspinall giving a party for himself to which guests were invited as 'extras' to fill the scene. There is no doubt that it was Aspinall who derived the most pleasure from the event, that it was designed above all to gratify himself rather than his guests. There was a tangibly theatrical air to the proceedings, as if the party were Aspinall's art-form, his mode of self-expression. As he readily admitted, the element of self-aggrandisement could not be ignored; he saw himself as a chieftain enhancing his prestige with an elaborate demonstration of disinterested generosity. Sir James Goldsmith was correct in his observation that Aspinall was decidedly 'a man divorced from his *époque*'.

Historically, too, the Torgamba dinner was notable. Not since the days of Philip Sassoon himself, or of the amazing Grace Vanderbilt at Newport, Rhode Island, at the beginning of the century, had such indifference to cost been evident in the organisation of an evening's entertainment. The bill was not far short of £400,000.

Aspinall had an additional private reason for making this celebration hyperbolic. A few months earlier he had suffered a stroke, short in duration but severe in degree. Lying in a hospital bed where he had been sent for observation after weeks of increasing weariness, he was suddenly paralysed the whole length of one side. Totally conscious throughout the minutes that his infirmity lasted (and which seemed like hours), he had time to reflect on an uncertain future. Although he was not one to lament his condition, still less to broadcast it in search of sympathy, Aspinall was aware that the Feast of Torgamba could be the last pagan entertainment he would be able to offer. He made plans for another five years hence, the optimist once again triumphant over the realist, but he began quietly to tidy up, to ensure plans for the future were secure, to consult his conscience and look objectively on his life. A message he received in his hospital bed from Mark Birley terminated a twenty-year squabble; in his new mood, Aspinall welcomed this with true warmth.

His recovery was fast and, according to all evidence, total. Doctors advised that it would be unwise for him ever to seek the company of gorillas and tigers again, as such might encourage dangerous excitement, but they did not appreciate that an hour with Djoum or a visit to Putra had quite the opposite effect upon this uncommon man. The company of gorillas and tigers provided moments of tranquillity, of union with the deepest calm of Nature; they offered relaxation, not turmoil and tension. After two weeks of compliance Aspinall resumed regular visits to his beloved animals, and the doctors had perforce to acquiesce.

The gorillas, the elephants, the African rhinoceroses, all had taken many years to establish colonies before their security was confirmed by the advent of a new generation. There was reason to hope that the Sumatran rhinoceros project would in time rejoice in similar continuity. To save the creature would be the culmination of John Aspinall's outlandish ambitions, ambitions which twenty years earlier would have been deemed absurd, presumptuous, pretentious. Now he knew they were reasonably pitched, and he knew furthermore that though he himself had nebulous antecedents, which in his youth he had countered by reverence for pagan forebears, his legacy would be the protection of not merely his own descendants but the descendants of scores of species which might otherwise have perished. It was compensation on a Gargantuan scale.

The less personal and more conscious motives that have moved Aspinall have been expressed in language so intemperate as to attract strong criticism, even obloquy. He makes no apology for bluntness. He considers the twin concerns which have dictated his course – the headlong destruction of the planet's variety and the chronic unstoppable spread of *Homo sapiens* – to be so vitally important that they must not be disguised by circumspection. Certainly the evidence supports him. Over 350 known species have vanished as the direct result of human greed or foolishness. It is a sour irony to reflect that the annihilation of wildlife has actually accelerated as 'civilisation' has progressed and developed more efficient methods of destruction.

The European lion was wiped out early, around AD 80. Since then, many species, some more famous than others, have perished. We have all heard of the dodo. The great auk was another flightless bird, helpless and unresisting. It was slaughtered to extinction, the last two killed in 1844 *on purpose, because* they were the last two. Steller's sea cow, an intelligent and affectionate creature, was first spotted in 1741. Only twenty-seven years later, in 1768, it was completely obliterated.

The discovery of America was a misfortune as far as the health of the planet was concerned. The entire continent was rich and teeming with life. Pumas, tigers, wolves, elk, buffalo, passenger pigeons, parakeets, the list of what has been lost is wearisome and sad. In the seventeenth century there were deer in profusion in Carolina; today, the only deer to be seen have been imported to provide targets for hunters. The greatest triumph of marauding man was the decimation of the bison, once the most populous mammal of its size to exist. Herds stretched as far as the eye could see, for miles in every direction. They were shot, even from trains, just for the fun of it, and also to deprive the Indians of their source of food and hides. In the space of a few years they had declined from

60 million to just over three thousand. Human progress in the United States, as elsewhere, has been a contamination.

Humankind has done more ecological damage to the world in the twentieth century than in the entire pre-ceding period of recorded history. There is now a serious possibility that half the total number of species on earth will be extinguished by the year 2000, only twelve years from now.

The tropical rain-forests are in the process now of being obliterated. Over half have been destroyed in the last thirty years alone, and the rest are soon to follow. Why does it matter? The rain-forests are the richest biological commu-nity on earth, harbouring millions of species of which barely 3 per cent are known to man. They will disappear before we have had a chance to explore them properly. Thus even our own advantage is neglected by this wholesale rape. Forty per cent of all the drugs we use come from the wild, and there is every reason to assume that the rain-forests may conceal cures for human ailments as yet undiscovered. Primitive Indian tribes are familiar with the curative prop-erties of their habitat; civilised man is simply wiping the habitat from the face of the earth, it seems without thought.

With his powers of analysis and foresight, man ought to be aware of the implications of his acts, yet in this, his most important influence upon the world, he shows signs of wilful obtuseness. Once most of the other species have been eradicated, evolution will doubtless adapt, as it has in the past, to new situations, but our interference will oblige it to adapt with speed and in distorted directions. The biosphere will be altered irreversibly, that is certain, but it is not yet known at what point the intricate interweaving web of life will be disrupted so violently that evolution 'gives up' and surrenders the fight. Eric Eckholm has written, 'Humans appoint themselves as the ultimate arbiters of evolution and determine its future course on the basis of short-term considerations and a great deal of ignorance.' John Aspinall has said much the same thing on many occasions, but he is not a scientist and can safely be disparaged.

Aspinall has been criticised for his high-handed and contemptuous opinions on the arrogance of mankind. They do not sit well with a man who is hardly modest. All too easily he provokes a denigratory response. This is to confuse dislike for the man's manner with discomfort at the truth. There is no longer any doubt that the arrogance of our own species makes us inimical to real progress. John Aspinall's grasp of this is affective rather than intellectual. One of his heroes, George Schaller, has written in a vein which is prescient of Aspinall's approach:

> With the same mentality that once enabled man to vanquish the lion and the bear, he is trying to subdue nature, sacrificing the eternal for the expedient. The destruction of the earth lies at his whim and cunning, yet he does not realise, does not feel, that he is not separate from but one with plants and animals, rock and water. He is as dependent on them as the protozoan, the tsetse, and the gorilla. By setting himself apart from the ecological community man has become a tyrant of the earth, but a tyrant who surely will fall if he succeeds in winning the struggle for existence.

That is the nub. Aspinall does *feel* that he is at one with all life, he does *feel* that he and his fellow humans are not at all separate from the rest of existence, and he does contemplate the blindness of *Homo sapiens* with despair. It is this feeling which made Howletts possible, and which some zoologists are now imploring him to disseminate and to share. Perhaps it is only when we as a species can disregard the brain which is leading us astray and heed the profound realities of our emotional knowledge, that disaster may be averted. John Aspinall's contribution has been the single-minded display of his passion, the springs of which are mysterious even to him but which are undeniably fundamental to the human condition.

Passions are habitually expressed in passionate language,

and this causes Aspinall some undeserved problems. To call the human race 'vermin' or 'a curse' as he does, is to raise the spectre of extremism and lose a potential audience. This in spite of the fact that the human race is quite clearly verminous in pure objective terms, being the only species which does not control its numbers. The annihilation of one group of *Homo sapiens* by another group, attempted even in the twentieth century, is frankly trivial in comparison with the threat to entire species of mammal. But I would be foolish to say so if I wanted to convince an audience of my sane and level thought. Each interlocutor must be approached gingerly, and assumed to have inherited the usual baggage of prejudices in favour of the inherent superiority and infallibility of man. Aspinall has never possessed a hint of this diplomacy.

His opinions on population control offer an example. In a long interview with Polly Toynbee of the *Guardian*, Aspinall was quoted as saying he would be happy to see large numbers of humans exterminated, and that the death of 200 million in the event of nuclear war would not be enough. 'Statistically, in terms of real population reduction, it would mean nothing more than a slight temporary dip in the world's population. It wouldn't solve the problem.' (Many learned international reports draw the same conclusions; the number of humans now exceeds 5,000 million.)

He was likewise quoted as suggesting the population of the United Kingdom be reduced from 58 million to 18 million, and spoke 'glowingly' of euthanasia, abortion and infanticide. Animals, and wiser, more primitive peoples, do not allow their populations to get so out of hand. Why should we? 'I do not wish to live in a world where there are no wild animals,' he said, 'yet that is what we are heading for.' The article confirmed Aspinall's reputation as a wild man of the lunatic fringe on the Right of politics, a joke at best, an embarrassment at worst. Nevertheless, what he said was sound good sense; it was only how he said it that was schoolboyish, and made him appear an apocalyptic prankster. He wrote a letter to the Editor of the *Guardian*, in subdued tones, challenging Polly Toynbee's version of their conversation:

> When she quotes me as wishing to reduce the population of Britain from 58 million to about 18 million, she fails to add that I suggested a period of about 200 years or more for the adjustment, by discouraging excess breeding through fiscal and other means. This does not seem too extreme a policy to me as the population of this country, only a thousand years ago, was a mere two and a half million.

Quite so. But no friend of Aspinall's can really doubt the essential truth of Miss Toynbee's impression, which accurately mirrors his ebullience and excitement in speech.

The notion that mankind will proliferate *ad infinitum*, conquer and colonise other planets, invent a method of sustaining life without food and of harnessing energy without fuel, is poppycock. No scientist subscribes to it, and no ethologist can countenance the idea without a shudder. There is no reason to suppose that we are the ultimate triumph of evolution, or that we shall not disappear one day as other species have disappeared long before us. 'Sooner or later we shall go', wrote Desmond Morris, 'and make way for something else.'

But before we go, we seem set to do an extraordinary amount of damage, to leave behind us a desolate and denuded home. Only a religious fanatic (Christian, Muslim, Marxist) can view this outcome without alarm and pity. The overwhelming richness of the earth's life-forms stands to be squashed, squeezed and flattened until all that is left is human. It will be a miserable achievement.

In the meantime, the burden rests with zoos to protect as best they can the vestiges of this richness. They are its trustees, and their responsibility is awesome and lonely. For many animals, they are the last place of refuge, the last sanctuary. No longer must animals be considered as exhibits or instruments of research, but as the sole carriers of genetic future. They must breed, they must thrive, they must continue, for there will be no others.

John Aspinall accepts the responsibility. He did not specu-
late and seek permission and dither. The success of Howletts
and Port Lympne is due to his impatience, his anger, his
vision, and his love for other creatures. As soon as he saw the
bleak prospects they faced, he vowed to be at their side. The
amazing breeding record at Howletts has ensured that at least
a few of the world's inhabitants will live to see another age and
not totter into the last darkness of their kind.

The zoo world has altered drastically in the last thirty years,
but Aspinall's antipathy towards it has remained constant. In
this he is probably wrong. He ought to play a much greater
role within the broader conservation fraternity, to consult,
contribute, and share in decisions. Because he is so incorrigibly impatient with bureaucracy, he keeps himself isolated,
which, in the long term, will not serve the best interests
of the species he has sought to help. He needs to be part
of a UK programme on conservation, not just a Howletts
programme.

His critics maintain that he has bred in an uncontrolled
fashion, without thinking ahead. The animal stock within
the zoo community *as a whole* needs to be managed carefully
as part of a long-term breeding intention which may last a
thousand years. His *laissez-faire* attitude to the problem of
genetic spread which the coming generation will have to
face is, say the critics, irresponsible, even selfish, and his
stubborn refusal to recognise the importance of scientific
study is an impediment. To take just one example, the
social relationships of clouded leopards must be closely
analysed if continued breeding success is to be achieved;
romantic notions are an inadequate substitute for technical
knowledge.

Similarly, Aspinall's fine herds of roan and sable antelope
used to suffer casualties because he refused to provide them
with protective housing in the winter. He resisted the idea
of 'domesticating' them in this way, of mollycoddling them,
because he cherished the vision of them wandering freely on
his domain. The price of romanticism was, in this case,

avoidable deaths. Aspinall has now retreated and zoological wisdom prevails at Howletts.

There are now well over four hundred captive gorillas in the world, with sufficient genetic variability to offer a viable population well into the future. In other words, there is a good captive stock well in advance of the animal's eventual disappearance in the wild, and if this stock is managed properly and co-operatively, there is no further need for any animals to be captured. The trade in gorillas ought now to cease. Aspinall's contribution to the captive population has been his most signal achievement.

His greatest failing, say the critics, is that he is too pessimistic. He must eventually recognise that the survival of other species has to be linked to the development of mankind. It is the only practical way. Conservation has to be useful to man, and Aspinall must one day swallow this uncomfortable truth and allow space in his gloomy philosophy for realism and pragmatism. One cannot exclude man from the formula. No one in the conservation world is in a position to dictate to countries what they should do with their human populations in order to protect the animal populations. The sudden disappearance of two billion people is not achievable.

Is there another way? At the time this book goes to press, John Aspinall is negotiating with the Australian government and aboriginal representatives to convert the island of Fantome into a haven for gorilla colonies. It is a scheme bound to appeal to him – large, idealistic and astonishing. It might even work.

The most recent chapter in Aspinall's mission occurred in 1987. Yvette Leroy, the lady in Brazzaville who had rescued Djala and sent him to Howletts, had another five orphans in her charge whom she could not hope to care for alone. She appealed once more to John Aspinall and met with a warm response. The Congolese government gave its support, going so far as to seek Aspinall's advice on the protection of gorillas in the wild, since the Minister of Forestry, Dr Ossebi Douniam, had visited Howletts and been deeply impressed.

Madame Leroy was concerned that no time should be lost, as she had earlier allowed another orphan to go to a zoo in Dakar (as a gift from the Congolese President), where it languished without proper food or adequate medical attention. Aspinall applied to the Department of the Environment for an import licence and was refused.

Much has been implied in these pages about John Aspinall's congenital idleness. He can, however, be roused to frenetic activity when the cause deserves, and this was one such occasion. He appealed against the decision, and brought Madame Leroy from the Congo to give evidence. He wrote to 10 Downing Street. He sent a film crew to Brazzaville to get pictures which would interest the television networks, and wrote copiously to newspapers. The result was that the plight of the orphans became known nationally, and the authorities could no longer deliberate in seclusion.

Two of the baby gorillas did not recover from Madame Leroy's apparent desertion. They died of alienation, what used to be called a broken heart. An army of objectors bombarded the D.o.E. with advice, virtually all of it urging that Aspinall be again refused. Led by Dr Alexander Harcourt of the University of Cambridge, they suggested that a permit for the gorillas' entry would encourage trade in gorillas and condemn the Congolese population to the threat of predation for profit. The argument was weak on obvious grounds. There was no 'trade', as the animals were not being bought. No money would be paid. Indeed, quite the opposite, as Aspinall had already sent his veterinary surgeon twice to Brazzaville and once to Dakar to provide urgent professional care. The villagers had for generations butchered for gorilla meat and tormented the young ones until they were old enough to cook; these people were unlikely to read of the decisions of the British government, and if they heard about it at all, they would conclude that it was pointless trying to sell gorillas when they were given away.

Nevertheless, Aspinall's application was opposed by the International Primate Protection League, by the World Wildlife Fund, by the Nature Conservancy Council, by the

Ape Advisory Panel, and many more. Only the Friends of the Earth supported him. The President of the Congo, due in London on a State visit, privately promised he would appeal to the Queen to allow the gorillas to come. Madame Leroy was frantic. She would never permit them to go to any African zoo; other reputable Western zoos were still talking about her problem in committee and getting nowhere; if the verdict went against Aspinall, she would be obliged to have the babies killed.

Eventually, the government bowed to pressure and reversed its earlier decision on 18 February 1987, making clear that this was an exceptional case, a 'rescue operation', and that it would not be repeated. For Aspinall it was a victory against all the might of established conservationists who still bridle at his independence. For Howletts it was a vindication of its unique status in the zoo world; one keeper told me it made him proud to be associated with Aspinall. And for the three gorillas – the male Kouillou aged two and a half, and two females Sangha (two years) and Sounda (eighteen months) – it was salvation. That, in a word, is what Howletts is about.

14
'Aspers'

It must by now be clear to the reader that John Aspinall is an unusual personality, resistant to rules, scornful of restraint, contemptuous of the bourgeois values of caution and *le juste milieu*. I hope it is also clear that these very characteristics, which make his more conventional and orthodox contemporaries grow red with indignation, have borne exotic fruit: they have overseen the restoration of five beautiful houses when there were no guaranteed (i.e. inherited or earned) funds to pay for it; they have forced the return of eighteenth-century elegance to the gambling world of London; and they have realised the entirely unreasonable dream that he should count wild animals among his friends and help rescue them from the obliteration to which human greed condemns them. 'The reasonable man adapts himself to the world,' wrote George Bernard Shaw. 'The unreasonable man persists in trying to adapt the world to himself. Therefore all progress depends upon the unreasonable man.'

It may well be that initially Aspinall's motives were not entirely laudable. From his earliest youth he has been by nature an incorrigible exhibitionist, a peerless show-off, a man who attracted attention to himself by conscious design. He has always made outrageous remarks in full knowledge of their effect, indeed usually with that effect in mind, and has in a sense spent his entire life acting the part of the character he has created. He is a performer who switches

into a well-rehearsed role at the promise of an audience.
This is not to say he is insincere, only that he is aware of
the power of hyperbole; what he says and what he does are
genuinely felt, but exaggerated for his audience. His personality has been described by a friend as 'an elaborate artifice
deliberately fashioned to yield anecdotes', and he makes no
secret of his admiration for other characters similarly prone
to extravagant expression. His adolescent desire to emulate
Oscar Wilde was founded on Wilde's courageous flashiness
and lofty disregard for middle-class reticence rather than his
sexual catholicism. In a letter to his friend, the financier Jim
Slater, Aspinall wrote, 'I like my friends more for their faults
than their virtues. I revel in your full repellent gloat just as I
like Jimmy [Goldsmith] when he is at his most outrageous.'

When Aspinall writes that he likes his friends for their
faults, it must be understood that he does not regard these
faults as blameworthy. He glories in any trait which sets his
friends apart from the common herd, and, short of cruelty or
left-wing bias (two hopelessly incompatible items), there is
very little which would excite his condemnation. He enjoys
Sir James Goldsmith's ruthlessness because it makes him a
'character', a personage, an individual, a glint among the
dross of mass humanity. Consequently, he is impatient with
bores and is a bad listener. On the other hand, when he is
released from the exigencies of the role (and when no one
is looking) he is compassionate towards the individual not
endowed with initiative or not blessed with the spark of
originality. He is not so extreme as to chastise a man for the
banality of his horizons, and will, on the contrary, give quiet
help when it is in his power to do so. I know several people
who receive unsolicited bounty many years after their last
meeting with Aspinall.

It follows that Aspinall may have discovered his mission
in life by accident. His first animals were an expression of
his extrovert nature; certainly no one else could compete
with a tiger roaming around the dinner-table or a Himalayan
bear tucked up on the sofa. Even as his interest in ethology
and animal husbandry developed, the element of display, of

exhibitionist indulgence, could never be entirely discounted. There are those even today who argue that his need for display vitiates the nobility of his purpose in so far as he might have done better to spend his energy protecting the natural habitat of wild animals rather than dragging them all the way to Kent. Had his endeavours taken this direction, however, their results would have been less visible. Aspinall could not have served wildlife at a distance, as his love for animals is personal, not abstract; he needs to be among them, to be surrounded by them, and for their happiness to be seen.

Nevertheless, once he decided that he would devote his time and income to the protection of wild animals, nothing would deflect him from his chosen aim. Despite setbacks, disappointments, obstructions, and appalling financial difficulties, Aspinall persevered, bolstered by an unusual degree of confidence in his own ability to see an ambition through to the end, in his own powers of recovery. When all about him urged surrender or at least counselled some curtailment of his grandiose plans, he would not give up. Perhaps it was precisely because advice ran counter to his wishes that he would not heed it, as he has never diluted an intention if he did not want to. This could be called stubbornness, or courage, but it derives from his conviction that the English are a warrior race who face difficulties with the determination to overcome them, and that he is a warrior by genetic inheritance. His view of himself simply will not allow him to accept defeat.

The corollary, that he must at all times succeed no matter how many casualties fall victim to his plans, is a view long held by newspapers enticed by the attraction of power and unable to imagine that its exercise can ever be anything but ruthless. He and his coterie have been depicted as 'savages', amoral and self-regarding. In fact, Aspinall does not conform to this facile image, despite his own avowals to the contrary. He has no malice, and cannot be cruel. Stories purporting to prove he has ruined scores of young men at the gaming-tables are mostly apocryphal, 'mostly' not because some are true, but because all are only half-true. Many are the occasions on which he has seen the danger of a fairly rich young man, son of a richer father, running the risk of self-destruction at the gaming-table, and has discreetly organised that someone should have a word with the father by way of warning; this though it would be far more in his business interest that the young man should lose his entire patrimony. Others who have owed Aspinall thousands of pounds for years have never felt the chill breath of pursuit and continue to enjoy his friendship and support to this day. He knows full well that he is unlikely ever to be repaid, and frankly does not give it a thought. Far from being pitiless or hard-hearted he has a marshmallow side which the truly brutal businessman finds risible. Some of his friends have the ruthlessness with which he is falsely credited and privately think him a fool for being soft. Far more, however, are alive to his inherent decency and proclaim him a force for good. The possibility exists that, in this regard at least, the great number of acquaintances may know him better than the small number of friends.

Aspinall's toughness, in other words, is called upon to see his plans to fruition. His sensibility comes into play to prevent his goals from harming others. He is like a Zulu king who alone knows that both qualities are necessary to a benign overlord, yet conceals the weakness less it be misunderstood by his less perceptive lieutenants.

He has never been known to forget a favour, whether it be a momentary display of trust, a good word, or a few thousand pounds. Moral support is acknowledged thirty years later with as much genuine delight (and more overt gratitude) as when originally offered. Many have been astonished to be reminded of an act or a gesture they had themselves long ago forgotten.

Aspinall's charm is well-attested. It has, in a sense, been the foundation of his success, not because he has used it cynically (though he is quite conscious of its power to manipulate), but because he has had the extraordinary knack of making everyone who comes into his ken feel gathered to the fold. Tradesmen, art dealers, architects, zoo-keepers, gamblers, waiters, all count themselves his friends, because he feels more natural dealing with friends than with strangers; *ergo*, he converts a stranger into a friend so that their dealings may continue. The charm has been known to fail with police officers and with inspectors from the Gaming Board, but it has worked wonders with the Inland Revenue, with bank managers, and with juries. It likewise imbues the zoos at Howletts and Port Lympne, even in his absence. One letter from an admiring visitor to Howletts may be allowed to stand for many; there was, said the writer, 'something in the atmosphere of Howletts which is wonderfully vital and beautifully human'.

Talking of which, Aspinall is not remotely embarrassed when visitors recognise him and pose questions. Quite the reverse. He welcomes enquiry, enjoys praise, and is secretly quite pleased to think he is something of a celebrity. That he should be pointed out and identified does not leave him indifferent, however much he may profess not to notice. He will converse amiably for half an hour with a perfect stranger about the latest events in gorilla husbandry or the present condition of one of the infants in the colony, especially if the questioner is seriously interested.

The other manifestation of the Aspinall charm is of course his ability as a 'bard'. One should remember, however, that the qualities required to tell a story with such guile that the listeners are drawn to the conclusion or inference that the teller intends do not include a strict adherence to factual accuracy. Aspinall knows well enough that truth does not reside in accuracy anyway, but in impression and impact. He will mould a story into the shape he needs for its moral to be clear, and though his audience knows the details have been invented they allow themselves to be seduced by the style. Aspinall is less masterful in this than he was; at Oxford he had legendary powers as a story-teller.

It is important also to remember that Aspinall is an initiator, what Lord Londonderry called 'an opener of roads'. Everything that happened at the Clermont Club, at Howletts, at Port Lympne, issued from his vision or impulse and was realised in deference to his ideas. On many occasions he has seen his purpose through despite general agreement that it was absurdly ambitious. It often happens that a man so bent on accomplishment is resentful of the success of others, as if he harbours a profound need to be the *only* man to do well. This is emphatically not true of Aspinall, who is quite devoid of envy. He is fond of quoting a remark by Gore Vidal as demonstrating the opposite of his own attitude – 'every time a friend succeeds I die a little'. It is an astute psychological observation, but not one Aspinall can comprehend. He is innocent of this kind of emotional treachery.

Similarly, the furnishing and decoration of his houses and clubs has largely been an expression of his own taste, the result of sudden initiatives and impulsive purchases. He has a fine eye for beauty and a coherent style, so much so that if he had never seen a wild animal he would be noteworthy for the interiors of his places alone. In furnishing, as in everything else, Aspinall has always bought the best of what is available, whether or not he could afford it. He is acquisitive, with the true collector's compulsion to pile things up irrespective of immediate need. Everything is *used*, however, not stored. This is why his lean period, when he was obliged to deplete weekly, was especially sad. He had to sell objects which were not tangential to his existence, but the very *décor* of his life; other, less personal, collectors would have regarded depletion as an irritation, not an affliction. Whatever he did was on the grand scale, there being nothing mean or small in any of his purchases as a collector, any more than there was in any of his other undertakings. Aspinall thinks, works, entertains, and possesses in a lordly manner.

It is somewhat difficult to adjudge wherein precisely lies the arrogance of which he is frequently accused. It is certainly not an arrogance of class, for he will treat the gardener with as much respect and courtesy as the most senior duke; nor will a duke earn inclusion at his table if he is boring or disloyal. He *is* arrogant in argument, for he does not possess the analytic mind which can appreciate the sense of another point of view. He assumes he is right, and an interlocutor

who disagrees must be either stupid or suspect. He can grow
so red-faced in conversational contest that it is often best to let
him have his way and calm down. His is the certainty born of
a conclusion which is reached emotionally, whereas the intellectual is ever aware of the equivocal nature of any conclusion
and protects his right to be wrong. Aspinall is honest, not
shifty or devious, and is incapable of saying what he wants
to say by a circuitous route. On the other hand, his stock of
information is immense, he has read widely, and is fascinated
by etymology and the correct use of English. There are few
subjects on which he cannot contribute a provocative piece of
esoteric knowledge.

When it comes to animal husbandry, its history as well as
its practice, Aspinall is now an expert, and only a fool would
attempt to gainsay him on this ground. Paradoxically, it is in
the field where he is pre-eminent that he is at his most modest. He does not parade his knowledge but shares it, and in his
zoo, surrounded by the evidence of his achievement, he is not
at all egotistical. When talking of past victories or future prospects in the zoo he always, invariably, uses the pronoun 'we'
to indicate that the venture belongs to his keepers as much as
to himself. He prefers to be thought of as a zoo-keeper, on
a level with his staff, more than a zoo-proprietor. His pride
is to be lowly. It is as if the propinquity of animals puts him
in his place, a place he happily welcomes. With Djoum, for
example, Aspinall is untypically self-effacing.

Of course, he views with horror the hubris which con-
sumes mankind in the twentieth century, but while others
loudly lament the wickedness of man's attitude towards the
rest of creation, Aspinall is one of the precious few who have
done anything about it. He has not talked, he has acted, and
in his own manner has done something, however little beside
the global catastrophe, to redress the evil of man's dominion.
It is this for which he will be remembered long after the
gambling stories have been relegated to their proper level
as amusing gossip.

Aspinall's colleagues in the zoo world are naturally indifferent to his worldly reputation. But Konrad Lorenz, the

doyen of ethologists, says that he 'knows more about animals than many learned people'. Dr Lester Fisher of Chicago calls him 'messianic' and Dr Kurt Benirschke of the world-famous San Diego Zoo says that if he were a gorilla there is nowhere he would rather be than with John Aspinall. Warren Thomas, director of Los Angeles Zoo, regrets that Aspinall is opinionated and undiplomatic, but admires the way he has solved difficult problems of animal husbandry with 'a mixture of folklore, intuition, and a few old wives' tales'. Some are alarmed by the risks he and his staff take while recognising the value of results. Most pay tribute to his uncanny knack with animals and wish he would overcome his abhorrence of scientific enquiry long enough to examine whence derives this knack, so that he could at least teach others, including some zoo-directors, how to cross the barrier between man and beast as only he knows how. In the long term, if man is to undo the damage he has done, he must 'feel' that kinship, and a proper study of Aspinall's emotional response towards his animals might show the way.

He is on less sure ground when he comes to apply his ethological observations to mundane human life. 'I am convinced', he wrote to Professor Roger Short, 'that the natural behaviour of social primates, which has only recently become known, can unlock the secrets of natural human behaviour.' This is almost certainly the case, but Aspinall's own conduct suggests that he draws parallels without much subtlety. The dominance of the male amongst all social primates has afforded him a superb excuse to treat women with the disdain which he would anyway have employed without the benefit of any ethological study. In the early days of the Clermont Club his gratuitously dismissive attitude towards women was a liability, as the English members who then predominated liked to bring wives or lady friends to the club. They soon learned not to when they could guarantee that Aspinall would ignore the women at best, or be downright rude to them at worst. He was particularly peremptory with weak women, and still cannot abide the presence of a woman with intellectual pretensions. In his view, women have wide and important roles and disgrace themselves if they attempt to break free of their confines. His three wives have coped in various ways with this prejudice; his mother was impervious to it; his daughter Amanda was already in her twenties before she came to terms with it. Lady Sarah Aspinall conforms to it by becoming a perfect example of a primate female, ready to serve the dominant male and make his life agreeable, careful not to challenge his position. Neither does he interfere with her role as châtelaine. Hence the marriage is hugely successful. One suspects that Aspinall would not ascribe this success to the subtle exercise of surreptitious power by the human female, a power easily recognised by novelists who study human behaviour rather more than they do the primate variety.

In the same way, the lessons he has learnt from animals have unduly coloured Aspinall's treatment of the rest of his family. Because his brother's sons are adopted, he feigns to believe they have no call upon family bonds. His aloofness with his eldest son Damian (the senior juvenile who had to earn his place in the primate hierarchy) caused the boy much loneliness which he did not conquer until he was himself a grown man. He subsequently went on to become a millionaire in his own right at a far earlier age than his father had done, a circumstance psychiatrists would understand more readily than ethologists. Aspinall's application of animal observation to human behaviour has therefore caused some avoidable disruption, which is a pity when one considers that he is a pre-eminently affectionate man for whom family life is of paramount importance. (He has forbidden his children only two sins: communism and drugs. They know with certainty that if ever they succumbed to drug-taking, their father would never speak to them again, and the certainty is a comfort.) Indeed, it is a truism worth repeating, in view of uninformed references to his 'coldness', that no one without a deep residue of affection could possibly commune with animals as Aspinall does. Animals do not respond to coldness, will not tolerate emotional distance, have no time for the heartless approach.

Another negative: Aspinall is not a pious ascetic willing to sacrifice everything to the cause. His disciples in the animal protection lobby would be disappointed to learn that he puts himself first, his family second, and the animals third, a system of priorities for which he feels no need to apologise. He is rather proud of his honesty in this regard, and is suspicious of those who pretend self-denial in the pursuit of an ideal. It is true, as we have seen, that during the six years of his relative penury he saw to it that the animals did not go wanting, and not one was sold. But he attributes this to his own ability to bounce back; the animals survived because he survived, and they have done well to back him. When he prospers, they prosper; when he tightens his belt, they trust him not to tighten theirs and they still prosper. This is a hopelessly anthropocentric view of animal motives, of course, and bears no relation to reality, but it is interesting that Aspinall interprets the situation with gambling metaphors. The hundreds of creatures that depend on his continuing to flourish are punters who have chosen a winner, and he likes to think of himself as a good bet. He is.

It must never be supposed, either, that Aspinall is moved by *pity* for animals. That way leads to selfish indulgence of human compassion (the solace of feeling pity being more important than the object pitied) and would never be permitted by any serious zoo-keeper. No, he is moved more by *admiration*, together with fury and incomprehension that this admiration is not shared by more people. It is a significant distinction.

Aspinall is thought by some to be naïve in his business dealings, naïve in his political views, naïve in his foolhardiness with the animals, naïve in his relationship with his closest friend, Sir James Goldsmith. As naïvety is an attractive trait, akin to boyishness and enthusiasm, and is often considered weakness by less subtle people, it is an accusation worth exploring.

With regard to business dealings, it is suggested that Aspinall is besieged by ideas, and leaves it to others to put them into operation. This is true in so far as he will not happily submerge himself in details, preferring to take the large view, but it belies his immediate and lasting grasp of the issues at stake. When others calculate at length the odds in favour and against an action, they are often astonished that he has worked them out for himself in a few seconds and already reached a conclusion. That he appears to be slapdash in business is his strength, for had he adhered to conventional business wisdom in his career he would never have been able to realise any of his ambitions. Taking the orthodox view, it was wrong to buy the Clermont Club when he did not have the fortune to sustain it, wrong to sell it when he did, wrong to buy Port Lympne when he was at his most impoverished, wrong to sink a vast amount of money in the Sumatran rhinoceros plan with only slim prospects of success, wrong to buy the Curzon House Club when it had been stripped of its licence. As it happened, they were all correct decisions (with the possible exception of the sale of the Clermont in 1972), because they were outlandish gambles which few other men would have the nerve to contemplate, and they paid off. A latent business sense is in the genes of Aspinall's family; brother Chips and his half-brother Sir Peter Osborne are both self-made millionaires, his son Damian is another. When John Aspinall appears not to know what he is doing (an impression he is content not to challenge), it is only on the surface. His calculations are fine, his confidence unassailable.

As for political views, it is usually thought that Aspinall exaggerates his right-wing radicalism in order to shock and watch reaction. He is certainly mischievous and enjoys the fuss which an outrageous argument can create, particularly if there are people present he knows will bridle, but it is a mistake to assume that acting plays the major part. In a letter to Kerry Packer in 1979 he wrote that in political and social terms, 'the UK is now in terminal decline, and only a right-wing counter-revolution, Francoesque in spirit and determination, can save us.' This was some months before the Conservative victory under Mrs Thatcher at the General Election. He does not bother to imagine what dire consequences for wildlife in general and for his own activities in particular might accrue under an extreme system, whether Fascist or Marxist, which sacrifices everything to the continued adoration of the human species. This is not so much naïvety as evasion.

In a typically outrageous speech to the Monday Club, Aspinall applauded the chimpanzee custom of dividing into rival armies which engaged in wholesale slaughter as a useful exercise in keeping down numbers. This was an instance of 'beneficial genocide'. He also said that dynasticism was 'deeply embedded in our simian past'. It has always been a dictum of his that right-wing 'gut instincts' are evolved from natural wisdom and are far more to be trusted than clever intellectualism. Left-wing 'gut instincts' he tends to ignore.

Aspinall's physical courage with his animals is beyond question, but is it adolescent? Does he take risks with his own life for the *frisson* it affords? Of course, danger is exciting and seductive, but in my opinion Aspinall does not court it; rather does he deny its authority to influence him. Besides which, his aim has always been to demonstrate that wild animals are our kin, not our enemy, and to admit they are dangerous would be to question his very premise. It is not danger which attracts him, but the challenge of proving that danger does not exist.

Sir James Goldsmith has been Aspinall's closest friend for nearly forty years. They are so unlike that their alliance holds a certain mystery, but an understanding of their influence upon each other is crucial to a proper assessment of Aspinall's character. Goldsmith is a self-confessedly aggressive man who has no objection to being described as ruthless. He might even be disappointed if he were not so depicted. Aspinall, on the other hand, lacks the harshness necessary to be entirely indifferent to the opinion of others. He wants to be liked, and to have his work acknowledged as beneficent. Goldsmith is incorrigibly litigious; Aspinall has a congenital preference for agreement. Aspinall tempers Goldsmith's more extreme obsessions, and Goldsmith injects steely realism into his friend's more extreme flights of fancy. Aspinall has quietly educated Goldsmith, who has been as ready to learn ethological principles from him as from his brother Teddy; and Goldsmith has educated Aspinall in the intricacies of financial leap-frogging and conquest. They admire each other almost (but not quite) unreservedly, each considering the other a giant among pygmies. They are fiercely loyal to one another, although this loyalty is expressed in different ways.

At the time of the Clermont sale, Jimmy Goldsmith was not the wealthy leviathan he subsequently became. His debt was the largest outstanding, and it was up to Aspinall to make special arrangements for the debt to be overlooked in order for the sale to proceed. There was never any hesitation that Aspinall would rescue the situation, mostly because money *per se* was not pre-eminently important as far as he was concerned. But for Goldsmith (who repaid, by the way, with scrupulous honour and speed), the pursuit of wealth has value in opening a route towards influence; he wants to improve society and seeks to do so with financial strength.

Later, when Aspinall returned to the gaming scene after an absence of six years and opened Little Aspinall's in Hans Street, he could only do so with Goldsmith's entire support. It was Sir James who made available the funds through a loan which he personally guaranteed, when other more cautious investors pulled away. However, the first year's trading did not produce the profits Sir James anticipated, whereupon he suspected collusion between staff and players and demanded the roulette wheels be removed and independently examined. (They were in proper condition and had not been touched.) Sir James prides himself on trusting few, whereas Aspinall is instinctively a trusting man who does not assume deceit. Goldsmith's loyalty is not in question, but it is bestowed sparingly. Aspinall's loyalty is more widely spread, given to everyone who has been part of his life; if a friend lets him down, he places a firm full-stop to the relationship against which there is no appeal, but is not recriminatory or vindictive. 'I wish', he has said, 'that I was a better grudge-bearer than I am.'

Goldsmith is unquestionably the more intelligent of the two, with a quicksilver brain of astonishing acuity. He is shrewd, analytical, probing, whereas Aspinall cannot be bothered to dissect the several strands of a problem and prefers the simple, startling idea to the complex, mysterious one which may yield jewels under examination. He has neither the patience nor the energy. Against Goldsmith's truly pulsing stream of energy, Aspinall seems as full of torpor as one of his tapirs.

Aspinall has confessed that he could never be a member of a club that he did not own. The need to shine, and further-more the need to be in a position where no one in authority can tell him what to do, are as strong now as they were in adolescence. The failing makes him a splendid host but a poor guest, and causes him to be myopic to the qualities of people he meets; he sees them as parts of a hierarchy, not as individuals. Sir James Goldsmith, in contrast, is keenly alert to talent and much more socially aware. He rejects the notion of hierarchies and aristocracies which Aspinall regards as inherent, and will encourage an individual talent to flourish.

Aspinall probably has a more profound understanding of Goldsmith's personality than any outside observer would imagine, and this knowledge affords him a secret advantage. He derives much entertainment from Goldsmith's extrava-gant behaviour, and when the latter is in the throes of an untrusting mood, Aspinall's response is to regard that as characteristic, without ever taking umbrage. In other words, his perception is subtle enough for him not to be surprised. It is a friendship based on the total inconceivability of betrayal, and if Aspinall is more loyal to one person than to any other, it is to Sir James.

Goldsmith has now amassed more wealth than Aspinall would ever want, but paradoxically Aspinall is the man who, many might say, lives better, with stable domestic routine and comfort. He is, by style and manner, a man from another era. Everything he has done, from his early twenties, fits him for elegant eighteenth-century living and passionate eighteenth-century commitment to an ideal. He is a benevolent Whig overlord living in the modern Tory world. Sir James Goldsmith is the perfect example of a creative entrepreneur in the twentieth-century mould. Aspinall is not. He is stranded in the wrong time.

The Aspinall Curzon Club is one of twenty-one casinos in London, compared with sixty-one which flourished, more or less, in the 1960s immediately after the new Gaming Act (the 'Aspinall Reform'). Of those sixty-one proprietors, John Aspinall himself was the only survivor in the 1980s. He sold the club at the end of 1987 for £90 million, retaining a seat on the board. Just over 20 per cent of Aspinall Holdings plc was publicly owned, the remaining 76 per cent divided equally between Sir James Goldsmith and Aspinall himself. As most of Aspinall's share was made over to the Howletts and Port Lympne Estates for the benefit of the animals, they thereby found themselves better off by £23 million. One might almost say that the 600-odd exotic animals living in Kent are the only ones of their kind to have their future invested in a gaming-den; their security has been assured by the number of rich men who have been prepared to lose a fortune on the turn of a wheel, their comfort and their future have come with the 'drop'.

Until 1987 Aspinall personally ran the club in Curzon Street, with much of the daily business left to his Number Two – his brother James Osborne. Number Three was his old gambling friend Dan Meinertzhagen, a veteran of Clermont days whose gambling instincts had sometimes served him ill. Meinertzhagen could not run the gambling business in the club, as the Gaming Board refused him a licence. He therefore looked after the rest of the house, including the restaurant. The Gaming Board had a similar opinion of Ian Maxwell-Scott, his even older friend from Oxford days who had occasionally slipped into damaging debt. He was employed at the club to manage the wine-cellar (and, incidentally, made it one of the choicest in London). Beyond these, there were 230 people employed in Curzon Street, including many, like Bert Payne, who had been with

Aspinall since the exciting days of the floating chemmy games in the 1950s. As a member of the board, John Aspinall is still frequently to be seen at the club which bears his name; it is difficult to imagine him anywhere else in London.

By a happy coincidence, the sale of Aspinall Holdings plc to Alfred Walker plc was agreed on 17 September 1987, the very day on which a dinner (planned long before) was given at the club to celebrate the arrival of the three orphan gorillas from the Congo – Kouillou, Sounda and Sangha, three amongst the many for whose ultimate welfare Aspinall agreed to the sale.

There are over 130 people working at either Howletts or Port Lympne, and this number is augmented during the high visiting season. Besides thirty keepers directly concerned with animals, there are twenty gardeners. Aspinall also has his own carpenters (four) and bricklayers (three), welders, painters, woodcutters and sixteen maintenance men; there is no week in the year that building of some sort is not in progress. Fourteen people work in administration.

In one year Howletts receives about 120,000 visitors, and Port Lympne 85,000. Between them they contributed nearly £800,000 in gate money in 1984-5 (£450,252 at Howletts, £338,823 at Port Lympne), representing about a third of the running-cost of the zoos. The remainder has to be raised from capital and profits on the sale of Aspinall Holdings, ultimately from gamblers. Most of the money goes on wages and salaries, some on food, but the zoos have their own farms in order to minimise expense. Aspinall bought 138 acres at Coombe Farm at the end of 1984 for £265,000; together with over 210 acres at Chilham and nearly 9 acres at Walmestone Nursery (owned jointly by himself and Lady Sarah), this enables the zoos to be self-sufficient up to a point. It would be tedious to list the entire crop, which is extraordinarily varied. At Chilham, for example, there are 30 acres set aside to grow nothing but herbal hay for the elephants. Mangold, lucerne, maize and kale are all grown at Port Lympne, for rhinos, elephants and hoof-stock, 150 tons of mangold alone from January to May. At Coombe Farm 30 acres provide a red clover mix for water buffalo and American bison.

Thousands of bales of hay are gathered every year at Port Lympne, yet it is still necessary to buy in some stock, as much as 500 bales or more of lucerne. The zoos also buy 30 bales a week of woodshavings (to provide bedding for the elephants), and branches in bundles for gorillas, rhinos and elephants. Three thousand bales of wheatstraw are used for bedding every year, and 4,000 bales of oatstraw for the gorillas. Fruit and vegetables which have to be bought from outside cost £150,000. These include unexpected items such as locust beans as well as vast quantities of pineapples, yams, leeks, kiwi fruit, figs and much else to make a gorilla's life pleasant. Visitors are sometimes amazed that such good quality produce should be provided, having assumed that animals would receive left-overs and flawed fruit deemed unsuitable for human consumption. Aspinall's answer to this is that there are no seconds in the jungle.

Sixty-seven different species of animal thrive at Howletts and Port Lympne, comprising nearly seven hundred individuals. When the human employees at both zoos and the London club are added, something over a thousand bodies now owe their livelihood or survival to John Aspinall. For a man born to the wife of a middle-class doctor in India, brought up as a boarder on a Sussex farm, more or less thrown out of Rugby, receiving an allowance of £1 a week at Oxford, degree-less, career-less and prospect-less when he came down, it is a remarkable denouement.

The last word might belong to Beryl Addley. Just as Susan Hunt, Aspinall's secretary in London, has been privy to the events of his professional life for years and is entrusted with the execution of decisions which shape it, so Beryl Addley knows everything of the private anguishes and joys which have attended the development of the zoos. For a man so proudly misogynistic as John Aspinall it is somewhat ironic that two women, virtually unknown to most of his friends, should be in positions of such confidence. Beryl has been with the family for twenty-five years and has therefore watched the emergence of Aspinall the renowned zoo-keeper from his beginnings as Aspinall the gregarious gambling man-about-town. She came in answer to an advertisement for a nanny to look after Amanda and was interviewed by Lady O., who frankly acknowledged there had already been seventeen nannies before her, some of them lasting only a day. Beryl has lasted for ever.

What is extraordinary is that Beryl Addley has brought up more wild animals at Howletts, with no training or even predilection for the task, than anyone else. It was she who hand-reared one of the first tigers, Zarka the one-eared, nearly a quarter of a century ago (the old tiger died in 1986 after a long quiet senility; elsewhere she would almost certainly have been put down). It was she who discovered a litter of three tigers born on Christmas Eve in intense cold, and saved their lives with hot-water bottles and undivided attention; they all survived, grew, flourished and bred. She brought up a wolf, Nushka, and several gorillas. Djoum, now the largest silverback in Britain, spent his earliest days with Beryl. As an infant Djoum had perforce to submit to his six months' quarantine, and as Amanda and Damian were old enough not to need a nanny's care so constantly, Beryl took on the task of rearing two gorillas, Djoum and Mushie. Djoum would climb into bed with her, and Mushie slept in a cot beside the bed. Djoum frequently became lively in the night, and wanted to play, so Beryl had to clout him rather harder than she might a human child. The old pram no longer used by Amanda and Damian served to transport the infant gorillas if Beryl had other jobs in hand and did not want to lose sight of them.

All of which is merely charming and intriguing to anyone who has not actually seen Djoum in charge of his group at Howletts. To watch the stately movements of this powerful giant, feel his dignity, see his grace, hear his mighty growl, observe the immense musculature of his back, and feel the searching mature intelligence of his glance beneath that heavy brow, then to reflect on his learning 'manners' from Nanny Addley and *still* retaining his essence as a gorilla rather than a human plaything, is to enjoy a momentary glimpse of the unique quality of Howletts and of the man who founded it. Djoum is a triumph. It would never have occurred to Beryl to treat him with anything but respect and she, now in charge of the tea-room open to visitors, must share some of the credit for that triumph. Having admired Djoum, pause to acknowledge Beryl.

Appendix

The following animals have all bred successfuly at either Howletts or Port Lympne Zoo.

Chimpanzee
Gorilla★
Siamang

Black-capped
   capuchin
Diana monkey
Emperor tamarin
Goeldis monkey
Golden lion
   tamarin
Humboldt's
   woolly monkey
Javan brown
   langur
White-faced saki
White-fronted
   capuchin

Black-and-white
   ruffed lemur

Canadian timber
   wolf

Hunting dog
Atlas lion
Black leopard
Cheetah
Clouded leopard
Fishing cat
Indian desert cat
Indian tiger
Leopard cat
Northern lynx
Ocelot
Serval cat
Siberian lynx
Siberian tiger
Snow leopard

Honey-badger

African elephant

Przewalski's horse

Black rhinoceros

Brazilian tapir

Axis deer
Barasingha
Calamian deer
Hog deer
Sambar
Wapiti

Blackbuck
Chousingha
Eland
Nilgai
Roan antelope
Sable antelope

American bison
Cape buffalo
European bison
Water buffalo

Wild boar

Parma wallaby

Peafowl
Jungle fowl

★In 1988 there are 34 individuals, 24 of whom were born at Howletts, an achievement unparalleled anywhere in the world.

Bibliography

W.C. Allee, *The Social Life of Animals*, Heinemann, London, 1939 (republished as *Co-operation among Animals with Human Implication*, Pitman, London, 1951)

Robert Ardrey, *The Territorial Imperative*, Collins, London, 1967

John Aspinall, *The Best of Friends*, Macmillan, London, 1976

——'Random Thoughts on the Human Animal', privately printed, London, 1967

——'Man's Place in Nature', in David Paterson and Richard Ryder (eds), *Animal Rights: a symposium* (Centaur Press, Arundel, 1979)

——'The Husbandry of Gorillas in Captivity', paper read at Franceville, Gabon, in 1979

——'Some Aspects of Gorilla Behaviour', paper read at Hanover in 1982

——'The Howletts Gorilla Bands', paper read at San Diego in 1985

David Attenborough, *Life on Earth*, Collins, London, 1979

F.W. Champion, *The Jungle in Sunlight and Shadow*, Chatto & Windus, London, 1933

Dian Fossey, *Gorillas in the Mist*, Hodder & Stoughton, London, 1983

Jane Goodall, *In the Shadow of Man*, Collins, London, 1971

H. Rider Haggard, *Nada the Lily*, Longman, London, 1892

Emily Hahn, *Zoos*, Secker & Warburg, London, 1968

H. Hediger, *Wild Animals in Captivity*, Butterworths, London, 1950

——*Man and Animal in the Zoo*, Routledge & Kegan Paul, London, 1970

C.W. Hume, *Man and Beast*, Universities Federation for Animal Welfare, London, 1962

W.E. Lecky, *History of European Morals*, Longman, London, 1869

Konrad Lorenz, *King Solomon's Ring*, Methuen, London, 1952

——*Man Meets Dog*, Methuen, London, 1954

——*On Aggression*, Methuen, London, 1966

Eugene Marais, *My Friends the Baboons*, Anthony Blond, London, 1971

Desmond Morris, *The Naked Ape*, Jonathan Cape, London, 1967

Vernon Reynolds, *The Apes*, Cassell, London, 1968

E.A. Ritter, *Shaka Zulu*, Longman, London, 1955

H.S. Salt (ed.), *The New Charter: a discussion of the rights of men and the rights of animals*, Bell, London, 1896

George Schaller, *The Year of the Gorilla*, Collins, London, 1965

C.F. Schoolbred, *The Law of Gaming and Betting*, Pitman, London, 1932

Ernest Thompson Seton, *Wild Animals I Have Known*, David Nutt, London, 1911

——*Lives of the Hunted*, David Nutt, London, 1911

Peter Singer (ed.), *In Defence of Animals*, Blackwell, Oxford, 1985

E.S. Turner, *All Heaven in a Rage*, Michael Joseph, London, 1964

Index